The T Programming Language:
A Dialect of LISP

27,153

Stephen Slade

Yale Artificial Intelligence Project
Yale Department of Computer Science

Prentice-Hall, Inc., *Englewood Cliffs, NJ 07632*

Library of Congress Card Number: 86-62148

Editorial/production supervision: Barbara Marttine Webber
Cover design: Diane Saxe
Manufacturing buyer: Gordon Osbourne

Printed in the United States of America

10 9 8 7 6 5 4 3 2 1

ISBN   0-13-881905-X   025

Prentice-Hall International (UK) Limited, *London*
Prentice-Hall of Australia Pty. Limited, *Sydney*
Prentice-Hall Canada Inc., *Toronto*
Prentice-Hall Hispanoamericana, S.A., *Mexico*
Prentice-Hall of India Private Limited, *New Delhi*
Prentice-Hall of Japan, Inc., *Tokyo*
Prentice-Hall of Southeast Asia Pte. Ltd., *Singapore*
Editora Prentice-Hall do Brasil, Ltda., *Rio de Janeiro*

Contents

iii

iv

x

Preface

In recent years, academic computer scientists have debated the role of programming in introductory computer science courses. Many have argued that an introductory science course should expose the student to the great ideas of the discipline. Thus, an introductory biology course should cover topics such as evolution and molecular genetics, but not how to build a microscope. Accordingly, a computer science course should emphasize the major intellectual issues of computing, not how to write programs.

We do not agree with this position. First, programming *is* a major intellectual issue in computer science. Second, the comparison of programming to building microscopes misses the point. Writing programs in computer science is more like building a living organism in biology. If biology had advanced to a stage that permitted introductory students easily to construct amoebas and clams and roses and hamsters, there would be little debate over the intellectual content of such exercises.

Programs are the organisms that populate the world of computing. This book presents some of these creatures and shows how to build them.

This book is not an introductory programming text. Rather, it is for students who have already learned to program in some language other than LISP. Given the ready access most students have to computers these days, it is rare to find a college student interested in computers who has not previously been exposed to programming. The odds are pretty good that a student's first programming language was not LISP.

Furthermore, we recognize that people who study a new programming language usually do so to apply it to particular problems. That is, the language should be a useful tool. The T language has been used in range of college courses, including artificial intelligence, data structures, computer systems, and compiler design. The present book is suitable as a companion text in such courses — a programmer's guide to a powerful software tool.

The T language is available on a variety of machines. Appendix A explains how to get a copy of T. For readers who have another version of LISP, appendix A discusses how to adapt other dialects of LISP to the style of programming afforded by T.

Programming is for participants, not spectators. This book is replete with examples and exercises. These sample programs demonstrate fundamental programming principles in familiar domains. The reader should execute these programs. The answers to most of the exercises are given in appendix C. Among the unanswered exercises are several large programs, such as the database management system assigned in later chapters, which are suitable as projects. We believe that learning to build large, complex programs is a worthy goal in any programming course. We suggest that the tools and materials supplied by the T language are well-suited to such an endeavor.

Stephen B. Slade
New Haven, Connecticut

Acknowledgments

I am most grateful for the intellectual infrastructure of the Yale Computer Science Department.

- For making critical comments and useful suggestions: Norman Adams, Douglas Baldwin, Eduard Hovy, Paul Hudak, Larry Hunter, Alex Kass, Michael Lebowitz, David Littleboy, David Littman, James Meehan, Nathaniel Mishkin, Alan Perlis, James Philbin, Kent Pitman, Frank Ritter, Christopher Riesbeck, Jonathan Rees, John Ramsdell, Michael Slade, Christopher Turk, and the many Yale undergraduates in Computer Science 170 (*Introduction to Artificial Intelligence*) who provided a superb run-time debugging environment for the textbook.

- For ideas regarding programming style and software engineering: John Ellis and Nathaniel Mishkin.

- For designing, implementing, and maintaining the DRAW graphics editor: James Firby.

- For keeping T_EX and L^AT_EX running: William Gropp and James Firby.

- For designing, implementing, and maintaining the T language: Norman Adams, Kent Pitman, and Jonathan Rees; and in recent years: James Philbin, Richard Kelsey, and David Kranz.

- For designing, implementing, and maintaining the U editor: Robert Nix, Nathaniel Mishkin, and James Philbin.

- For nurturing T and U at Yale: John O'Donnell.

- For his support and skill in fostering computer science and AI at Yale: Roger Schank.

Many of the people who reviewed drafts of this book are ardent supporters of T and expressed vehement opinions on such matters as selection of topics, order of presentation, diction, and typography. I always found their comments salutary. I adopted their suggestions wherever possible. However, there were occasions in which competing points of view were irreconcilable. In those cases, I remain sole arbiter, and accept responsibility for any shortcomings that may result.

I am grateful to Nicholas Fox Weber, Director of the Albers Foundation, for his stimulating advice and solicitous assistance in selecting the cover art.

Furthermore, I appreciate the professional expertise of the people at Prentice-Hall, especially John Wait and Barbara Marttine Webber.

This book was written under the auspices of the Yale Artificial Intelligence Project, which receives support from numerous sources, including the Advanced Research Projects Agency of the Department of Defense, the Office of Naval Research, the Air Force Office of Scientific Research, the Army Research Institute, the National Science Foundation, the National Library of Medicine, the Sloan Foundation, and the Systems Development Foundation.

Finally, I have repeatedly borrowed on the patience of my wife, Daniela Ioan. In time, I hope to be able to reimburse her calm endurance and encouragement.

Chapter 1

LISP and T

High thoughts must have high language.

◇ ARISTOPHANES, *Frogs (405 B.C.)*

Brekekekex, ko-ax, ko-ax.

◇ ARISTOPHANES, *Ibid.*

Thank God for tea! What would the world do without tea? – how did it exist? I am glad I was not born before tea.

◇ SIDNEY SMITH, *Lady Holland's Memoir, Recipe for Salad (1855)*

This book presents the T programming language, which is a dialect of the LISP programming language. LISP was developed in the late 1950's by John McCarthy, and is one of the oldest computer languages in current use. Initially, LISP evolved as the primary language for research in artificial intelligence (or AI), and has matured as a very general purpose language for a wide variety of applications.

LISP, which stands for LISt Processing, was developed as a language for manipulating symbols. LISP's symbolic manipulation can be contrasted with other languages, such as FORTRAN, which are primarily used for numeric calculations.

LISP has been used for many AI applications, including programs to perform tasks such as natural language understanding, game playing, learning, planning, theorem proving, problem solving, and speech recognition. LISP is now being used more and more by computer scientists outside AI.

T is a modern version of LISP. It is derived from Scheme, a version of LISP developed by Gerald Sussman and Guy Steele at MIT [24,18]. T was designed by Jonathan Rees, Kent Pitman, and Norman Adams at the Yale Department of Computer Science, and implemented by Jonathan Rees and Norman Adams.

Researchers at Yale have used T to write text editors, circuit design tools, graphics editors, compilers, and numerous artificial intelligence programs. T has also been used for several years in a wide range of undergraduate computer science courses, at Yale as well as at other universities.

There are many other dialects of LISP, including INTERLISP, MacLISP, Franz Lisp, Lisp Machine LISP (ZetaLISP), Common LISP, and Portable Standard LISP. While this book concentrates on T, many of the features of T can be found in other LISP dialects. There are strong family resemblances among the various dialects. Appendix A discusses other LISP dialects, and compares them with T.

LISP has several features which recommend it as a desirable programming language:

- *Simple syntax.* The canonical form of LISP is the same for both programs and data – they are both lists of items enclosed by parentheses. This seemingly trivial matter has significant ramifications. LISP programs can easily analyze, modify, and generate other LISP programs. This is extremely important not only for automatic programming research, but also for many other complex artificial intelligence applications where dynamic program manipulation comes into play.

- *Extensible.* LISP is extensible. The programmer can easily add new procedures and even make syntactic alterations through macros. This allows the programmer to develop special-purpose tools that are well integrated into the normal LISP environment. Over the years, numerous utilities have been developed and added to various LISP implementations, including in-core editors, database retrieval systems, window packages, cross-reference packages, spelling correctors, and undo facilities.

- *Adaptable.* Not only can the programmer extend the language by adding new procedures and macros, but he can redefine existing ones. This ability to tailor the language can be useful in translating code from one LISP dialect to another.

- *Memory management.* LISP (like most interpreted languages) performs dynamic memory allocation and reclamation. The programmer does not need to allocate or free storage explicitly, although primitives are available for such explicit control in the rare case where the programmer feels it is appropriate.

The T language has all the features of regular LISP listed above, plus several others.

- *Procedural arguments.* T allows procedures to be used as arguments to other procedures and returned as values. This feature can be viewed as a higher-level, well-defined mechanism for using programs as data.

- *Debugging and error checking.* T procedures perform extensive argument checking. Furthermore, T provides the programmer with a variety of error-checking routines that can be incorporated into the user's own programs, thus facilitating the debugging of code. For programmers more concerned with speed of execution, T allows the programmer to turn off the error checking.

- *Data abstraction.* T provides direct methods for implementing and manipulating new data structures. Abstract data structures allow the programmer to focus on the conceptual aspects of programming, without regard to the underlying representation and implementation.

- *Object-oriented programming.* Every entity in T is viewed as an object – numbers, lists, symbols, procedures, and so on. In addition to the approach of having procedures act on data objects, T allows the programmer to create objects that themselves respond to operations. This object-oriented programming methodology was pioneered in the languages Simula [5] and Smalltalk [9]. T provides the programmer with a seamless combination of procedural and object-oriented programming.

- *Locales.* The dichotomy of global and local reference is refined into a hierarchy of nested environments through the use of contours, created implicitly with lambda expressions or explicitly with locales.

- *Optimizing compiler.* T has been implemented with an optimizing compiler which produces efficient object code. The compiler employs several different optimizing techniques, including source-to-source transformations and sophisticated register allocation. Furthermore, T is lexically scoped and properly tail-recursive, providing additional opportunities for generating efficient code.

- *Uniform semantics for interpreted and compiled code.* The T language has been designed with a semantics that allows the interpreted and compiled code to be true to the same language description. The implementation of T provides for programs to produce the same results in both interpreted and compiled versions.

This book is in two parts. The first is an introduction to LISP, or rather, T qua LISP. We present those aspects of T which are found in most LISP implementations. We assume that the reader already knows how to write computer programs, but does not know LISP.

The second part covers the T programming language in particular — T qua T. Here we present those features which are unique to T. The programmer who already knows LISP should skim part one and then more closely examine part two. The dividing line between parts one and two occurs at chapter 7 ± 2.

Throughout the book, we provide extensive examples of T programs in a variety of areas, such as text formatting and spelling correction. These examples illustrate both basic and advanced programming techniques using T. The examples are chosen to focus on programming issues, not theoretical concerns. Thus, the reader is not expected to have special knowledge of artificial intelligence, mathematics, or molecular biology. On the other hand, the reader should not expect to gain any new insights about those topics either.

Appendix A provides a comparison of T with Scheme and several other LISP dialects. This appendix should be particularly useful to those readers who have access to some other version of LISP, but not to T.

It is recommended that the programmer who wishes to pursue T in greater detail refer to the T release notes and *The T Manual* [16], by Rees, Adams, and Meehan, which documents the many features of T, not all of which are covered by this present volume. The programmer should appreciate that T is a living language. T continues to evolve.

Finally, it is most important that the reader of this book also write programs. The reader should have access to a computer running LISP and try the examples and exercises given in the book. Learning a computer language requires practice and application. Fortunately, this practice should not prove onerous. Given the fervor with which T programmers extol and defend their chosen language, for many programmers learning T is its own reward.

1.1   Chapter Summary

- LISP is a computer language developed in the 1950's for manipulating symbols.

- T is a modern version of LISP, based on Scheme. T was designed and implemented at the Yale Computer Science Department.

- LISP's key features include:

  - simple syntax
  - extensibility
  - adaptability
  - memory management

- T's enhancements to LISP include:

  - procedural arguments
  - debugging and error checking
  - data abstraction
  - object-oriented programming
  - locales
  - optimizing compiler
  - uniform semantics

- The reader of this book should use a computer to try the examples and exercises.

Chapter 2

A Tutorial Introduction

"Reeling and Writhing, of course, to begin with,"
the Mock Turtle replied, "and the different branches of
Arithmetic – Ambition, Distraction, Uglification, and Derision."

◇ LEWIS CARROLL, *Alice's Adventures in Wonderland (1865)*

The imagination ... gives birth to a system of symbols,
harmonious in themselves, and consubstantial with the truths
of which they are the conductors.

◇ SAMUEL TAYLOR COLERIDGE, *The Statesman's Manual (1816)*

Disputes over the merits of various programming languages are chronic in computer
science. The outside observer or programming neophyte is often bewildered by
the arguments. Why should one programming language be different in kind from
another? Don't all languages do the same things?

A programming language is a means for constructing programs. When we
build a program, we create an artifact. The choice of programming language can
determine the nature of that artifact. By comparison, consider the construction of
a more tangible artifact: a building.

In designing a building, an architect is aware of numerous goals: function,
capacity, aesthetic appeal, efficiency, stability, and the time and cost required for
the design, construction, and maintenance of the building. There may be optimal
ways of satisfying these various constraints. For example, Aladdin's genie from
the lamp could construct the world's most glorious palace instantly, at no cost to
Aladdin. Outside the land of imagination, however, the architect must recognize
the practical limitations of his resources and abilities. Still, he strives to satisfy as
many of the design goals as possible.

In each decision, the architect faces trade-offs between competing goals. The
architect has a variety of construction materials to choose among, such as concrete,

6

wood, glass, brick, and steel. The choice of material constrains many factors, such as cost, stability, and appearance, which will then affect the way the architect makes other decisions. Some materials are good for skyscrapers, and other materials are better for homes. Certain materials may be well-suited for very specific applications. Asphalt is terrific for paving, but not for walls. Concrete can be used for both. Which is better? It depends.

Which programming language is best? It depends. Computer languages differ on many dimensions:

- Speed of program development and speed of program execution often depend on the programming language.

- Program cost is commonly measured in terms of time (speed of development, execution, and maintenance), and space (size of the program).

- Efficiency is the inverse of cost in terms of time and space.

- Capacity for a programming language might refer to the size of programs and problems for which the language is practical.

- Stability in a programming language is reflected in a program's ability to accommodate changes or unexpected events.

- Appeal and function are related properties. A programming language which is well-suited for function X will have many supporters among those who require function X.

Many of these factors are often more related to a language's implementation for a specific machine than to any intrinsic property of the language.

LISP is one of the older computer languages, and has become the primary language for artificial intelligence research. To continue with the construction analogy, the languages BASIC or Pascal might be viewed as the bricks and lumber languages for the do-it-yourselfer, due to their popularity and availability for microcomputers. The home hobbyist can build the equivalent of a deck and patio in his backyard. LISP was rarely used for mundane applications, since it required the more elaborate hardware found in artificial intelligence labs. Who would want to build a picnic bench out of titanium? However, as the price of more powerful hardware continues to decline, there is greater demand for more powerful computer programming languages. LISP has proven to be a language of great power and sophistication.

T has been implemented with an optimizing compiler to be fast and efficient. We discuss T's speed and efficiency at length in chapter 16.

2.1   The LISP Interpreter

LISP is primarily an interpreted language. By comparison, the languages BASIC and APL are also interpreted, and FORTRAN, COBOL, C, and Pascal are compiled.

One important difference between different types of languages is the manner of programmer interaction. Interpreter-based languages are *conversational.* They assume that the programmer has a computer terminal or personal computer and is able to type interactive responses. With compiler-based languages, there is a delay between entering and executing a program.

From the programmer's perspective, the difference between an interpreter and a compiler is like the difference between a conversation and a correspondence. An interpreter provides more immediate feedback, like a dialog between two people. A compiler has a longer time between action and response, like an exchange of letters through the mail.

One might also contrast interpreted and compiled languages with interactive and batch computer systems. With interactive systems, such as personal computers or time-sharing systems, the programmer has frequent contact with the computer. The computer can prompt for more information or print out error messages. The programmer can respond and often proceed from error conditions. With batch processing, the programmer prepares a program and then submits it to be processed without any further intervention. The batch job may be submitted on punch cards, magnetic tape, or from disk. The important distinction is that the program will execute without any additional feedback or data from the programmer. Interactive systems are then more similar to interpreted languages, while batch processing seems to parallel compiled languages.

Interpreted languages are most useful for developing and debugging program prototypes. They allow the *programmer* to interact quickly and easily with the computer. Compiled languages are most useful for the producing the application version of a program to be used by someone else. The *end user* of an application program is more concerned with speed of execution than with ease of modification.

Many LISPs, including T, are both interpreted and compiled. This means that the programmer can develop a program very conveniently using the interpreter, and then, when the program is complete, the programmer may compile the program to produce a more efficient, production version of the program. When it is executed, the compiled version of the code will still require the interpreter itself as an execution environment. That is, the interpreter for compiled code acts like a run-time library found in other languages, such as C.

For most of this book, we will focus on the interpreted side of LISP. The compiler will be discussed in chapter 16.

From this point on, we shall focus specifically on the T dialect of LISP. The examples and exercises given will refer to T, but in most cases, will also apply generally to other dialects of LISP. The specific names of procedures will vary from one dialect to another, and the reader who is using another version of LISP should refer to appendix A, which outlines the main differences between T and other LISPs. This appendix shows how the reader might change another LISP dialect to resemble T.

2.2 Running T

To use T, one invokes the T interpreter at the operating system shell by typing T or whatever name is given to the dialect of LISP on your computer.

At this point, the T interpreter will begin execution. It will typically print a greeting and a prompt. The greeting displays information such as the name and version number of the interpreter. The prompt is a character, or a set of characters, printed to indicate that the interpreter is awaiting input from the programmer.

Here are a typical greeting and prompt.

```
T 3.0 (2) MC68000/AEGIS  Copyright (C) 1985 Yale University

>
```

There are three basic actions the T interpreter will take:

1. **READ.** It will read each expression the programmer types.

2. **EVALUATE.** It will determine what the given expression means and calculate its value.

3. **PRINT.** It will print out that value for the expression.

Most expressions yield values that are printed, though sometimes these values may be undefined.

This basic cycle of the interpreter is often called the READ-EVAL-PRINT loop or REPL. You might think of this as a conversation with the T interpreter: you ask a question, which it READs; it determines the answer to the question by EVALuating it; and then it responds to the question by PRINTing its answer. We don't wish to personify the computer – however, it seems fairly natural to understand this process as being analogous to dialog.

2.3 Simple Arithmetic

We will now use T to do some simple arithmetic and then review some of the principles of how T works. Here are examples of addition, subtraction, negation, and multiplication. The programmer input is right of the prompt and the T output is below the prompt. Thus, in the first example, the prompt is **>**, the input expression is **(+ 1 2)**, and the output value is **3**. The addition procedure "+" is applied to the arguments 1 and 2. You should try these examples yourself. Generally, you must type a carriage return after the closing right parenthesis.

```
> (+ 1 2)
3

> (+ 2 3 4)
9

> (- 5 1)
4

> (- 30)
-30

> (* 12 4)
48

> (* 2 3 4)
24

> (exit)
$
```

The last expression, **(exit)**, terminates the T session and returns the programmer to the shell, indicated here with a $ prompt.

We'll continue with some more arithmetic examples. This time we'll intersperse comments with the examples. T, like most programming languages, allows one to place comments in the midst of programs by preceding the comments with a special character, often called a *comment character*. In T, the semicolon is the comment character. All text to the right of a semicolon is disregarded by the interpreter.

```
> (add1 8)                          ;  addition of 1
9                                   ;  equivalent to: (+ 8 1)

> (subtract1 100)                   ;  subtraction of 1
99                                  ;  equivalent to: (- 100 1)

> (/ 48 12)                         ;  division returning quotient
4

> (remainder 49 12)                 ;  division returning remainder
1

> (remainder -49 12)
-1
```

```
> (mod 49 12)                 ; modulus arithmetic
1

> (mod -49 12)                ; always returns non-negative integer
11
>

> (->integer 4.5)            ; returns the integer part of a number.
4                             ; note: the procedure name is ->integer

> (->integer -4.5)           ; "->" in a T procedure name indicates
-4                            ; conversion of a data type

> (->integer 12.0)
12

> (max 1 3)                   ; maximum value
3

> (min 1 3)                   ; minimum value
1

> (abs -17)                   ; absolute value
17

> (abs -17 4)                 ; example of a mistake

** Error: wrong number of arguments to procedure (ABS -17 4)

>> (reset)                    ; the double prompt >> indicates a
                              ; break loop (to be explained later).
                              ; reset returns to the normal
                              ; read-eval-print loop.

T: Top level
> 45                          ; numbers evaluate to themselves
45

> -7
-7
```

These few examples exhibit some major points about the way T works.

- T uses prefix notation. The procedure name appears to the left of its arguments. Thus, in T one writes (+ 1 2) instead of (1 + 2).

- Parentheses are used to delimit expressions. A left parenthesis precedes the procedure name in these examples. The last argument to the procedure is followed by a right parenthesis, which matches or balances the opening left parenthesis.

- Some T procedures, such as addition and multiplication, have a variable number of arguments. The addition and multiplication examples have both two and three arguments, and the subtraction examples have both one and two arguments. Other procedures, such as **abs** (absolute value), take a fixed number of arguments.

- In T, as in most LISP's, procedures will produce an error message if given the wrong number of arguments. The second absolute value example demonstrates this.

- T allows you to recover from errors. In the case above, we merely start over again using the **reset** procedure. However, T provides a facility which enables the programmer to correct a mistake from a breakpoint caused by an error in the middle of execution. This is useful for debugging, and will be discussed in chapter 10.

- Some procedures have no arguments. **(reset)** is an example of this. Another important procedure which takes no arguments is **(exit)**, which is used to terminate a T session.

- Numbers evaluate to themselves. This feature is quite intuitive. The last two examples demonstrate this.

Here are some other examples.

```
> (min 1 (min 3 0))            ;  another way to calculate (min 1 3 0)
0

> (max (+ 3 5) (abs (* -2 5)))
10

> (abs (min (remainder -13 4) (+ 3 5 (max 2 4))))
1

> (* (+ 30 40) (max 12 (abs -11)))
840

> (->integer (/ 48 2))
24
```

These examples show that procedural expressions can have other procedural expressions as arguments. Notice that each procedural expression is surrounded by its own set of parentheses.

This nesting of parentheses can lead to a large number of closing right parentheses, as seen in the third example. There are four right parentheses that match the left parentheses in the `max`, `+`, `min`, and `abs` procedural expressions, respectively.

2.4   Objects

As we stated earlier, programming languages allow you to build programs. This process of construction involves materials and techniques. Just as buildings are composed of elements such as bricks, lumber, and nails, T programs are made from language elements. T also provides techniques for combining elements. In T, the materials used for building programs are called *objects*. Some objects are primitive, and others are composed of other objects.

In the preceding section, we saw examples of several T objects, including numbers and procedures. These objects can be combined to form expressions. Throughout this book, we shall see examples of many kinds of objects, such as characters, strings, ports, structures, and files, and ways of manipulating these objects. From this perspective, a program is simply a tool for manipulating some object.

2.5   Symbols and Variables

Like any other computer language, T allows the programmer to create symbolic names for identifying and referencing variables and procedures. Unlike some other languages, T allows these names to be arbitrarily long. The normal rules for creating symbols are these:

- You may use a sequence of letters, digits, and punctuation marks, including:
  `* $ % ! ^ = & | ~ < > - _ ? + :`

- You should not use the other punctuation characters, including: `' " # , ;
  ( ) [ ] { } . ' / \` or the space character.

- The identifier should not correspond to an existing T symbol, such as `min`, `max`, or `remainder`, unless you intend to redefine that symbol, which T allows you to do. If you redefine a T procedure, it will not necessarily do what it did previously. *Caveat programmer.*

- You may use both upper- and lowercase letters. T will automatically convert to uppercase. This means that `VAR` and `var` and `Var` are the same symbol in T.

- You should not use a number as a symbol. `FOUR-POINT-OH` is a symbol, but `4.0` is a number.

Here are some acceptable symbols:

```
x
y
Variable-1
3RD-BASE
ANSWER592
*GOAL*
Just-try-to-type-this-the-same-way-twice-without-an-error!
john_loves_mary
love+marriage
slot:filler
```

And here are some unacceptable symbols (with reasons following the semi-colon):

```
3                    ;  number
.700                 ;  number
"SYMBOL"             ;  contains  "'s
(x)                  ;  contains ( and )
```

2.6 Defining Variables and Procedures

Now that we can create symbols, we can use them to identify objects, such as variables or procedures. A symbol's value can be specified using the T special form **define**.

```
> (define x 7)            ;  the symbol x  is defined and given the value 7
7

> (define y 4)
4

> (+ x y)
11

> (- x y)
3

> (define my-add +)       ;  the symbol my-add  is defined to be the
#{Procedure 61 ADD}       ;  same as +
```

```
> (my-add 3 4 5)
12
```

The last two examples show how one can define synonyms, giving another name to an existing procedure. Many T procedures already have synonyms. For example, **add** is equivalent to **+**. T synonyms are listed in the summaries at the end of each chapter.

In T, you can also use **define** to create your own procedures or even change the definitions of existing procedures. Here are some examples.

```
> (define (square x) (* x x))
#{Procedure 62 SQUARE}

> (square 4)
16

> (square -5)
25

> (define (square-sum x y) (+ (square x) (square y)))
#{Procedure 64 SQUARE-SUM}

> (square-sum 3 4)
25

> (square-sum 5 12)
169
```

Here we have defined two new procedures: **square** and **square-sum**. There are several things to notice.

- The names of the procedures, **square** and **square-sum**, are T symbols.

- **define**'s first argument is an expression which contains the name of the new procedure followed by the names of the arguments to that procedure.

- The names of the arguments to the new procedure are *local* to that procedure. Thus, the x in **square** is not related to the x in **square-sum**. Local variables are discussed at length in chapter 5.

- A new procedure can have as many or as few arguments defined as necessary: **square-sum** has two arguments, x and y; and **square** has only one, x.

- A new procedure can call any procedure, including another programmer-defined procedure: **square-sum** calls **square** twice.

- The value returned by **define** is *undefined*. Some value may be returned, but the language does not specify what that value is. The implementation used to generate the examples in this book prints: `#{Procedure <number> <name of procedure>}` to represent the data structure that holds the procedure.

One other feature of T is that, unlike languages like Pascal, the order in which procedures are *defined* doesn't matter. What is important is the intuitive notion that a procedure must be defined before it is actually called. So, in the above example, we could have *defined* the procedure **square-sum** prior to defining the procedure **square** which it called. However, we have to define **square** before we call **square-sum**, since **square** is called by **square-sum**.

The programmer should note that T does not make a distinction between procedures and functions. T procedures return values that may be used by other procedures. Throughout this book we uniformly refer to these objects as procedures, though in many instances they seem to behave like things that are called functions in other languages.

T does distinguish between procedures and special forms, such as **define**. Special forms are also known as macros, and are discussed in detail in chapter 11. We will identify special forms as they are introduced in each chapter.

2.7   File Input

By this time, you may have discovered that typing procedure definitions to the interpreter is a tedious and error-prone task. This is especially true if you wish to use some procedure in more than one terminal session. You want to avoid having to type the same definition repeatedly.

The answer to this problem is simple: disk files. You can use a text editor to create a file containing T procedure definitions. Then, you start up T, and tell the interpreter to load in the procedure (or any T expression) from the file.

There is a convention that T disk files have particular file extensions, such as `.t`. So, suppose that you created a file named **convert.t**, which contains the definitions of two procedures for converting Fahrenheit and Celsius temperatures. That file might look like this:

```
(herald convert)
;;;     convert.t

;  (f-to-c ftemp)  returns the corresponding Celsius temperature.
;                  The formula is:  C = 5/9 (F - 32)
(define (f-to-c ftemp)
    (/ (* 5
          (- ftemp 32))
       9))
```

```
;  (c-to-f ctemp)  returns the corresponding Fahrenheit
;                      temperature. The formula is:  F = (9/5 C) + 32
(define (c-to-f ctemp)
   (+ (* 9
         (/ ctemp 5))
      32))
```

There are several things to note at this point. First, the line (herald convert) which appears at the top of the file is used to provide information about the contents of the file for other T programs that may process the file. There are several advanced features associated with the herald form. For now, all you need to include is a file identifier following herald.

Second, the semicolons that appear in the file are comment characters. T ignores everything else on that line (including other comment characters) and skips to the next line. It is a good idea to add comments for every procedure that you define. The comments don't make the code run faster (or slower), but they do help the humans who have to read the code.

Third, the procedures are formatted in the file with progressive indentation to indicate the levels of nesting. This indentation, like the comments, is solely for the benefit of the programmer – not the T interpreter. T would work just as well if the procedures in convert.t were written:

```
(define (f-to-c ftemp) (/ (* 5 (- ftemp 32)) 9)) (define (c-to-f
ctemp) (+ (* 9 (/ ctemp 5)) 32))
```

but chances are that you would have some difficulty understanding the code.

The basic issue here is one of programming style. As a programmer, you need to realize that sooner or later someone will have to read your code and try to understand how it works (or why it doesn't). That someone could be you, six months after you first wrote the program. Therefore, you should take pains to make your code, as it appears in a file, as comprehensible as possible. Clarity of exposition is sometimes more important than getting the program to work in the first place.

Your program should be visually clear and clean. The file should be broken up into a series of procedure definitions, each with appropriate comments. Each procedure definition should be formatted in the file in a consistent and logical way. Here is a set of guidelines for formatting a procedure definition:

- Start procedure definitions at the left margin.

- Try to put a procedure definition all on one line, if not more than half a line long (40 characters), e.g.,
  `(define (plus2 x) (+ x 2))`

- If the procedure won't fit on one line, put the procedure name and argument list on the first line, and then one expression per line thereafter until the end of the procedure definition.

- Increase indentation on a new line if the previous line has an open left parenthesis. You may wish to indent to the second left parenthesis on the preceding line. Otherwise, four spaces provides adequate indentation.

- Decrease indentation on a new line if the previous line has a right parenthesis which closes a left parenthesis from an earlier line.

- Otherwise, align the new line with the previous line.

These guidelines should help make the appearance of your procedure definitions reflect the logical structure of the procedure. For example,

```
(define (complex-procedure x y z)
    (+ (square x)
       (* (min y z)
          (max (abs x)
               (remainder y z)))
       (- z x)))
```

By virtue of the indentation, one can see at a glance that **square**, *, and − are at the same level of nesting and thus are all arguments to +; that * has two procedural arguments (**min** and **max**), and that **max** also has two procedural arguments (**abs** and **remainder**). Compare this with the following, and you should be convinced of the utility of indentation.

```
(define (complex-procedure x y z) (+ (square x) (* (min y z) (max
(abs x) (remainder y z))) (- z x)))
```

We can now return to the **convert.t** file example. We enter T and read in this file using the **load** procedure:

```
> (load "convert.t")
;Loading "convert.t" into USER-ENV
F-TO-C C-TO-C #{Procedure 97 C-TO-C}

> (f-to-c 32)
0

> (c-to-f 100)
212
```

The procedure **load**, with a filename in "double quotes" as its argument, enters a READ-EVAL-PRINT loop taking its input from the given file. It READs in each expression, it EVALuates the expression, and it PRINTs the resulting value. When it reaches the end of the file, it usually returns the value of the last expression that it evaluated. Generally, **load** is used for its side-effects, not the value returned.

The programmer should realize that **read**, **eval**, and **print** are actual T procedures. We discuss **read** and **print** in chapter 7, and **eval** is presented in chapter 15.

When T starts up, it looks for a user file called **init.t** and automatically loads that file if it exists. Thus, it is convenient to put procedure definitions that you use frequently in your **init.t** file.

Files can also load other files. So, you could have your **init.t** file load other files, simply by including the appropriate command, such as (**load "utilities.t"**) if you have a file with that name.

If you find an error in a procedure after you have loaded it into T from a file, you can leave T temporarily, modify the procedure definition in the file, and then return to T. You can use the **stop** procedure, which will return you to the monitor level, from which you can edit your file, exit the editor, and then resume T by typing T. This will return you to your previous state in T. At this point, you can reload your file into T. Of course, on a workstation with multiple windows, you should be able to edit a file window without stopping the T process window.

2.8 Predicates

Predicates are procedures that answer *yes/no* or *true/false* questions like the following:

- Is the argument a number?

- Is the argument greater than zero?

- Is the first argument equal to the second argument?

- Is the argument negative?

Predicates, in answering such questions, will return the value *true* or the value *false*.

In the T language, *true* is given as the value of the symbol **T**, and is notated as "**#t**." That is, the letter T is a symbol which has the value of true. The value *false* is indicated by the empty list: (), or notated as "**#f**." In the language T, the empty list () is also represented by the symbol NIL. The quoted empty list '() evaluates to the regular empty list, which has the logical value of false. (See section 3.1 for a discussion of the role of quote marks.) In most situations, anything non-NIL will be equivalent to true.

```
> T                          ; T  evaluates to true: #t
#t

> nil                        ; the value of nil  is ()
()

> '()                        ; the value of '()  is ()
()

> '#f
()

> '#T
#t
```

There is a morphological convention in T regarding predicates: most predicates are named by symbols which end in a question mark. Here are some examples of numeric predicates. Their names are perspicuous.

```
> (equal? 4 4)
#t

> (equal? 4 5)
()

> (less? 4 5)
#t

> (greater? 4 5)
()

> (not-equal? 4 5)
#t

> (not-less? 4 5)
()

> (not-greater? 4 5)
#t

> (zero? .01)
()

> (negative? .01)
()
```

```
> (positive? .01)
#t

> (number? 45)
#t

> (integer? 4.5)
()

> (float? 4.5)
#t

> (ratio? 5/2)        ;  A ratio is the quotient of two integers.
#t

> (odd? 5)
#t

> (even? 5)
()
```

By now it should be obvious that there are different types of numbers in
T, including integers, floating point numbers, and ratios. These differences are a
reflection of computer implementation efficiencies, and can be exploited by the programmer on occasion. However, T allows the programmer to ignore the difference.
Usually, T will convert one type of number to another type if needed. This process
is called *coercion*. The procedure **->integer** presented above would convert a ratio
or floating point number to an integer. The procedure **->float** converts integers
and ratios to floating point.

For example,

```
> (equal? 17 17.0)
#t

> (equal? 17 17.00000001)
()

> (* 3.2 10)
32.0

> (/ 5.0 2)
2.5
```

```
> (/ 5 2)
5/2

> (quotient 5 2)                    ;  integer division
2

> (->float 5/2)
2.5

> (->integer 5/2)
2

> (->integer (->float 5/2))
2
```

There is a hierarchy of generality for numbers, given by the following simple list. The symbol > should be read as "includes all the."

    numbers > reals > rationals > integers > small integers

In T, reals are floating point numbers, rationals are ratios, integers are fixed point numbers, and small integers are termed *fixnums*. Other arithmetic operations which distinguish among these types are discussed in chapter 16.

2.9   Conditionals

Predicates are normally used in tests in computer programs for conditional execution of code. For example, IF `<predicate-1>` is true THEN execute `<expression-1>` ELSE execute `<expression-2>`. This IF-THEN-ELSE conditional construct which prevails in computer languages corresponds to T's special form `if` and the more general `cond` form.

The `if` form takes two or three arguments. In either case, the first argument is a predicate. If the predicate is true (actually, just non-NIL), then the second argument is evaluated. What objects are non-NIL? Numbers, symbols, procedures — anything except `nil` and `()`. If the predicate is false, then the third argument, if present, is evaluated. If the predicate is false and the third argument is missing, then the value of `if` is undefined. Here is an example.

```
> (if t 1 2)
1

> (if nil 1 2)
2
```

```
> (if (odd? 3) 1)
1
```

The **if** form has the virtue of brevity. However, the **cond** form provides greater generality. The syntax of **cond**, with its paired predicate-expression clauses, is a bit different from other T expressions. Here is a syntactic outline of **cond**:

```
(cond ( <predicate-1> <expressions-1> )
      ( <predicate-2> <expressions-2> )
      . . .
      ( <predicate-n> <expressions-n> ) )
```

The semantics of **cond** is fairly simple. Predicate clauses are evaluated in sequence from top to bottom until one of them is found to be true, or until there are no more predicate clauses. If one of the predicate clauses has a non-NIL value, the corresponding expression clauses are evaluated, and the rest of the predicate and expression clauses are ignored.

There can be any number of expression clauses (including zero) following a predicate clause. If a predicate is evaluated to be non-NIL, but has no expression clause following it, then **cond** returns the value of the predicate clause itself. Otherwise, **cond** returns the value of the *last* expression clause.

The **cond** construct is a very general form of the normal IF-THEN-ELSE constructions found in most programming languages. The IF-THEN-ELSE form of **cond** would be

```
(cond ( <IF-PREDICATE> <THEN-EXPRESSION> )
      ( else          <ELSE-EXPRESSION> ) )
```

The **else** beneath the IF-PREDICATE above indicates a predicate which always evaluates to true. So, if IF-PREDICATE is true, then the THEN-EXPRESSION will be performed. If IF-PREDICATE is false, then the ELSE-EXPRESSION will be evaluated since **else** is always true. That is, the symbol **else** is defined to have a non-NIL value.

Here are two examples using **cond**.

We shall define the signum procedure, which returns -1 for negative numbers, 1 for positive numbers, and 0 for zero.

```
> (define (signum x)
    (cond ((positive? x) 1)
          ((negative? x) -1)
          ((zero? x) 0) ))
#{Procedure 28 SIGNUM}

> (signum 5)
1
```

```
> (signum  -23.67891)
-1

> (signum (+ 1 -1))
0
```

The procedure **interest-rate** shows how return on investment might be indexed to the size of the investment.

```
> (define (interest-rate money)
     (cond ((less? money 0) 0)
           ((less? money 1000) 5)
           ((less? money 10000) 8)
           ((less? money 100000) 10)
           (else 15)))
#{Procedure 29 INTEREST-RATE}

> (interest-rate 99)
5

> (interest-rate 5000000)
15
```

In addition to the IF-THEN-ELSE conditional construction afforded by **if** and **cond**, T provides several other basic conditional functions, including **and**, **or**, and **not**. Here are examples of these functions.

```
> (and 3 4 5)                  ; if no argument is (), and  returns the
5                              ; value of the last argument

> (and 3 (even? 5))            ; and  takes a variable number of
()                             ; arguments

> (or 3 4 5)                   ; or  returns the first non-NIL argument,
3                              ; evaluating from left to right

> (or (even? 3) (equal? 2 1))
()

> (not (or 3 4 5))             ; not  returns the opposite truth value
()                             ; of its argument

> (not (or (even? 3) (equal? 2 1)))
#t
```

```
> (not (not (or 3 4 5)))
#t
```

The behavior of **and**, **or**, and **not** is fairly plain:

- **and** returns () if any argument is false, otherwise, it returns the value of the last argument.

- **or** returns () if all arguments are false, otherwise, it returns the value of the first non-NIL argument.

- **not** negates the truth value of its argument, returning () if the argument is true, and T if the argument is false.

There is one additional feature of which to be aware. Both **and** and **or** are different from regular T procedures in one important respect: they don't always evaluate all their arguments. In this respect, they are like **define** and **cond**. In fact, one could simulate most of the behavior of **cond** using **and** and **or** as follows.

cond construction:

```
(cond  ( <predicate-1> <expression-1> )
       ( <predicate-2> <expression-2> )
       . . .
       ( <predicate-n> <expression-n> ) )
```

and/or version of cond construction:

```
(or    (and <predicate-1> (or <expression-1> T ))
       (and <predicate-2> (or <expression-2> T ))
       . . .
       (and <predicate-n> (or <expression-n> T )) )
```

This example bears some analysis. In the **cond** case, each predicate clause is evaluated from top to bottom until one of them yields a value which is not false. At that point, the respective expression clause is evaluated, after which its value is returned and no further clauses are evaluated. We see the analogous behavior with the **and/or** version. If `<predicate-i>` has a non-NIL value, then the corresponding expression clause, `<expression-i>`, is evaluated. The clause `(or <expression-i> T)` will always return a non-NIL value, thus the surrounding `(and ...)` clause will return a non-NIL value, which will then satisfy the top-level `(or ...)` clause. At that point, none of the subsequent clauses are evaluated. The reader should note that this definition of **cond** does not always behave like the true **cond**. See exercise 2.11.7.

This demonstrates a significant property of **and**, **or**, and for that matter, **cond**, namely that they sometimes avoid evaluating some of their arguments. By virtue of this important property, they are special forms and not procedures. They act as syntactic keywords. The T interpreter treats these functions differently from procedures such as `remainder`, `abs`, or `not`, which always evaluate all their arguments. The procedures which you create with the special form `define` will evaluate all their arguments. In chapter 11 we shall see how to create new special forms.

Here is another example of creating a conditional procedure, this time without the use of the `cond` construction. The predicate `go-to-movie?`, defined below, shows how `and`, `or`, and `not` might be combined.

```
> (define (go-to-movie? age cash)
    (or  (and (less? age 12)             ;  child rates
              (greater? cash 2.00))
         (and (not-less? age 12)         ;  adult rates
              (less? age 65)
              (greater? cash 4.00))
         (and (not (less? age 65))       ;  senior citizen rates
              (greater? cash 2.50))))
#{Procedure 36 GO-TO-MOVIE?}

> (go-to-movie? 8 3.00)            ;  an 8-year-old with $3
#t

> (go-to-movie? 16 3.00)          ;  a 16-year-old with $3
()
```

Note in the above example that `(not-less? ...)` and `(not (less? ...))` are logically equivalent.

2.10   Dot Notation

In this chapter we have covered a lot of ground: the T interpreter, arithmetic, symbols, procedure definition, file input, indentation, comments, predicates, and conditional expressions. We shall close with one brief topic: dot notation.

As mentioned above, some procedures and special forms take an indefinite number of arguments. For example, the addition and multiplication procedures will work for any number of numbers. Similarly, the `define` and `cond` special forms allow an arbitrary number of clauses in the expression body. To notate an expression argument which may occur zero or more times, we place a dot surrounded by spaces – " . " – before the name of that argument. Thus, the addition and multiplication procedures may be notated as follows.

```
(+ . numbers)
(* . numbers)
```

indicating that each procedure takes zero or more numbers as arguments. Similarly, **define** and **cond** may be notated in a like manner.

```
        (define (variable . arguments) . expressions)
        (cond . clauses)
;       where each clause has the form
        (predicate . expressions)
```

This notation for **define** indicates that there may be zero or more arguments in a procedure definition, and that the body of the definition will consist of zero or more expressions. A **cond** form may have zero or more clauses, each of which consists of a predicate followed by zero or more expressions.

In the next chapter, we shall examine the list structure that underlies this notational convention.

2.11   Exercises

At the end of most chapters, the reader will find a set of exercises which employ the concepts presented in that chapter. Following the heading for each exercise is a number in brackets, such as [5], with an optional asterisk, such as [7*]. The number indicates the relative difficulty of the exercise on a 10-point scale, where a [1] is trivial ("What color is an orange?") and a [10] is quite challenging ("Write a T predicate **halts?**, which returns true if a given T procedure halts, otherwise, false.") The asterisk indicates that the answer to the given exercise appears in appendix C.

2.11.1   Expression Drill [2]

Evaluate all of the following expressions by hand. Then check your answers with the help of your T interpreter.

```
(+ 5 (- 7 2))
(+ 5 (+ 7 2))
(+ 5 (+ 7 (+ 1 1)))
(* (+ 1 6) (* 2 3))
(* (* 3 2) (+ 6 1))
(/ 30 (- (+ 7 3) (max 1 (max 2 (max 5 (max 3 4))))))
(/ 30 (+ (+ 7 2) (min 1 (min 2 (min 5 (min 3 4))))))
(remainder 25 (- (+ 7 3) (max 1 (max 2 (max 5 (max 3 4))))))
(remainder 25 (+ (+ 7 2) (min 1 (min 2 (min 5 (min 3 4))))))
(abs (remainder -7 (min 1 (min 2 (min 5 (min 3 4))))))
(+ (->integer 4.4) (->integer -3.5))
(->integer (+ 4.4 -3.5))
```

2.11.2   Defining New Procedures [2*]

Write definitions for the new T procedures demonstrated below. Then check your results with the T interpreter.

For these and subsequent exercises, you should create a file using a text editor and define the appropriate procedures, using proper indentation and comments. Then, start up T and read the file in using **load**.

```
> (add2 5)              ;  add 2 to argument
7

> (add5 5)              ;  add 5 to argument
10

> (double 7)            ;  double argument
14

> (min-abs4 3 5 -2 -8)  ;  find the minimum of the absolute value
2                       ;  of four numbers

> (max-abs4 3 5 -2 -8)  ;  find the maximum of the absolute value
8                       ;  of four numbers
```

2.11.3   Foreign Procedure Names [1*]

It is possible to give new names to existing T procedures. Define the foreign language versions of T procedures as demonstrated below.

```
> (ajoutez 2 5)         ;  French addition
7

> (retranchez 7 2)      ;  French subtraction
5

> (hochstmas 4 7)       ;  German maximum
7

> (multiplizieren 5 3)  ;  German multiplication
15

> (njia-ya-kutokea)     ;  Swahili exit for T

$                       ;  monitor prompt returned after exiting T
```

2.11.4 Zeller's Congruence [3]

We shall now ask you to write a more complicated procedure, based on a formula called Zeller's congruence, which computes the corresponding day of the week for a given date, after the year A.D. 1582. For a date, such as September 1, 1983, one breaks the date up into five separate numbers:

- N: the number of the day of the month. Here, $N = 1$.

- M: the number of the month, *using March as the first month*. This is used to allow for the extra day in February on leap years. Here, $M = 7$ for September.

- C: the hundreds of the year. Here, $C = 19$.

- Y: the year of the century. Here, $Y = 83$.

- L: 1 for a leap year, 0 otherwise. Here, $L = 0$.

The formula returns a number, d, between 0 and 6 corresponding to the day of the week, where $d = 0$ is Sunday, $d = 1$ is Monday, etc.

Here is the formula:

$$d = (N + [2.6M - 0.2] + Y + [Y/4] + [C/4] - 2C - (1 + L)[M/11]) \, mod \, 7$$

- where $[x]$ indicates *greatest integer not greater than x*, so $[3.14159] = 3$

- and where *mod x* indicates *remainder after division by x*, so $29 \, mod \, 7 = 1$

Write a T procedure which calculates Zeller's congruence, given the five numbers.

```
> (zeller 1 7 19 83 0)      ;    1 September 19 83 no leap year
4                           ;    4 = Thursday
```

Optional thought exercise. If you wish to convince yourself that this formula actually works, you might try a simple inductive proof. First show that if the formula is correct for any given date, then it is correct for the next succeeding date. For example, if it correctly identifies some date as occurring on a Wednesday, then it will accurately identify the next date as a Thursday. Second, show that it is correct for some date. Given these two features, you may conclude that the formula is correct for all dates, since the formula (1) accurately cycles through successive dates, and (2) is correct for a specific date.

If you are more ambitious, you might try a derivation of the formula.

2.11.5 signum and interest-rate Redefined [3]

Redefine the **signum** and **interest-rate** procedures given above, but use the **and, or,** and **not** constructions instead of **cond.**

2.11.6   go-to-movie? Redefined [3]

Redefine the `go-to-movie?` predicate given above, but use **cond** instead of the **and, or,** and **not** constructions.

2.11.7   cond vs. and/or [4*]

On page 25, we simulated **cond** using **and** and **or**. Under what conditions will the **and/or** version behave differently from the real **cond**? Give specific examples.

2.11.8   and/or Redefined [3]

Rewrite the following expressions using only **cond** instead of **and** and **or**, respectively.

```
(and predicate-1 predicate-2 predicate-3 predicate-4)

(or  predicate-1 predicate-2 predicate-3 predicate-4)
```

2.11.9   floor and ceiling [3*]

Create two procedures, **floor** and **ceiling**. **floor** returns the largest integer less than or equal to its argument, and **ceiling** returns the smallest integer greater than or equal to its argument. Here are some examples.

```
> (floor 5)
5

> (floor 5.2)
5

> (floor -5.2)
-6

> (ceiling 5)
5

> (ceiling 5.2)
6

> (ceiling -5.2)
-5
```

2.11.10   Leap Year [3*]

February 29th appears in years that obey the following conditions: the year is divisible by 4 and the year is not divisible by 100, unless the year is also divisible by 400. Thus, 1984 is leap year. 1900 is not a leap year, but 2000 is.

Write a predicate `leap-year?` which answers the question *Is this year a leap year?* For example,

```
> (leap-year? 1983)
()

> (leap-year? 1984)
#t

> (leap-year? 1900)
()

> (leap-year? 2000)
#t
```

2.11.11   Zeller Revisited [3*]

Rewrite the procedure to evaluate Zeller's congruence (exercise 2.11.4, page 29) using the `leap-year?` procedure described above. The procedure `son-of-zeller` will take only three arguments: day, month number (using the Zeller numbering of months), and year.

```
> (son-of-zeller 1 7 1983)   ;  1 September 1983
4                            ;  4 = Thursday
```

2.12   Chapter Summary

- T is an interpreted or conversational language.

- The T interpreter cycles through a READ-EVAL-PRINT loop.

- T arithmetic procedures (with synonyms given in brackets):

```
+           ;  addition [add]
add1        ;  addition of 1
subtract1   ;  subtraction of 1
-           ;  subtraction and negation [subtract] [negate]
*           ;  multiplication [multiply]
/           ;  division [divide]
remainder   ;  remainder from division
mod         ;  modulus arithmetic
quotient    ;  integer division
->integer   ;  convert to integer
max         ;  maximum value
min         ;  minimum value
abs         ;  absolute value
```

- Other T procedures and special forms:

```
exit        ;  leave the T interpreter
stop        :  temporarily leave T
reset       ;  return to top-level
define      ;  create a procedure
herald      ;  identifier at the top of a file
load        ;  input a file to the interpreter
```

- T uses prefix notation with parentheses as delimiters.

- T allows the programmer to recover gracefully from errors.

- The generic type in T is the *object*. Objects encountered so far include numbers (integers, ratios, and floats), symbols, and procedures.

- Symbolic names can be arbitrarily long, allowing for meaningful identifiers.

- Values may be assigned to symbolic names using **define**.

- New procedures may be created and existing procedures modified using **define**.

- T procedures may be loaded in from disk files.

- It is important to indent and comment your programs to make them easier for humans to grasp.

- Predicates are procedures that answer true/false questions.

- True and false are given as the values of **T** and **()**, respectively, and notated as **#t** and **#f**.

- T predicates (with synonyms given in brackets):

```
(equal? number1 number2)           ;   [=]
(less? number1 number2)            ;   [<]
(greater? number1 number2)         ;   [>]
(not-equal? number1 number2)       ;   [N=]
(not-less? number1 number2)        ;   [>=]
(not-greater? number1 number2)     ;   [<=]
(zero? number)                     ;   [=0?]
(negative? number)                 ;   [<0?]
(positive? number)                 ;   [>0?]
(number? object)
(integer? object)
(float? object)
(ratio? object)
(odd? integer)
(even? integer)
```

- T conditional constructs:

```
(if test consequent alternate)
(cond . clauses)
(and . tests)
(or . tests)
(not object)
```

- Special forms are different from procedures. Special forms might not evaluate all their arguments. Examples of special forms encountered so far are **cond**, **and**, **or**, and **define**.

- T uses a dot surrounded by spaces – " . " – to indicate an expression argument which may occur zero or more times.

Chapter 3

Lists

As some day it may happen that a victim must be found,
I've got a little list – I've got a little list.

◇ WILLIAM SCHWENCK GILBERT, *The Mikado (1885)*

I reckon – when I count at all –
First – Poets – Then the Sun –
Then Summer – Then the Heaven of God –
And then – the List is done –

◇ EMILY DICKINSON, *No. 569 (c. 1862)*

In the previous chapter, we introduced the basic READ-EVAL-PRINT cycle of the T interpreter using familiar arithmetic procedures. We saw how to define procedures and load procedure definitions into the T interpreter from disk files.

We now turn our attention to the fundamental motif of T: the list data structure. Lists have a very simple notation: sequences of objects, such as numbers, symbols, or other lists, enclosed by parentheses. Here are some examples of lists.

```
(1 2 3 4 5)
(this is a list)
((this) (is) (a list) (of lists))
()                                    ; the empty list, also known as NIL
(define (add1 x) (+ x 1))
(+ (abs (remainder 29 7)) (* 17 8))
```

The last three lists could also be evaluated directly as expressions, demonstrating that lists can represent either programs, data, or both. This is one of the most important properties of T. It allows one to create programs which can create and modify other programs. This principle is fundamental in many artificial intelligence applications of T.

34

3.1 List Operations: car, cdr, and cons

There are numerous operations one can perform on lists. Most involve *selectors* and *constructors*. A selector takes a list and returns a specified part of it. A constructor makes a new list from other lists or symbols. The primary selectors are **car**, which returns the first element of a list, and **cdr** (pronounced *COULD-er*), which returns all *but* the first element of a list. The **car** of a list is often called the *head*, and the **cdr** is called the *tail*.

The names **car** and **cdr** are vestigial artifacts. They come from the machine language acronyms used on the initial implementation of LISP: **car** was the Contents of Address part of Register, and **cdr** was the Contents of Decrement part of Register. One might expect that such arcane argot would fade over the years and be replaced by more appealing and perspicuous terms such as **head** and **tail**. This has not happened. The terms **car** and **cdr** are alive and flourishing and likely to outlive the author of this book, and perhaps the readers as well.

The primitive list constructor is **cons**, which simply takes two arguments and joins them to form a new structure which is notated as a list indicated by a surrounding pair of parentheses. The first argument to **cons** becomes the **car** of the new structure, and the second argument becomes the **cdr**.

Another very useful function for dealing with lists is the special form **quote**, which merely returns its argument without evaluating it. Thus, the value of **(quote x)** is the symbol **x**, regardless of what the value of **x** is. A programmer will often want to suppress evaluation of certain arguments, such as when passing data to a procedure. In these (frequent) cases, the programmer may use **quote** to keep the data from being evaluated.

T provides an abbreviation for **quote**, namely the single quote mark: **'**, so **'x** is the same as **(quote x)**. Note that the single quote mark (**'**) is different from the double quote mark (**"**), which is likewise different from two single quote marks (**''**).

Here are some examples.

```
> (quote (a b c))
(A B C)                          ;  Note: T converts symbols to uppercase

> '(a b c)
(A B C)

> '()
()

> (define x (+ 2 3 5 7 11))  ;  the +  expression is evaluated
28

> (define y '(+ 2 3 5 7 11)) ;  the quote  prevents the evaluation
(+ 2 3 5 7 11)               ;  of the +  expression
```

```
> (car y)
+

> (cdr y)
(2 3 5 7 11)

> (car (cdr '(a b c)))          ;  you can nest  car's and  cdr's, just
B                               ;  as you can nest any expression


> (cdr 'a)                      ;  car  and  cdr require the argument
                                ;  to be a list
 ** Error: some argument didn't answer true to LIST? as expected
   (CDR ... A ...)

>> (reset)                      ;  leave break loop

Top level

> (cons 'a '(b c))
(A B C)

> (cons (car '(a b c)) (cdr '(a b c)))  ;  a list is just its
(A B C)                         ;  car cons 'd to its cdr

> (cons 'a '())
(A)

> (cons 'a 'b)
(A . B)
```

The last two examples demonstrate the difference between a *list* and a *proper list*.
A proper list always ends with the empty list. That is to say that the final **cdr** of
a proper list is always NIL. If the final **cdr** of a list is non-NIL, then it is printed
out using the dot notation of the last example above. The list in the last example
is called a *dotted pair* or an *improper list*. The dot indicates that what follows is
the final **cdr**. In the other examples, it was implicit that the lists ended with the
empty list.

It's important to realize that **cons** creates a new list, without modifying the
values of the **car** or **cdr**. That is, the expression   (cons x y) yields a new result
without changing either x or y, just as   (+ x y) produces a new value without
modifying x or y.

By convention, the **car** and **cdr** of nil are **nil**.

```
> (car nil)
()

> (cdr nil)
()

> (car '())
()

> (cdr '())
()
```

3.2   List Predicates

T distinguishes among numerous types of expressions: symbols, numbers (integers, floating point numbers), lists, and others. We have already used some predicates for detecting different types of numbers, such as **integer?** and **float?**. There are similar predicates for lists and symbols. Also, just as there are predicates for comparing numbers, such as **greater?** and **equal?**, there are predicates for comparing lists.

```
> (symbol? 'x)        ; true if argument is a symbol
#t

> (symbol? 34)
()

> (symbol? '(x))
()

> (symbol? 'NIL)      ; NIL  is a symbol whose value is ()
#t

> (symbol? '())       ; ()  is the empty list which is often called NIL
()

> (number? 'x)        ; true if argument is an integer or float
()

> (pair? 'x)          ; true if argument has a car and cdr
()
```

```
> (pair? '(x))
#t

> (atom? 'x)          ; (not (pair? x))
#t                    ;   an  atom is any object that is not a pair,
                      ;   including symbols, numbers, and ()

> (pair? '())         ;  ()  is not a pair – it doesn't point to a car and cdr
()                    ;  ()   is a list (see below)

> (list? '(x y))      ;  true if argument is a list
#t

> (list? '())         ;  ()  is a list – the empty list
#t

> (proper-list? '(x y)) ;  true if argument is a list and ends in NIL
#t

> (proper-list? '())
#t

> (proper-list? (cons 'x 'y))
()

> (null? '())         ;  true if argument is the empty list
#t                    ;  null?  is logically equivalent to not
```

The above predicates are all *type* predicates. That is, they check the data type
of the given object. Type predicates take only one argument. There are also
comparison predicates, which check to see if some relation holds between the two
given arguments. The arithmetic predicates **greater?** and **less?** were examples
of comparison predicates. Here are two important comparison predicates for lists
and symbols.

```
> (eq? 'a 'a)         ;  eq?  is a comparison predicate which returns
#t                    ;  true if arguments are  exactly the same objects

> (eq? 1.5 1.5)       ;  use  equal? for comparing numbers
()
```

```
> (eq? '(a) '(a))      ;  two lists have different memory addresses, but
()                     ;  may point to some of the same objects
                       ;  See Section 3.7 below

> (eq? (car '(a)) (car '(a)))    ;  a symbol always points to exactly
#t                               ;  one memory location

> (eq? (cdr '(a b c)) '(b c))
()

> (alikev? '(a b c) '(a b c))    ;  true if arguments have elements which
#t                               ;  are equivalent, but not necessarily
                                 ;  having the same memory locations

> (alikev? '(+ 2 2) 4)           ;  the list  (+ 2 2) is not the same
()                               ;  as the number  4

> (alikev? (+ 2 2) 4)            ;  the value of  (+ 2 2) equals 4
#t

> (equal? (+ 2 2) 4)             ;  the value of  (+ 2 2) equals 4
#t

> (alikev? (cdr '(a b c)) '(b c))
#t
```

3.3   More Selectors

We now have a set of basic predicates and operations for dealing with list expressions. There are more advanced list operations that we can use for manipulating lists.

First, T provides a shorthand for dealing with nested **car**'s and **cdr**'s.

(car (car x))	=	(caar x)
(car (cdr x))	=	(cadr x)	(Pronounced *CAD-er*)
(cdr (car x))	=	(cdar x)	(Pronounced *cuh-DAR*)
(cdr (cdr x))	=	(cddr x)
(car (caar x))	=	(caaar x)
(cdr (caar x))	=	(cdaar x)
. . .		
(car (cadar x))	=	(caadar x)
(cdr (cadar x))	=	(cdadar x)
. . .		

The letters **a** and **d** are embedded between **c** and **r** to reflect a sequence of nested car's and cdr's. It should be apparent how one would define these procedures. In T, they are supported up to four levels of nesting, e.g., **(cadddr x)**, but not five.

There are additional operators for picking out specific parts of lists.

```
> (nth '(a b c d) 2)        ; (nth list i)  picks the  ith element
C                           ; of  list, starting with 0 from
                            ; left to right. (Pronounced ENTH)

> (nth '(a b c d) 0)
A

> (nth '(a b c d) 4)

  ** Error: illegal index into a list
   (NTH (A B C D) 4)
>> (reset)

T: Top Level

> (nthcdr '(a b c d) 2)     ; (nthcdr list i)  picks the  ith tail of
 (C D)                      ; of  list, starting with 0 from left
                            ; to right. (Pronounced ENTH-could-er)

> (nthcdr '(a b c d) 0)
(A B C D)

> (last '(a b c d))         ; (last list)  returns the last
D                           ; element of list.

> (last '(a b c . d))       ; but  last assumes that lists end in ()
C                           ; caveat programmer
```

```
> (lastcdr '(a b c d))        ; (lastcdr list)  returns the last pair of
(D)                           ; list.

> (lastcdr '(a b c ()))
(())

> (lastcdr '(a b c . d))
(C . D)

> (sublist '(a b c d) 1 2)    ; (sublist list start count)  returns a
(B C)                         ; copy of  list of length  count
                              ; beginning with the  start element from
                              ; the left (where 0 is the first one).

> (sublist '(a b c d) 0 1)
(A)
```

It is important to notice that these procedures index the top-level elements of the list from left to right starting with 0. So a five-element list, either simple or complex, would be indexed as shown below:

```
(a  b  c  d  e)
 0  1  2  3  4

((a)  (b b b b)  ((c)  c)  (((d)))  e)
 0     1          2        3        4
```

So if the latter list were bound to x, then   (nth x 0) would be (A), and   (nth x 1) would be   (B B B B), and so forth.

3.4   More Constructors: list and append

T also provides some more constructors in addition to **cons**. The main ones are **list** and **append**, demonstrated below.

```
> (list 'a 'b 'c)             ; returns a proper list of its arguments
(A B C)


> (list)                      ; list  takes a variable number of arguments
()
```

```
> (list 1 2 3 4 5)
(1 2 3 4 5)

> (list 'a)
(A)

> (cons 'a (list 'b 'c))        ;   contrast with next example
(A B C)

> (list 'a (list 'b 'c))
(A (B C))

> (list '(a b) '(c d) '(e f))
((A B) (C D) (E F))
```

; append   constructs a new list whose elements are from the argument lists
```
> (append '(a b) '(c d) '(e f))
(A B C D E F)

> (append 'a '(b c))

  ** Error: expected a list, but got an atom instead
    (... . A)

>> (reset)

T: Top Level

> (append '(a) '(b c))
(A B C)

> (list 'a '(b c))
(A (B C))
```

Both list and append can take a variable number of arguments. Using the dot notation introduced in the preceding chapter and discussed above, we can produce a simple definition of list

```
(define (list . objects)
    objects)
```

That is, list simply returns a list consisting of its arguments.

The definition of append requires recursion and the apply procedure. We present it in section 8.3, on page 136.

3.5   Other List Operations and Predicates

Often, we want to determine certain properties of a list or its elements, and also modify the list. Here are some other useful procedures for list examination and manipulation. Many of these procedures take predicates as arguments, which perform tests on the elements of the lists. One procedure given below, map, applies a procedure (map's first argument) to the elements of a set of lists (the other arguments). This is an extremely powerful procedure. It is useful for applying another procedure over an entire list or set of lists.

```
> (length '(a b c d))        ; (length list)  returns the number of
4                            ; top-level elements in list

> (length '())
0

> (length '((a b) (c d) (e f)))
3

> (length '((a b c d e f g )))
1

> (reverse '(a b c d e))     ; (reverse list)  reverses the order of the
(E D C B A)                  ; top-level elements of a copy of list

> (reverse '((a b c) (d e f)))
((D E F) (A B C))

> (define x '(1 2 3 4 5 6))
(1 2 3 4 5 6)

> (reverse x)
(6 5 4 3 2 1)

> x                          ; the value of  x has not changed
(1 2 3 4 5 6)                ; reverse  produced a reversed copy of x

; (any? predicate list)  returns true if predicate  is true for at least one
;  top-level element of list
> (any? number? '(a b c d))
()
```

```
;   Note that  predicate is not quoted.
;   The value of  number?, not the symbol number? , is a predicate.
> (any? number? '(a b c 3))
#t

> (any? zero? '(1 2 3 4 0))
#t

> (any? number? '(a b c d (3)))
()

; (every? predicate list)  returns true if predicate  is true for all
;   top-level elements of list
> (every? number? '(1 2 3 4 5))
#t

> (every? number? '(a b c d 3))
()

; (memq? object list)  returns true if object  is  eq? to some top-level
;   element of list
> (memq? 'c '(a b c d))
#t

> (memq? 'c '((a b c d)))
()

> (memq? '() '(a b c d))
()

> (memq? '(a) '((a) (b) (c)))    ; because  '(A) is not  eq? to  '(A)
()

; (mem? predicate object list)  returns true if the comparison predicate
;   is true between  object and some top-level element of list
> (mem? alikev? '(a) '((a) (b) (c)))
#t

> (mem? greater? 5 '(1 2 3 4))    ; is 5 greater than some element
#t                                ;  of the list?

> (mem? equal? 5 '(1 2 3 4))
()
```

```
> (mem? less? 5 '(1 2 3 4))
()
```

; (delq object list) returns a copy of **list** with all top-level elements **eq?**
to
; object deleted.
```
> (delq 'c '(a b c d))
(A B D)
```

```
> (define x '(1 2 3 4 3 2 3 4))
(1 2 3 4 3 2 3 4)
```

```
> (delq 3 x)
(1 2 4 2 4)
```

```
> x                        ; the value of  x has not changed.  delq
(1 2 3 4 3 2 3 4)          ; produced a modified copy of x.
```

; (del predicate object list) returns a copy of **list** but deleting
; all top-level elements that satisfy the comparison predicate with **object**
```
> (del greater? 5 '(1 2 3 4 5 6 7))
(5 6 7)
```

```
> (del not-equal? 3 '(1 2 3 4 3 2 3 4))
(3 3 3)
```

```
> (del alikev? '(a) '((a b) (a) (b)))
((A B) (B))
```

; (map procedure . lists) returns a list of the results of applying
; procedure to the respective elements of each **list**.
;   The length of the result is the same as the length of the shortest list.
;   In this example, each element is negated.
```
> (map - '(1 3 4 5 6 -9))
(-1 -3 -4 -5 -6 9)
```

```
> (map + '(1 2 3 4) '(5 6 7))    ; adds the respective elements of each
(6 8 10)                ; list and returns the results as a list.
                        ; Equivalent to (list (+ 1 5) (+ 2 6) (+ 3 7))
```

```
> (map equal? '(1 2 3 4) '(5 4 3))   ; compares respective list elements
(() () #t)                ; for equality
```

```
> (map less? '(1 2 3 4) '(2 3 4))
(#t #t #t)

> (map list '(joe mary sue) '(22 34 23))
((JOE 22) (MARY 34) (SUE 23))

; (subst predicate new old tree) returns an object which is the same as
; tree  but with all occurrences (not just top-level elements)
;  satisfying predicate with old  replaced by new.
> (subst alikev? 5 0 '(0 1 2 0))
(5 1 2 5)

> (subst eq? 'aa 'a '(a b (a b c) d e))
(AA B (AA B C) D E)

> (subst eq? 'aa 'z '(a b (a b c) d e)))
(A B (A B C) D E)

> (substq 'a 'b '(a b (a b c) d e)) ; (substq new old tree)
(A A (A A C) D E)                    ;  is the same as
                                     ; (subst eq? new old tree)
```

The **map** and **del** procedures are very useful for performing an operation repeatedly for all the elements of a list. Here is an example which combines these two procedures in a new procedure, **div-by-3**. The argument is a list of numbers, and the result is the subset of the given list whose elements are divisible by 3. Notice that a second procedure, **div-by-3-single**, is defined which can then be applied directly by **map** in **div-by-3**. It is very common in T to define secondary procedures to handle some sub-problem. It is often desirable to break up a program into several modules, each of which is a separate procedure. This approach is one aspect of the accepted practice of *structured programming* and is easily accomplished in T.

```
> (define (div-by-3 number-list)
      (delq nil (map div-by-3-single number-list)))
#{Procedure 22 div-by-3}

;;  returns number if it is divisible by 3, otherwise, ()
> (define (div-by-3-single number)
      (cond ((zero? (remainder number 3))
               number)
            (else nil)))
#{Procedure 23 div-by-3-SINGLE}
```

```
> (div-by-3 '(1 2 3 4 5 6 7 8 9 8 7 6 5 4 3 2 1))
(3 6 9 6 3)

> (div-by-3 '(2 4 8 16 22))
()
```

```
;; Here are the results without removing the  nil's with delq
> (map div-by-3-single '(1 2 3 4 5 6 7 8 9 8 7 6 5 4 3 2 1))
(() () 3 () () 6 () () 9 () () 6 () () 3 () ())

> (map div-by-3-single '(2 4 8 16 22))
(() () () () ())
```

3.6   Using Lists as Stacks: push and pop

The *stack* is a pervasive data structure in computer science. As its name implies, a stack allows you to add things to or remove them from the (figurative) top of a set of objects. It is a form of *last-in first-out* (or *LIFO*) data retrieval. That is, when you remove something from a stack, it is guaranteed to be the most recently added element in the stack.

The two basic stack operations are *push*, to add something to the top of the stack, and *pop*, to remove the top item. One can use a list in T as a virtual stack, and use the special forms **push** and **pop** to manipulate the stack. Both functions change the actual value of the stack, as shown below.

```
> (define x '())
()

> (push x 'c)            ; push the value  C to the front of x
(C)

> (push x 'b)
(B C)

> (push x 'a)
(A B C)

> (push x 'd)
(D A B C)

> x                      ; the value of  x has been modified by push
(D A B C)
```

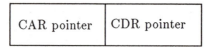

Figure 3.1: CONS cell

```
> (cons 'e x)
(E D A B C)

> x                     ; cons  does not modify the value of x
(D A B C)

> (pop x)               ; pop   returns the car of its argument
D

> x                     ; pop   also has modified the value of x
(A B C)
```

We will look at **push** and **pop** again in chapter 11, which deals with macros.

Both **push** and **pop** result in *side effects*. That is, not only do they return a value, they also modify an existing value. The **define** form similarly performs side-effects. In fact, we usually do not care at all about the value returned by **define**.

3.7   List Representation

We have seen numerous instances of lists and ways of manipulating lists. We now present how those lists are represented, both schematically and in the computer.

The primitive building block of a list is a pair of pointers, or addresses. One address points to the head of the list (the **car**), and the other address points to the tail (the **cdr**). Since the constructor procedure **cons** is used to create these pointer pairs, the pairs are often called *CONS cells*.

Figures 3.1 and 3.2 illustrate the structure of lists in T.

For those readers who are curious about how lists might actually be implemented in a computer, we now briefly discuss the internal representation of lists. Others may skip to the next section with impunity.

The addresses within CONS cells can point to several different types of objects, including symbols, numbers, and other lists. Figure 3.3 is a hypothetical list of memory addresses together with their types and contents – both as they might appear in the computer and as T would print out the contents. These addresses represent the objects depicted in figure 3.2. In this example, we show sequential

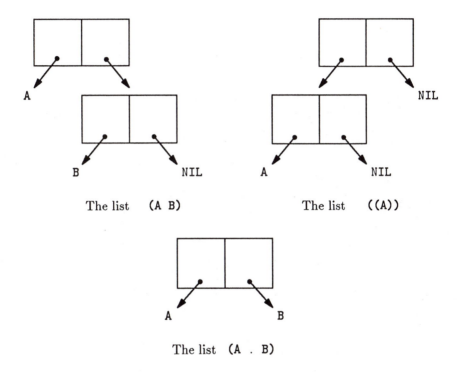

The list   **(A B)**   The list   **((A))**

The list   **(A . B)**

Figure 3.2: Several lists

Address	Type	Contents	Printed Version
1000	list	1001,1002	(A B)
1001	symbol	A	A
1002	list	1003,1004	(B)
1003	symbol	B	B
1004	nil	1004,1004	()
1005	list	1001,1003	(A . B)
1006	list	1007,1004	((A))
1007	list	1001,1004	(A)

Figure 3.3: Hypothetical memory contents

memory locations, with one CONS cell per memory location. In an actual T implementation, it is more likely that the addresses would be distributed throughout memory. Also, some implementations require more than one memory location for a single CONS cell.

Address 1000 contains a CONS cell, the head of which points to 1001, which contains the symbol A, and the tail of which points to 1002, which is another list. Address 1002 has a head which points to the symbol B in address 1003, and a tail which points to (), which lives in address 1004. Note that the **car** and **cdr** of () are both ().

A second list begins at address 1005. The head of this list points back to address 1001, which is the symbol A, and the tail points to the symbol B at 1003. This is a dotted pair, or improper list.

The final list at address 1006 has a **car** which points to the list **(A)** at 1007.

This example should give the reader some appreciation for how T's list structures can be implemented in a computer. Below is a partial diagram of the example given above, with the memory address noted at the side of each CONS cell or symbol.

3.8   Association Lists

We have seen how lists can be used to implement a simple stack structure. Another useful structure is the *association list*, or simply, *a-list*. Association lists are often used as tables for maintaining a correspondence between one piece of information and another. Thus, you might have a list of people's names with their respective ages, and want to retrieve an age, given the name.

```
> (define name-age-list '((joe 22) (jane 21) (john 12)))
((JOE 22) (JANE 21) (JOHN 12))
```

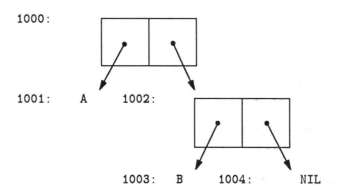

1000:

1001:   A   1002:

1003:   B   1004:   NIL

Figure 3.4: Diagram of memory addresses 1000-1004

```
> (assq 'john name-age-list)     ; (assq object a-list) returns the
(JOHN 12)                ; top-level list whose car is eq? to object

> (assq 'jim name-age-list)      ; returns nil if no match
()
> (assq 3.0 '((1 one) (2 two) (3 three)))
()

> (ass = 3.0 '((1 one) (2 two) (3 three)))
(3 THREE)
```

The **ass** procedure, with its indelicate name, takes an explicit predicate argument in addition to the object key and the association list. Thus, **assq** would be equivalent to (**ass eq? object alist**).

Association lists are merely lists of lists. The key is the **car** of each given sublist.

Association lists are often convenient mechanisms for handling simple tables. Here is an example with a price list for a grocery store. We first define an association list **food-price-list** which contains prices for various foods. Then we define a procedure **get-price** for retrieving a price, given the food. This is a very elementary table look-up scheme.

```
> (define food-price-list
        '((apples 60) (bananas 70) (cabbages 55) (dates 89)
          (eggplants 79) (figs 75) (garlic 33)))
((APPLES 60) (BANANAS 70) (CABBAGES 55) (DATES 89) (EGGPLANTS 79)
(FIGS 75) (GARLIC 33))
```

```
> (define (get-price food)
    (cadr (assq food food-price-list)))
#{Procedure 16 GET-PRICE}

> (get-price 'apples)
60

> (get-price 'figs)
75

> (get-price 'oranges)          ;  oranges weren't in the list
()
```

The association lists **name-age-list** and **food-price-list** given above are examples of *global variables*. In chapter 5, we will discuss the dangers of global objects as well as the alternatives.

3.9   Property Lists

Another type of data organization scheme is afforded by *property lists*, which are easily implemented in T. Most T systems provide a package for property lists. We present a simple version of property lists in section 14.3.

With property lists, one can associate arbitrary data with symbols, and retrieve and modify that data. Property lists are global, and as such, form a type of data base accessible from any level of T.

Property lists can easily be modified and accessed. Due to their convenience and simplicity, property lists often seduce programmers into sloppy and wasteful habits. Programmers may put arbitrary data on property lists in lieu of using more efficient and manageable data structures. Often, a programmer will use a property list in the initial design stage of a program when it is not yet clear what form the data will ultimately take. A good programmer should be prepared to go back later and review all uses of property lists to see if another data structure might be more appropriate.

Property list entries comprise a pair: the property name and its value, which are stored on a list associated with the given identifier.

```
> (put 'john 'age 37)          ; (put id property value)
37                             ; John is 37 years old.

> (put 'john 'weight 160)
160
```

```
> (get 'john 'age)              ; get   retrieves the value
37

> (put 'john 'wife 'mary)       ;   John's wife is Mary
MARY

> (put 'mary 'age 35)           ;   Mary is 35 years old
35

> (get (get 'john 'wife) 'age)  ;   How old is John's wife?
35
```

The object **nil** has no property list.

As you might imagine, property lists provide a flexible (and undisciplined) way to organize data. We can reimplement our grocery store price list using property lists. Here we assign a **price** property to each food, and redefine the **get-price** procedure to retrieve this property's value.

```
(put 'apples    'price 60)
(put 'bananas   'price 70)
(put 'cabbages  'price 55)
(put 'dates     'price 89)
(put 'eggplants 'price 79)
(put 'figs      'price 75)
(put 'garlic    'price 33)

> (define (get-price food)
      (get food 'price))
[Redefining GET-PRICE] #{Procedure 17 GET-PRICE}

> (get-price 'garlic)
33
```

3.10   Exercises

3.10.1   Expression Drill, Part 1 [3]

Evaluate the following T expressions by hand. Check your answers with the help of your T interpreter. (From sections 3.1 through 3.2.)

```
(cons 3 4)
(cons 3 '(4))
(define x (cons 'a (cons 'b (cons 'c '() ))))
(define x (cons 'a (cons 'b (cons 'c 'd))))
```

```
(car (cdr x))
(car (cdr (cdr x)))
(car (cdr (cdr (cdr x))))
(cons x y)
(define z (cons y x))
(cdr (car z))
(symbol? (car x))
(symbol? (car z))
(atom? (car x))
(pair? x)
(list? y)
(proper-list? y)
(list? (car (cdr z)))
(define w '(cons z (cons x y)))
(car (cdr w))
(eq? (car w) 'cons)
(eq? w (cons (car w) (cdr w)))
(alikev? w (cons (car w) (cdr w)))
(alikev? (+ 4 3) (- 9 2))
(eq? (+ 4 3) (- 9 2))
(alikev? '(+ 4 3) '(- 9 2))
(eq? '(+ 4 3) '(- 9 2))
```

3.10.2   Expression Drill, Part 2 [3]

Evaluate the following T expressions by hand. Check your answers with the help of your T interpreter. (From sections 3.3 through 3.6.)

```
(define x '(a b c d e))
(cadr x)
(caddr x)
(cadddr x)
(cddddr x)
(nth x 4)
(nth (cdr x) 2)
(nthcdr (cdr x) 2)
(last (sublist x 1 2))
(lastcdr (sublist x 1 2))
(list 1 2 3 '(+ 2 2))
(list 1 2 3 (+ 2 2))
(list (cons x '()))
(define y (reverse x))
(append x y)
(append y x)
(reverse (append x x))
```

```
(length (append x (nthcdr x 2)))
(any? positive? (define z '(-2 -1 0 1 2)))
(every? number? z)
(every? positive? z)
(memq? 0 z)
(mem? less? 3 z)
(delq 'a x)
(delq  1 z)
(del equal? 1 z)
(map + z z)
(map * z z)
(map cons x y)
(map list x y)
(substq 3 1 (map abs z))
(+ (pop z) (pop z))
(cadr (push z 7))
```

3.10.3   New List Procedures [4*]

Define the procedures **no-zeros**, **collect-numbers**, and **verb-find**, which are described below.

```
> (no-zeros '(1 0 2 0 3))          ; removes all top-level zeros
(1 2 3)

> (no-zeros '(a b c d e))
(A B C D E)

> (collect-numbers 1 '(2 3 4 5))   ; puts numbers on the front of list,
(1 2 3 4 5)                        ; but not other data types

> (collect-numbers 'a '(2 3 4 5))
(2 3 4 5)
```

verb-find returns a list of the verbs contained in the given sentence. You may need to define a secondary procedure. Also, you will find it convenient to use a defined list of verbs, such as **verb-list**.

```
> (define verb-list  '(is am are have has go went gone))
(IS AM ARE HAVE HAS GO WENT GONE)

> (verb-find '(tom went to the store))
(WENT)
```

```
> (verb-find '(tom went to the store and mary went to town))
(WENT WENT)

> (verb-find '(have you gone to the store))
(HAVE GONE)
```

3.10.4 Association List Personnel File [4*]

Define a procedure called **make-person** which takes six arguments: name, age, weight, sex, astrological sign, and a list of children's names. This procedure will return an association list with the respective pairings of keywords with data elements, as shown below. Then, define six selector procedures, one for each keyword: **get-name**, **get-age**, **get-weight**, **get-sex**, **get-sign**, and **get-children**. Note that the elements of the a-list are dotted pairs.

```
> (define joe (make-person 'joe 35 150 'male 'taurus
  '(irving mabel)))
((NAME . JOE) (AGE . 35) (WEIGHT . 150) (SEX . MALE)
 (SIGN . TAURUS) (CHILDREN IRVING MABEL)))

> (get-age joe)
35

> (get-children joe)
(IRVING MABEL)

> (get-sign joe)
TAURUS
```

3.10.5 Property List Personnel File [4*]

Define a procedure called **make-person2** which takes six arguments: name, age, weight, sex, astrological sign, and a list of children's names. This procedure will add the five latter items to the property list of the given name. Then, define five selector procedures, one for each keyword: **get-age2**, **get-weight2**, **get-sex2**, **get-sign2**, and **get-children2**. Each of these procedures takes the name as the only argument.

```
> (make-person2 'beth 23 110 'female 'cancer '())
BETH

> (get-age2 'beth)
23
```

```
> (get-children2 'beth)
()

> (get-sign2 'beth)
CANCER
```

3.10.6 More List People [4*]

Define two more procedures for retrieving information about people using either the association list or property list representation in the two preceding exercises. First, define a procedure called **get-name+age** which returns the obvious information as a list.

```
> (get-name+age 'beth)
(BETH 23)
```

Then, use the **get-name+age** procedure to define a second procedure called **age-of-children** which will return a list of name-age pairs of the children of the person given. You will first need to enter additional information about the children via the regular **make-person** procedure. Thus, suppose you had entered information about Joe's two children, Irving and Mabel, who are 12 and 10 years old, respectively. You could then make the following query.

```
> (age-of-children joe)
((IRVING 12) (MABEL 10))
```

The procedure **age-of-children** should not depend directly on whether the data is represented as an association list or in property lists. The selector procedures should take care of those details.

3.10.7 Daughter of Zeller [4*]

Building on your previous work at converting dates into days of the week, write a procedure **daughter-of-zeller** which is given the date with a quoted month name and returns the text for the day of the week. For example,

```
> (daughter-of-zeller 'september 1 1985)
SUNDAY
```

3.11 Chapter Summary

- The pervasive data structure of T is the list.

- List selectors and constructors:

```
(car list)              ;  select the first element of a list
(cdr list)              ;  select the tail of a list
(cons obj1 obj2)        ;  construct a list from two objects
```

- The special form **quote** returns its argument without evaluating it. **quote** may be abbreviated with the single quote mark: '

- T type and comparison predicates:

```
(symbol? object)
(number? object)
(pair? object)
(atom? object)
(list? object)
(proper-list? object)
(null? object)
(eq? object1 object2)
(alikev? object1 object2)
(equal? object1 object2)
```

- More list selectors and constructors:

```
(caar list)
(cadr list)
(cdar list)
(cddr list)
(nth list integer)
(nthcdr list integer)
(last list)
(lastcdr list)
(sublist list start count)
(list . objects)
(append . lists)
```

- More operations and predicates:

```
(length list)
(reverse list)
(any? predicate . lists)
(every? predicate . lists)
(memq? object list)
(mem? predicate object list)
(delq object list)
(del predicate object list)
(map procedure . lists)
(subst predicate new old tree)
(substq new old tree)
```

- Lists can be used as stacks with the special forms **push** and **pop**.

- List structure can be diagrammed using paired boxes and pointers.

- List structure can be represented in a computer memory using pairs of addresses pointing to other parts of memory.

- Association lists and property lists are useful data structures, especially for certain kinds of table look-up.

- Operations for association lists and property lists:

```
(assq object a-list)
(ass predicate object a-list)
(put object1 object2 value)
(get object1 object2)
```

Chapter 4

Recursion

100 bottles of beer on the wall,
100 bottles of beer,
Take one down, pass it around,
99 bottles of beer on the wall ...

⋄ ANON., *Traditional*

Recursion entails self-reference.

⋄ STEPHEN SLADE, *The T Programming Language (1986)*

Just as the list is the prevalent T data structure, so *recursion* is the typical T programming style. The verb from which the word *recursion* is derived is *recur: to happen again or repeatedly.* The programmer may at times suspect the spurious derivation from *recurse: to curse again or repeatedly.* Before we look at recursion in programming, it may be helpful first to explore the idea in general.

Recursion entails self-reference. A definition or a pattern which includes itself as a part is recursive. This may initially seem implausible. How can something include itself? Some examples may be illustrative.

If you place two mirrors opposite one another, they will each reflect the other. Furthermore, they will reflect the reflections of themselves as seen in the opposing mirror. In fact, the images of mirrors within mirrors can seem to be infinite. Each mirror's image contains an image of itself. It is a recursive image.

Writers and artists have occasionally used recursive structures in works of art. A simple example is Shakespeare's play-within-a-play in *Hamlet.* The Luis Buñuel movie *The Discrete Charm of the Bourgeoisie* contains numerous dream sequences in which the dreamer wakes up from a dream to continue as a part of someone else's dream. These dreams within dreams imbue the film with a recursive absurdity. Douglas Hofstadter discusses the role of recursion and self-reference in art, music, mathematics, and computer science at great length in *Gödel, Escher, Bach: An Eternal Golden Braid* [10].

A more formal example of recursion can be found in a simple definition of the list data structure:

1. A list is composed of a left parenthesis, zero or more objects, and a right parenthesis.

2. An object is either an atomic value or a *list*.

The second part of the definition of a list itself refers to the concept of list. This is a recursive definition. One might wish to argue that it is a circular definition, like saying *A list is a list*. That is not the case though. The first part of the definition serves to limit and focus the applicability of the second. The important fact about lists which this definition imparts is that *lists may contain lists*. The list is a recursive data structure.

4.1 Recursive Programs

In computer programming, recursion is simply the ability for a procedure to call itself – either directly or indirectly. Recursion offers a simple and elegant way of solving a problem by progressively reducing it to a simpler form.

A recursive procedure generally reflects some inductive aspect of the problem.

1. There is a test for a boundary condition.

2. There is a method for reducing the problem in such a way that it converges to the boundary condition.

We can use the recursive definition of *list* to define a recursive procedure for building a list. The `replicate` procedure, which we shall define below, takes two arguments: an expression and a number. It returns a list containing the expression copied the given number of times. For example,

```
> (replicate 'a 3)
(A A A)

> (replicate '(1 2) 5)
((1 2) (1 2) (1 2) (1 2) (1 2))

> (replicate '(as if by magic) 0)
()
```

The boundary condition for `replicate` is given in the last example: if the number is 0, the procedure returns the empty list. Otherwise, `replicate` will `cons` the given expression to the result of `replicate` called with the same expression and one less than the given number. Here is a detailed expansion of the first example.

```
(replicate 'a 3)
    = (cons 'A (replicate 'a 2))
    = (cons 'A (cons 'A (replicate 'a 1)))
    = (cons 'A (cons 'A (cons 'A (replicate 'a 0))))
    = (cons 'A (cons 'A (cons 'A nil)))
    = (cons 'A (cons 'A '(A)))
    = (cons 'A '(A A))
    = (A A A)
```

Here is a recursive definition of **replicate**.

```
(define (replicate expr num)
    (cond ((zero? num) nil)
          (else (cons expr (replicate expr (- num 1))))))
```

The **replicate** procedure exemplifies the use of recursion in processing lists. We also encounter recursion in processing numbers.

The epitome of mathematical recursive functions is factorial, which is the product of a positive integer with all other smaller positive integers. The factorial of 4, written 4!, is $4 * 3 * 2 * 1$ or 24. $3! = 3 * 2 * 1$ or 6.

We can give a recursive definition of factorial: the factorial of a positive integer is the product of that number and the factorial of one less than that number. The boundary condition is that the factorial of 0 is equal to 1.

This recursive definition can be applied to 4! as follows:

```
4! = 4*3!
 3! = 3*2!
  2! = 2*1!
   1! = 1*0!
    0! = 1
   1! = 1*1 = 1
  2! = 2*1 = 2
 3! = 3*2 = 6
4! = 4*6 = 24
```

Here is a recursive T procedure **fact** to calculate the factorial of a given positive integer.

```
> (define (fact n)
    (cond ((zero? n) 1)
          (else (* n (fact (- n 1))))))
#{Procedure 26 FACT}

> (fact 4)
24
```

```
> (fact 5)
120
```

We use the **trace** operation below to print out the intermediate results, show-ing multiple calls to the factorial procedure, with the respective returned values of the embedded calls. Note that **trace** indents one space for each level of recursion. A counter at the left also indicates how deep the current level is.

```
> (trace fact)                    ; trace  is useful for debugging procedures
[Assigning FACT] #{Traced 27 #{Procedure 26 FACT}}

> (fact 4)                        ; the following 10 lines are trace  output
;0 Calling FACT with arguments (4)
; 1 Calling FACT with arguments (3)
;  2 Calling FACT with arguments (2)
;   3 Calling FACT with arguments (1)
;    4 Calling FACT with arguments (0)
;    4 Returned from FACT with value 1
;   3 Returned from FACT with value 1
;  2 Returned from FACT with value 2
; 1 Returned from FACT with value 6
;0 Returned from FACT with value 24
24

> (untrace fact)                 ; untrace  turns off trace
#{Procedure 26 FACT}

> (fact 3)
6
```

The factorial procedure has little intrinsic interest, but it is illustrative of the process of recursion. The procedure keeps on calling itself until it reaches the boundary condition. At that point, it starts returning values, and pops back up to the top again. (Note: Recursion is often implemented with a stack, as was discussed in section 3.6, page 47. Pending computations are pushed on the stack until results start being returned, at which point the stack is popped.)

What would happen if we tried to execute (**fact** -1) or (**fact** 1.5)? The argument to **fact** is suppose to be a positive integer, but that supposition does not guarantee that the argument will, in fact, be a positive integer. Thus, the programmer should be on guard for such errors. We discuss error checking and debugging at length in chapter 10. See also exercise 4.7.1.

4.2   Recursive Money Changing

You can view the process of making change as recursive. You first see if any dollars are required, subtract them from the total, and then make change for what remains. The following procedure implements such a recursive approach to making change. The procedure **make-change** converts a given number of cents into dollars, half-dollars, quarters, and so forth. The alert programmer will see that this is an inefficient algorithm, since the tests for higher denominations of coins and currency must be made repeatedly in most cases.

Note that there can never be more than one half-dollar, quarter, or nickel in a given set of change.

```
> (define (make-change money)
    (cond ((not-less? money 100)
            (cons (list (quotient money 100) 'dollars)
                (make-change (remainder money 100))))
          ((not-less? money 50)
           (cons (list (quotient money 50) 'half-dollar)
                (make-change (remainder money 50))))
          ((not-less? money 25)
           (cons (list (quotient money 25) 'quarter)
                (make-change (remainder money 25))))
          ((not-less? money 10)
           (cons (list (quotient money 10) 'dimes)
                (make-change (remainder money 10))))
          ((not-less? money 5)
           (cons (list (quotient money 5) 'nickel)
                (make-change (remainder money 5))))
          ((greater? money 0)
           (cons (list money 'pennies)
                '()))
          (else '()))))
#{Procedure 37 MAKE-CHANGE}

> (make-change 123)
((1 DOLLARS) (2 DIMES) (3 PENNIES))

> (make-change 125)
((1 DOLLARS) (1 QUARTER))

> (make-change 97)
((1 HALF-DOLLAR) (1 QUARTER) (2 DIMES) (2 PENNIES))
```

```
> (make-change 292)
((2 DOLLARS) (1 HALF-DOLLAR) (1 QUARTER) (1 DIMES) (1 NICKEL)
(2 PENNIES))
```

4.3   Recursive Roman Numerals

Here is another example of recursion which converts Roman numerals into decimal notation. The two previous examples, **fact** and **make-change**, took a single number as an argument. This time we'll take a list as an argument. The Roman numerals are represented as a list of letters. For example, the numeral XXIV would be represented as (X X I V). We shall use an association list to keep the correspondence between Roman numerals and decimal numbers. The procedure **numeral->decimal**, defined below, performs the simple table look-up.

The procedure **roman->decimal** takes the list of letters which represents a Roman numeral. It first checks to see if the list is empty, in which case the procedure returns 0. This is the termination condition for the recursion.

If the list is not empty, it calculates the value of the current Roman letter which it adds to the remainder of the Roman letters through a recursive call to the **roman->decimal** procedure with the **cdr** of the input list.

The value of a Roman numeral depends very much on the order of the individual letters. The numeral XI is 11, but the numeral IX is 9. In the first case, the value of I is added to the value of X $(1 + 10 = 11)$, and in the second case, the value of I is subtracted from the value of X $(-1 + 10 = 9)$. In general, the value of the current Roman letter is negative if its value is less than the next letter. In that case, the current letter's value is subtracted from, rather than added to, the total. The procedure does this first by checking to see if the **cdr** is not empty, that is, if there are at least two letters. If there are, then it checks to see if the current letter's absolute value is less than the absolute value of the next letter. If it is, then the current letter's numerical value is negated. Otherwise, the positive value is added to the result of converting the rest of the list. For example, (I V) would yield $-1 + 5$, or 4, whereas (V I) would yield $5 + 1$, or 6.

```
> (define roman-number-a-list '((I 1) (V 5) (X 10) (L 50) (C 100)
(D 500) (M 1000)))
((I 1) (V 5) (X 10) (L 50) (C 100) (D 500) (M 1000))

> (define (numeral->decimal numeral)
     (cadr (assq numeral roman-number-a-list)))
#{Procedure 26 NUMERAL->DECIMAL}
```

```
> (define (roman->decimal num-list)
    (cond
     ((null? num-list) 0)
     (else
      (+ (cond
           ((and (cdr num-list)
                 (less? (numeral->decimal (car num-list))
                        (numeral->decimal (cadr num-list))))
            (- (numeral->decimal (car num-list))))
           (else (numeral->decimal (car num-list))))
         (roman->decimal (cdr num-list))))))
#{Procedure 25 ROMAN->DECIMAL}

> (roman->decimal '(M C C C X X I I I))
1323

> (trace roman->decimal)
#{Traced 28 #{Procedure 25 ROMAN->DECIMAL}}

>  (roman->decimal '(M C M L X X X I V))

;0 Calling ROMAN->DECIMAL with arguments ((M C M L X X X I V))
; 1 Calling ROMAN->DECIMAL with arguments ((C M L X X X I V))
;  2 Calling ROMAN->DECIMAL with arguments ((M L X X X I V))
;   3 Calling ROMAN->DECIMAL with arguments ((L X X X I V))
;    4 Calling ROMAN->DECIMAL with arguments ((X X X I V))
;     5 Calling ROMAN->DECIMAL with arguments ((X X I V))
;      6 Calling ROMAN->DECIMAL with arguments ((X I V))
;       7 Calling ROMAN->DECIMAL with arguments ((I V))
;        8 Calling ROMAN->DECIMAL with arguments ((V))
;         9 Calling ROMAN->DECIMAL with arguments (())
;         9 Returned from ROMAN->DECIMAL with value 0
;        8 Returned from ROMAN->DECIMAL with value 5
;       7 Returned from ROMAN->DECIMAL with value 4
;      6 Returned from ROMAN->DECIMAL with value 14
;     5 Returned from ROMAN->DECIMAL with value 24
;    4 Returned from ROMAN->DECIMAL with value 34
;   3 Returned from ROMAN->DECIMAL with value 84
;  2 Returned from ROMAN->DECIMAL with value 1084
; 1 Returned from ROMAN->DECIMAL with value 984
;0 Returned from ROMAN->DECIMAL with value 1984
1984
```

4.4 Recursive List Operations

The more common use of recursion in T is not for arithmetic procedures like factorial or making change, but for list operations. The preceding Roman numeral example showed a simple way to traverse a list of items using recursion. In fact, many of the list operations presented in the preceding chapter can be given simple recursive definitions. Here is a recursive definition of **length**.

```
> (define (length l)              ; length   traverses the top level of a list
    (cond ((null? l) 0)           ; assuming that the list ends in NIL
          ((atom? l)
           (list 'error:improper-list l))
          (else (+ 1 (length (cdr l))))))
[Shadowing LENGTH] #{Procedure 30 LENGTH}

> (length '(a b c))
3

> (length '(a b . c))            ; We'll see better ways of signaling errors
(ERROR:IMPROPER-LIST (A B . C)) ; in later chapters. This method is not
                                 ; very useful except at the top level.

> (trace length)
[Assigning LENGTH] #{Traced 31 #{Procedure 30 LENGTH}}

> (length '(a b))
;0 Calling LENGTH with arguments ((A B))
; 1 Calling LENGTH with arguments ((B))
;  2 Calling LENGTH with arguments (())
;  2 Returned from LENGTH with value 0
; 1 Returned from LENGTH with value 1
;0 Returned from LENGTH with value 2
2
```

Since the **length** procedure is already defined in T, you will be overwriting the existing definition with the above code. There are times when you may wish to change a system procedure, and T lets you do this quite easily. However, you should be careful not to destroy or redefine a system procedure by accident. T will print a warning message whenever you redefine any procedure – either a predefined system procedure or one originally defined by the programmer. The new definition will remain in effect until either the end of the session or when the procedure is defined yet again.

It should be obvious from the definition, but bears emphasizing that the **length** procedure does not look at the elements of the list it is traversing. Hence, elements which are lists themselves are not thought of as *longer* than elements which are atoms. For example, the following three expressions yield the same result, namely, 4.

```
(length '(a b c d))
(length '(a (b) c d))
(length '(a (b e f g h) c d))
```

This type of recursion is often called cdr recursion, since the cdr selector procedure is used to traverse the top level of the list.

The use of cdr recursion can also make your code more modular. The **make-change** procedure given in section 4.2 above can be rewritten in a more flexible fashion using cdr recursion.

```
(define (new-make-change money currency-list)
    (cond ((null? currency-list) nil)
          ((zero? money) nil)
          ((not-less? money (caar currency-list))
           (cons (list (quotient money (caar currency-list))
                       (cadar currency-list))
                 (new-make-change (remainder money
                                             (caar currency-list))
                                  (cdr currency-list))))
          (else
           (new-make-change money (cdr currency-list)))))
```

```
;  Currencies are defined as simple lists in descending denominations
;    giving the value and name for each denomination.
(define *us-currency* '((100 dollar) (50 half-dollar)
    (25 quarter) (10 dime) (5 nickel) (1 penny)))
```

```
> (new-make-change 236 *us-currency*)
((2 DOLLAR) (1 QUARTER) (1 DIME) (1 PENNY))
```

One may easily introduce new currencies. For example, suppose that in the solar system of the binary star Algol, there is a currency which uses base 2, instead of base 10. We can use the same functions as before, but simply change the currency list.

```
(define *algol-currency* '((64 grumpy) (32 dopey) (16 sneezy)
    (8 sleepy) (4 happy) (2 bashful) (1 doc)))
```

```
> (new-make-change 87 *algol-currency*)
((1 GRUMPY) (1 SNEEZY) (1 HAPPY) (1 BASHFUL) (1 DOC))
```

In this new version of `make-change`, we have separated the denomination data from the change calculations. The result is a procedure which is more versatile and more efficient.

4.5   car/cdr Recursion

Often, one would like to delve deeper into the structure of a list, going beyond the top level. A form of recursion called car/cdr recursion allows you to do just that. At each stage, one examines the `car` and the `cdr` of the list; if either is a list, then the procedure is applied recursively to the respective `car` or `cdr`. Treated this way, a list can be considered a *tree*, where the embedded lists are branches and the atoms are leaves.

The next example, `count-atoms`, is similar to `length`, but tallies every atom in a list whether or not it is at the top level. Thus, `count-atoms` treats the list as a tree and counts all its leaves. Note how the use of car/cdr recursion appears to divide and conquer.

```
> (define (count-atoms l)
    (cond ((null? l) 0)
          ((atom? l) 1)
          (else
           (+ (count-atoms (car l))
              (count-atoms (cdr l)))))))
#{Procedure 69 COUNT-ATOMS}

> (count-atoms '(a b c d))
4

> (count-atoms '(a (b e (f g) h) (c d)))
8
```

Manipulating lists often requires taking them apart and putting them back together after making some changes. Here is an example of a procedure which takes the tree apart with car/cdr recursion to examine the branches and joins it back together again with `cons`. The procedure `subst` (which was described in section 3.5, page 46 above) travels down the various branches the tree. It replaces those nodes which satisfy the given `predicate` with the `new` value, and returns the newly constituted tree as a result.

`subst`, like `count-atoms`, traverses all branches of the tree, not just the top level ones. The argument `predicate` is passed as a variable and then called as a procedure.

```
(define (subst predicate new old tree)
    (cond ((predicate old tree) new)
          ((atom? tree) tree)
          (else (cons (subst predicate new old (car tree))
                      (subst predicate new old (cdr tree))))))
```

```
> (subst alikev? 3 1 '(1 2 (1 2 (1 2))))
(3 2 (3 2 (3 2)))
```

This definition of **subst** also shows the use of a procedure as an argument to another procedure. The argument **predicate** is itself a procedure which is called with **subst**.

Recursion is a very important and powerful programming technique. Most of the examples and exercises in the remainder of this book will further illustrate recursion. The reader should expect to be immersed in a flood of recursion.

4.6   Recursive Subfunctions

There are certain problems which cannot be solved using direct recursion. The procedure may need to keep more information around than is contained in the original argument. In these cases, you can create a secondary procedure which is called by the primary procedure and then calls itself recursively. An example may help to illustrate this point.

Consider the common task of getting the average of a list of numbers. There is a fairly simple way to do this in T:

```
> (define (average num-list)
    (/ (total num-list) (length num-list)))
#{Procedure 14 AVERAGE}
```

```
> (define (total num-list)
    (cond ((null? num-list) 0)
          (else (+ (car num-list)
                   (total (cdr num-list))))))
#{Procedure 15 TOTAL}
```

```
> (total '(1 2 3 4 5 6 7))
28
```

```
> (length '(1 2 3 4 5 6 7))
7
```

```
> (average '(1 2 3 4 5 6 7))
4
```

So far, there is nothing special about this example. The procedure **average** simply divides the sum of the numbers from **total** by the number of numbers from **length**. The **total** procedure uses simple cdr recursion, as does the **length** procedure as defined before.

Is there anything wrong with this approach? Yes. The **average** procedure requires that the number list be traversed *twice*: once for **total** and once for **length**. This is really not much of an issue for short lists such as the one given in the example, but it could be real efficiency problem for very long lists.

For example, consider a census taker who has to visit 10,000 homes and ask ten questions at each household. Which method is preferred?

1. Visit each household ten times, asking one question each time.

2. Visit each household once, asking ten questions each time.

Those readers who selected the first method should do the taxpayers a favor and avoid careers in public administration.

What we would like to do is combine the **total** and **length** procedures into one operation that keeps both a running count and subtotal as it cdr's down the list. Here is one way to do that.

```
> (define (above-average num-list)
    (below-average num-list 0 0))
#{Procedure 16 ABOVE-AVERAGE}

> (define (below-average num-list count total)
    (cond ((null? num-list) (/ total count))   ;  done? return average
          (else (below-average (cdr num-list)  ;  go to next number
                               (+ count 1)      ;  increment count
                               (+ (car num-list)
                                  total)))))    ;  update total
#{Procedure 17 BELOW-AVERAGE}

> (above-average '(1 2 3 4 5 6 7))
4

> (trace below-average)
[Assigning BELOW-AVERAGE]
#{Traced 18 #{Procedure 17 BELOW-AVERAGE}}
```

```
> (above-average '(3 4 5 6 7 8 9))
;0 Calling BELOW-AVERAGE with arguments ((3 4 5 6 7 8 9) 0 0)
; 1 Calling BELOW-AVERAGE with arguments ((4 5 6 7 8 9) 1 3)
;  2 Calling BELOW-AVERAGE with arguments ((5 6 7 8 9) 2 7)
;   3 Calling BELOW-AVERAGE with arguments ((6 7 8 9) 3 12)
;    4 Calling BELOW-AVERAGE with arguments ((7 8 9) 4 18)
;     5 Calling BELOW-AVERAGE with arguments ((8 9) 5 25)
;      6 Calling BELOW-AVERAGE with arguments ((9) 6 33)
;       7 Calling BELOW-AVERAGE with arguments (() 7 42)
;       7 Returned from BELOW-AVERAGE with value 6
;      6 Returned from BELOW-AVERAGE with value 6
;     5 Returned from BELOW-AVERAGE with value 6
;    4 Returned from BELOW-AVERAGE with value 6
;   3 Returned from BELOW-AVERAGE with value 6
;  2 Returned from BELOW-AVERAGE with value 6
; 1 Returned from BELOW-AVERAGE with value 6
;0 Returned from BELOW-AVERAGE with value 6
6
```

The procedure **above-average** calls the secondary procedure **below-average** with the original list of numbers and zero values for the running count and total. Then, the procedure **below-average** uses cdr recursion to traverse the number list while doing the necessary bookkeeping for the running count and total. When it reaches the end of the list, the **below-average** procedure simply divides its running total by its running count, and returns the result to the main procedure, **above-average**.

4.7 Exercises

You may find it helpful to use **trace** (and **untrace**) to help debug these procedures.

4.7.1 Checking Facts [3]

The definitions of **replicate** and **fact** given above have a nasty problem when given improper arguments. What is the result of (**replicate** 'A 1.5) or (**fact** -2)?

Redefine both procedures to check their arguments and catch these errors.

4.7.2 Legal Roman Numerals [5]

What happens if **roman->decimal** is given improper data? For example, '(C I I C). Redefine **roman->decimal** to ensure that illegal Roman numerals are disallowed.

4.7.3   Making Changes [3*]

The `make-change` procedure defined above had problem with numbers agreement. That is, it sometimes used a plural denomination for a singular instance. Modify the procedure so that it knows singular from plural.

```
> (make-change 123)
((1 DOLLAR) (2 DIMES) (3 PENNIES))

> (make-change 211)
((2 DOLLARS) (1 DIME) (1 PENNY))
```

4.7.4   Making More Changes [4]

Modify the `new-make-change` procedure to handle number agreement. The currency list should be changed to include irregular plural forms as a third element of the inner lists. For example:

```
(define *us-currency* '((100 dollar) (50 half-dollar)
  (25 quarter) (10 dime) (5 nickel) (1 penny pennies)))
```

Regular plurals can be formed by adding an S to the end of the singular form. In T, you can construct new symbols using (`concatenate-symbol` ...).

```
> (concatenate-symbol 'a 'b 'c)
ABC

> (define (mis x)
    (concatenate-symbol 'mis x))
#{Procedure 13 MIS}

> (mis 'take)
MISTAKE

> (mis 'sissippi)
MISSISSIPPI
```

4.7.5   Recursive reverse [4]

Write a recursive version of `reverse`.

4.7.6   Recursive append [4*]

Write a recursive version of `append`. Assume only two arguments.

4.7.7   Recursive nth [4]

Write a recursive version of nth.

4.7.8   Recursive lastcdr [4]

Write a recursive version of lastcdr.

4.7.9   Recursive remove-duplicates [4*]

Write a procedure remove-duplicates, which takes a list and removes all the top-level duplicate symbols, as shown below.

```
> (remove-duplicates '(a b c d a b f g))
(C D A B F G)

> (remove-duplicates '(a b c d (a b) f g))
(A B C D (A B) F G)
```

4.7.10   Recursive Check Balancing [5*]

Write a procedure check-book which takes two arguments: a balance and a list of transactions. The balance is simply a number. A transaction is either a credit (positive number), a debit (negative number), or an interest rate (a positive number enclosed in parentheses). The procedure returns the net balance, by adding credits, subtracting debits, and compounding the interest. The interest is given as a multiplier; thus, a 10% interest rate would be given by (1.1). Interest is compounded by multiplying the current balance by the given interest rate. So if the balance is \$100 and the interest rate is 10% (or 1.1), the resulting balance would be \$110. The procedure should also verify the form of its input, making sure that the balance is a number, the transactions are a list, and that the interest rate is a list of exactly one number.

```
> (check-book 100 '(100 50 -75))
175

> (check-book 100 '(-17.50 -1.73 -7.5))
73.27

> (check-book 100 '(100 50 -50 (1.1)))
220.0

> (check-book 100 '((1.1) 100 50 -50 (1.1)))
231.0
```

```
> (check-book 100 -17.50)
(ERROR:ATOM-INSTEAD-OF-LIST: . -17.5)

> (check-book 'balance '(-17.50 -1.73 -7.5))
(ERROR:NON-NUMERIC-BALANCE: . BALANCE)
```

4.7.11 Recursive NOW Account [5*]

Write a modified version of `check-book` called `now-account` to incorporate the following two rules:

1. If the balance drops below $500, then charge $0.10 for every check (debit) on the account.

2. Interest is compounded only if the balance is $500 or more.

```
> (now-account 100 '(100 50 -50 (1.1)))
199.9

> (now-account 500 '(100 50 -50 (1.1)))
660.0
```

4.7.12 Simple Pattern Matcher [6*]

One of the pervasive functions in artificial intelligence is pattern matching. The T predicate `alikev?` might be thought of as a type of pattern matcher. Here we present a very basic pattern matcher that allows wild cards in the pattern. The wild card patterns provide a way of making approximate matches based on the more important aspects of the given pattern.

Write a predicate `match?` which takes two arguments: a pattern and an input list. The predicate returns true if the top-level items in the input list match the corresponding items in the pattern according to the following rules.

1. All lists and patterns are flat. That is, there are no embedded lists.

2. A pattern symbol must match a respective symbol in the input list.

3. A pattern wild card, given by *wild*, may match any (possibly empty) set of adjacent symbols in the input list.

4. Every item in the input list must match either a literal or a wild card in the pattern.

As you might imagine, `match?` should be written as a recursive procedure. Furthermore, since it only has to deal with flat lists and not trees, `match?` will only require CDR recursion – not CAR/CDR recursion.

Here are examples.

```
> (match? '(a b c) '(a b c))
#t

> (match? '(a b c) '(a b c d))         ;  extra  d on input list
()


> (match? '(a b c d) '(a b c))         ;  extra  d on pattern list
()

> (match? '(a *wild*) '(a b c))        ;  matches any list starting with  a
#t

> (match? '(a *wild*) '(a))
#t

> (match? '(a *wild* b) '(a b c d b))  ;  must start with  a
#t                                     ;  and end with  b

> (match? '(a *wild* b) '(a b c d e))  ;  second list doesn't end in  b
()

> (match? '(*wild* b *wild*) '(a b c d e))  ;  matches any list
#t                                          ;  containing  b

> (match? '(*wild*) '(a b c))          ;  (*wild*)  should match any list
#t
```

Hint on implementing *wild*: There are basically two cases for *wild*.

1. Empty match. Ignore the *wild* and match the rest of the pattern list with the current input list.

2. Match one (or more) input elements. Ignore the next input element and match the rest of the input list with the current pattern list.

4.7.13   Count Occurrences [4*]

Write a procedure count-occurrences that finds how many times something occurs in a tree. The procedure returns the number of times that the value of its first argument (an atom) occurs in the value of its second argument. This procedure, like count-atoms, uses CAR/CDR recursion.

```
> (count-occurrences 'a '(a ((a b)) d c (a)))
3
```

```
> (count-occurrences 'z '(a ((a b)) d c (a)))
0
```

4.7.14 Tree Addition [4*]

Write a procedure **tree-addition** which adds a given number to every number (or leaf) of a tree of numbers. Like the preceding problem, this procedure uses CAR/CDR recursion. However, in this case, you must return an entire tree as a value, not simply a number. Thus, it is more similar to **subst** than to **count-atoms**.

```
> (tree-addition 2 '(5 4 3 2 1))
(7 6 5 4 3)

> (tree-addition 3 '(1 2 (3 (4 (5) 6) (7)) 8 (9)))
(4 5 (6 (7 (8) 9) (10)) 11 (12))

> (tree-addition 5 '(((((((1))))))))
(((((((6)))))))
```

4.7.15 Tree Average [5*]

Write a procedure **tree-average** which computes the average of a tree of numbers. *You should traverse the tree only once.* That is, you should create a secondary recursive procedure which both counts the number of leaves in the tree and adds up their values, similar to the **above-average** example before. This secondary procedure will return a pair of values as a list (the total and count) to **tree-average**, which will then calculate the average.

```
> (tree-average  '(1 2 (3 (4 (5) 6) (7)) 8 (9)))
5

> (tree-average  '(((((((1))))))))
1
```

4.8 Chapter Summary

- Recursion is the typical T programming style.

- One can find examples of recursion and self-reference in art, literature, and especially mathematics.

- Recursion as used in programming helps to solve problems by progressively reducing the problem to a simpler form.

- Recursion provides a convenient way to traverse a list by examining the successive cdr's.

- Embedded lists, or trees, can be traversed using car/cdr recursion.

- Sometimes it is useful to create a recursive subfunction, as in the averaging examples.

- New symbols can be created using `concatenate-symbol`.

Chapter 5

Local vs. Global Reference

> *...as imagination bodies forth*
> *The forms of things unknown, the poet's pen*
> *Turns them to shapes, and gives to airy nothing*
> *A local habitation and name.*

◇ WILLIAM SHAKESPEARE, *A Midsummer-Night's Dream (1595-1596)*

> *Much of what Mr. Wallace calls his global thinking is,*
> *no matter how you slice it,*
> *still Globaloney.*

◇ CLARE BOOTH LUCE, *Speech, House of Representatives (February 9, 1943)*

Where do variables come from? Where do they live? When do they die?

The alert and prescient reader may have noticed that we have been using variables in programs in two distinct ways. The two separate ways in which variables have been introduced or created are

- as an initial argument of a **define** expression. For example,

```
(define x 100)        ; the symbol  x is created and given
                      ; the value of 100.
```

```
(define (plus2 y)     ; the symbol  plus2 is created and given
    (+ y 2))          ; the value of a procedure which adds 2 to
                      ; its argument.
```

- as an element of an argument list in a **define**d procedure. For example, in the above **plus2** definition, the symbol **y** is created, but not given any value until the procedure is called.

79

The first type of variable is called *global*, and the second type is called *local*. Thus, in the examples above, x and plus2 are global symbols, and y is a local symbol.

In the Roman numeral example in the preceding chapter (page 66), the defined procedure names (roman->decimal and num->dec) are global, as is the name of the association list for converting roman numerals, roman-number-a-list. The variable names defined as arguments to the procedures are local (num-list and numeral).

What's the difference between global and local variables? The terms *global* and *local* are actually quite descriptive of the difference which hinges on the range or scope of a variable's definition. Local variables are accessible only within the scope of their definition, such as within a particular procedure definition. A local variable resides in a contained neighborhood. A local variable lives its entire life in the same block.

Global variables are jet-setters. They are accessible from anywhere, at any time, *except when preempted by a local variable of the same name.*

For example, imagine you have a cat named George Washington. Your cat having the same name as the first President should not generally cause confusion. Usually, the context will provide sufficient means to resolve any ambiguity. The questions "Did you feed George Washington this morning?" and "Did George Washington sign the Declaration of Independence?" are not likely to be misinterpreted. However, you might adopt another more technical method for resolving the reference. You could assume that whenever the words "George Washington" are said inside your house, they refer to your cat. If the words "George Washington" are said anywhere *except* inside your house, they refer to the President. In this sense, George Washington the cat is local to your house, and George Washington the President is global.

Let's look at some programming examples.

```
> (define x 25)                 ; x  is a global variable
25

> (define (plus2 y)             ; plus2  is global
     (+ y 2))                   ; y  is local to the procedure plus2
#{Procedure 60 PLUS2}

> x
25

> (plus2 x)                     ; x 's value of 25 is passed to the
27                              ;   local variable y

> (define y 30)                 ; y  is a global variable different from
30                              ;   the local variable  y in plus2
```

```
> y
30
```

```
> (plus2 y)          ; y 's global value of 30 is passed to
32                   ;   the local variable y
```

```
> y                  ; y 's global value is unchanged
30
```

The y within the procedure **plus2** was local; it was an argument to the procedure. It is possible to have a global variable within a procedure, as we can see below.

```
> (define (plus-z n)   ; plus-z  will add the global value of z
    (+ z n))           ;   to the local value of n
#{Procedure 61 PLUS-Z}
```

```
> (define z 10)        ; create and initialize the global z
10
```

```
> (plus-z 5)           ; 5  is passed to the local variable n
15                     ;   which is added to the global value of z
```

```
> (define z 20)        ; Give a new value to z
[Redefining Z] 20
```

```
> (plus-z 5)           ; Voilà.  A new result.
25
```

We thus created a procedure that depended on the value of a global variable, and the behavior of that procedure changed dramatically when that global variable was changed. There is an important moral lesson to be derived from this brief example.

- Refrain from using global variables within procedures. The results can become unpredictable.

5.1   Modifying Values of Objects: set

Another point to notice about the preceding section is the line of text [Redefining Z] which follows the second (define z ...) example. This is a warning to let the programmer know that the symbol z had previously been defined. All we really want to do is change the value of **z**. There is a T special form for modifying the values of objects, both local and global: **set**.

```
> (set z 3)
3

> z
3

> (set zz 8)
[Binding ZZ] 8
```

As the last example shows, you can also use **set** to create and initialize objects, but T prints a warning message in this case. The preferred usage is **define** for object creation and **set** for object modification.

The programmer can use **set** within procedure definitions to create more readable code. For example, the recursive subfunction **below-average** given in the preceding chapter was presented in typical T programming style, with procedure calls nested as arguments to other procedures.

```
(define (below-average num-list count total)
  (cond ((null? num-list) (/ total count))    ;  done? return average
        (else (below-average (cdr num-list)    ;  go to next number
                             (+ count 1)       ;  increment the count
                             (+ (car num-list);  add current number
                                total)))))     ;  to total
```

Everything is happening in the recursive call at one time. In other languages, programmers often change the values of local variables before passing them as arguments. Using **set**, we could adopt this style.

Example using set with local variables. NOT RECOMMENDED.

```
(define (below-average num-list count total)
  (cond ((null? num-list) (/ total count))     ;  done? return average
        (else (set count (+ count 1))          ;  increment the count
              (set total (+ (car num-list)
                            total))            ;  update total
              (set num-list (cdr num-list))    ;  get remainder of list
                                  ;  make the next recursive call
              (below-average num-list count total)  )))
```

This second version of **below-average** is less efficient than the first, and does not represent accepted T idiomatic style. Notice that here **set** is used to assign new values to the *local* variables **count**, **num-list**, and **total**.

For further contrast, let's see how we might have solved the average problem using global variables instead of local variables.

Example using global variables. **NOT RECOMMENDED.**

```
(define (above-average num-list)
  (set count 0)                        ;  create and initialize count
  (set total 0)                        ;  create and initialize total
  (below-average num-list))
```

```
(define (below-average num-list)
  (cond ((null? num-list) (/ total count))    ;  done? return average
        (else (set count (+ count 1))         ;  increment the count
              (set total (+ (car num-list)
                            total))           ;  update total
              (set num-list (cdr num-list))   ;  get remainder of list
                                              ;  make the next recursive call
              (below-average num-list) )))
```

This global-variable version of **above-average** and **below-average** will work pretty much the same as the local-variable version. Why choose one over the other? The reason is simple: safety. When you use a local variable, you can be certain that no other outside procedure will mess around with its value. With a global variable, there is no such assurance. If you get into the habit of using global variables, you very quickly have a bookkeeping problem to make sure that no procedure accidentally clobbers the value of a global variable. For example, if we implement **above-average** using the global variables **count** and **total**, we have to make sure that no other procedure will have conflicting uses of these variables. There is no such concern for the local-variable version of **above-average**. Two local variables of the same name won't conflict the way two identical global variables will.

One further aspect of the global versus local conflict stems from the precedence of local variables over global variables in the event of name conflicts. That is, if you have a global variable and a local variable with the same name, the local variable will win out within its own context. Here are some examples.

```
> (define x 10)
10

> (define (plus3 x) (+ x 3))
#{Procedure 75 PLUS3}

> (plus3 11)              ;  The local value of x  is
14                        ;  bound to 11, not 10

> (define (double 1)      ;  The local variable 1  does
    (list 1 1))           ;  not conflict with any global value
#{Procedure 77 DOUBLE}
```

```
> (double '(7 8))
((7 8) (7 8))

> (define (triple list)          ;  The local variable list
    (list list list list))       ;  has an obvious conflict
#{Procedure 79 TRIPLE}

> (triple '(7 8))

** Error: attempt to call a non-procedure
   ((7 8) (7 8) (7 8) (7 8))
>>
```

In T, if you recall, procedures can be passed as arguments. In the **triple** example, the local variable **list** takes precedence over the procedure definition for **list**, and an error occurs. The T interpreter tried to treat the list   **(7 8)** as a procedure and failed. The lesson then is not to give local variables names that conflict with global variables, including procedure names.

5.2   Creating Local Variables: let

We have been trying to convey the virtue of local variables. So far, we have only seen one way to create local variables, namely, as arguments in procedure definitions. There is another very useful method: the special form **let**.

Like **define** and **set**, **let** assigns values to objects. However, since **let** is for defining local variables, there must be a means for specifying the range or scope of the variables' definitions. This is accomplished by the special syntax of **let**.

```
(let ((variable-1 value-1)
      (variable-2 value-2)
         . . .
      (variable-n value-n))
  body-of-expression)
```

The **let** clause works as follows: each **variable** is created as a local variable with its respective initial **value**. The **body-of-expression**, which may consist of any number of expressions, is then executed within the scope of all the local variables. That is, each expression within **body-of-expression** may refer to and access the value of any of the local variables just instantiated. When the last expression is completed, the **let** expression is exited and the local variables are no longer accessible.

Here is a procedure (of no apparent use) which shows how **let** can simplify a calculation.

```
> (define (square-sum a b)
    (let ((a-square (* a a))
          (b-square (* b b))
          (a-b      (* a b)))
        (cond ((odd? a-square) b-square)
              ((even? b-square) a-square)
              ((equal? a-square b-square) a-b)
              (else (- a-b)))))
#{Procedure 82 SQUARE-SUM}

> (square-sum 3 4)
16

> (square-sum 2 4)
4

> (square-sum 3 3)
9

> (square-sum 4 3)
-12
```

This procedure demonstrates a way in which local variables can be used to avoid repeated calculations. Here, the values of the squares and products of the two arguments **a** and **b** are needed several times. To avoid recalculating these values, we use **let** to assign them to local variables which can then be accessed directly. Thus, we save repeated multiplications.

5.3 Indirect set

One final note on **set**. It is actually more general than previously indicated. Its form is *not* simply

(**set** symbol value)

It can be used to modify the value of any specified location, with a symbol being merely one way to indicate a location. Accessor or selector procedures may also be used to specify a location.

```
> (define x 1)              ;  The symbol  x is created and initialized
1

> (set x '(a b c d))        ;  A new value is assigned to x
(A B C D)
```

```
> x
(A B C D)

> (set (car x) '(1 2 3))     ; A new value is assigned to (car x)
(1 2 3)

> x                          ; x 's value has been modified
((1 2 3) B C D)

> (set (cdr x) '(4 5 6 7))   ; A new value is assigned to (cdr x)
(4 5 6 7)

> x                          ; x 's value has been modified again
((1 2 3) 4 5 6 7)

> (set (nth x 4) '())        ; A new value is assigned to (nth x 4)
()

> x                          ; x 's value has been modified again
((1 2 3) 4 5 6 ())
```

These examples should demonstrate the great versatility of **set**. The programmer should be aware that the use of **set**, both directly and indirectly, *destructively* modifies the object. That is, the object's previous value cannot be retrieved. Normally this is not a concern, since the intended effect is to change the value of the object. However, when you have one object that points to the value of another object, and you indirectly change the value of the second object, you have also changed the value of the first object. Here are some examples.

```
> (define x '(1 2 3 4))      ; x  is created and given an initial value.
(1 2 3 4)

> (define y x)               ; y  is created and given  x's value.
(1 2 3 4)

> (set x '(2 2 2))           ; x 's value is changed.
(2 2 2)

> y                          ; y  still points to the old value of x.
(1 2 3 4)

> (set y x)                  ; Now set  y to the new value of x.
(2 2 2)                      ; (See figure 5.1.)
```

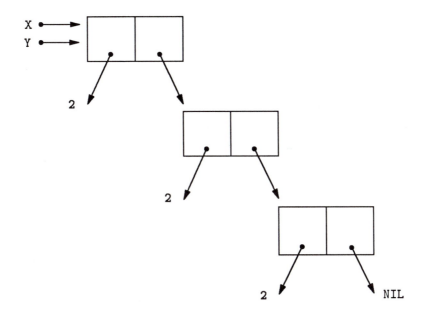

Figure 5.1: Shared list structure

```
> (set (car x) 5)          ; x 's value is modified indirectly.
5

> x                        ; x  has a new value.
(5 2 2)

> y                        ;  and so does y.
(5 2 2)

> (set (last y) 7)         ;  By modifying  y now, we also change x.
7

> y                        ;  y  has a new value.
(5 2 7)

> x                        ;  and so does x.
(5 2 7)                    ;  (See figure 5.2.)
```

From these examples, the programmer should see that one should be especially wary when dealing with shared structures, for it may produce unintended

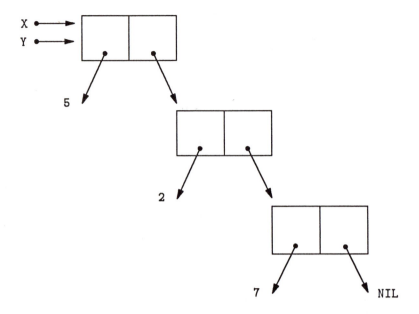

Figure 5.2: Shared list structure, after indirect changes

results. To appreciate how disastrous shared structure can be, consider the following example.

```
> (define x '(1 2 3))
(1 2 3)

> (set (car x) x)                ; Don't do this!
(((((((((((((((((((((((((   ; (lots more left parens ...)

** Error: horrible stack overflow - top of stack is trash
>>
```

The last statement resulted in a *circular list*, which causes a problem for the print routine when it tries to print something infinitely long. See figure 5.3, which depicts the result of the expression **(set (car x) x)**.

It is very easy to create circular lists.[1] The hard part is to print them.[2] In this example, the **car** of **x** is **x** itself.

It should be clear that one should avoid circular lists. It is important, however, that the programmer be aware of their existence, just as the prudent person can

---

[1]Circular lists embody the more general phenomenon of circular reference. (See next footnote.)

[2]Circular reference is exemplified by circular lists. (See preceding footnote.)

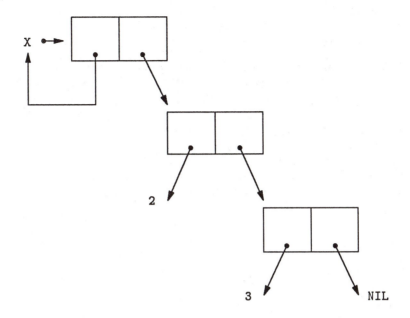

Figure 5.3: Circular list example

recognize poison ivy and rattlesnakes.[3]

We can avoid these unwanted interactions by using copies of lists instead of shared structure.

```
> (set x '(2 2 2))
(2 2 2)

> (set y (copy-tree x))
(2 2 2)

> (set (car x) 5)
5

> x
(5 2 2)

> y
(2 2 2)
```

The procedure **copy-tree** recursively makes a copy of its argument.

---

[3]Actually, there are rare occasions when circular lists are very useful, e.g., implementing a cyclical data structure.

5.4   Exercises

5.4.1   Expression Drill [3]

Evaluate all of the following expressions by hand in order. Calculate the value of x after each expression is evaluated. Then check your answers with the help of your T interpreter.

```
(define x '(1 2 3))
(set (car x) '3)
(set (cdr x) '(2 3))
(set (last x) '4)
(define (add-to-x n) (set (car x) (+ n (cadr x))))
(add-to-x 5)
(add-to-x 3)
(define (add-to-x n) (set (car x) (+ n (car x))))
(add-to-x 5)
(add-to-x 5)              ;  Yes.  Do it twice.
(set y x)
(set (car y) 0)
```

5.4.2   Identifying Local and Global Variables [3*]

In the preceding exercise, identify all occurrences of global and local variables, specifying which is which.

5.4.3   Local Variables and Making Change [4*]

The **make-change** procedure defined in the preceding chapter (page 64) was fairly inefficient. With each recursive call, it would repeat checks for the higher denomination currency.

   Rewrite **make-change** using local variables, so that no test is performed more than once. You should find that you no longer need to use recursion.

5.4.4   Niece of Zeller [4*]

The answer to exercise 3.10.7 could have been written more clearly using local variables for both the list of days of the week and the association list for the months of the year. Rewrite **daughter-of-zeller** using these local variables.

5.5   Chapter Summary

- Variables which are accessible from all procedures are called *global*.

- Variables which are accessible only from the procedure in which they are created are called *local*.

- Use **define** to create and initialize global objects.

- Use **let** to create and initialize local objects.

- Use **set** to modify objects, globally or locally.

- Accessor or selector procedures may be used to specify indirect locations to be changed by **set**.

- Indirect structure modification can cause problems in shared structures, especially with circular lists. The **copy-tree** procedure provides a way to avoid shared structure.

Chapter 6

Characters and Strings

The hell to be endured hereafter, of which theology tells,
is no worse than the hell we make for ourselves in this world
by habitually fashioning our characters in the wrong way.

⋄ WILLIAM JAMES, *The Principles of Psychology (1890)*

Harp not on that string.

⋄ WILLIAM SHAKESPEARE, *King Richard III (1592 - 1593)*

The chief defect of Henry King
Was chewing little bits of string.

⋄ HILAIRE BELLOC, *Cautionary Tales (1907)*

Thus far, we have dealt with numbers and symbols, which in turn were used to compose lists. We now look at more building blocks: characters and strings.

Strings are composed of characters linked together, just as a string of beads is composed of single beads threaded together. Characters are to strings what symbols and numbers are to lists. A string is merely a sequential set of characters, just as a list is a sequential set of objects. However, lists can also include other lists through embedding. Strings cannot be embedded.

In T, strings are denoted by characters surrounded by − no, not parentheses − double quotes. The string: `"a string"` is the sequence of characters a, *space*, s, t, r, i, n, and g. Note that the space between **a** and **s** is explicitly represented as a character.

Characters in T are a data type in their own right. They are denoted by the character itself, in the case of graphical characters, preceded by # and \, such as #\A, #\a, #\3, and #\∗. Note that upper- and lowercase characters are distinct.

Non-printing characters, such as tab, space, and newline (which moves to the beginning of the next output line), have symbolic names preceded by #\ as in #\tab, #\space, and #\newline.

Characters and strings are self-evaluating in T, just like numbers. They need not be quoted. Here are some examples.

```
> "a string"                     ;  strings are self-evaluating
"a string"

> (define x "This is a string."); strings can be bound to variables
"This is a string."

> x
"This is a string."

> (cons "hello" "there")         ;  strings can be used in lists
("hello" . "there")

> #\A                            ;  characters are self-evaluating
#\A

> (define y #\t)                 ;  characters can be bound to variables
#\t

> (define z #\tab)
#\TAB

> (cons #\A #\Z)                 ;  characters can be used in lists
(#\A . #\Z)

> (list #\A "mixed" 'list)       ;  you can mix data types in lists
(#\A "mixed" LIST)
```

Note that #\a, #\A, and 'A are three different things, namely, the character a, the character A, and the symbol A.

6.1   String and Character Predicates

Characters and strings are important when writing programs that deal with text, such as formatters, editors, or natural language processing programs. Just as we had a wide variety of procedures for dealing with lists and symbols, there is an abundance of string and character manipulation procedures.

We shall first look at the predicates that deal with strings and characters.

```
> (char? 3)                    ;  true if argument is of type character
()

> (char? #\3)
#t

> (char? #\tab)
#t

> (string? #\3)               ;  true if argument is of type string
()

> (string? "3")
#t

> (alphabetic? #\a)           ;  true if argument is an alphabetic character
#t                            ;  that is, an uppercase letter  A-Z, or a
                              ;  lowercase letter  a-z

> (alphabetic? #\A)
#t

> (alphabetic? #\1)
()

> (alphabetic? #\space)
()

> (digit? #\3 10)             ;  true if first argument is a digit character
#t                            ;    under the radix, or base, specified by the
                              ;  second argument

> (digit? #\3 2)              ;  3  is not a digit in base 2
()

> (digit? #\A 16)             ;  A  is a digit (10) in hexadecimal (base 16)
#t

> (uppercase? #\A)            ;  true if character is an uppercase letter
#t

> (lowercase? #\A)            ;  true if character is a lowercase letter
()
```

In addition to the type predicates given above, there are a large number of comparison predicates. These correspond quite directly with the arithmetic comparison predicates such as greater than, or not equal to. The basis for comparing characters is their numeric representation, which is commonly implemented in T with the ASCII[1] code. Each character, both graphical and non-printing, has a unique numeric code which provides a simple method for sorting characters. This collating sequence corresponds in large part to normal alphabetical order.

Here are T's character comparison predicates.

```
> (char= #\a #\A)          ; true if characters are the same
()

> (char= #\a #\a)
T

> (char< #\a #\b)          ; true if first is alphabetically less than the
T                          ; second

> (char> #\a #\b)          ; true if first is alphabetically greater than
()                         ; the second

> (charN= #\a #\b)         ; true if characters are different
T

> (char>= #\a #\b)         ; greater than or equal
()

> (char<= #\a #\b)         ; less than or equal
T
```

It is helpful to have a chart of the ASCII codes for reference. One appears in appendix B and in *The T Manual*.

The predicates for strings are quite simple.

```
> (string-empty? "")       ; the empty string is denoted by "",
#t                         ; just as the empty list is ()
                           ; Note: There is no space between the
                           ; double quotes for the empty string.

> (string-empty? "no")
()
```

---

[1] American Standard Code for Information Interchange. Pronounced *ASK-ey*.

```
> (string-equal? "s1" "s2")  ;  true if the strings are congruent
()                           ;  that is, they correspond exactly

> (string-equal? "s1" "s1")
#t

> (define x "string")
"string"

> (define y "string")
"string"

> (string-equal? x y)        ;  the strings are congruent
#t

> (eq? x y)                  ;  they do not have the identical memory
()                           ;  locations

> (equiv? x y)               ;  equiv? uses string-equal?
#t                           ;  thus, it returns true for congruent strings

> (alikev? x y)              ;  alikev? uses equiv?
#t                           ;  it also returns true for congruent strings

> (define x #\a)             ;  now, we'll try the same thing
#\a                          ;  with characters instead of strings

> (define y #\a)
#\a

> (eq? x y)                  ;  characters, like symbols but unlike strings,
#t                           ;  are uniquely instantiated

> (eq? #\space #\space)
#t
```

6.2   Character Operations

There are fairly few operations one uses with characters. The character operations either convert lowercase characters to uppercase, or vice versa, or convert characters to their ASCII code value, or vice versa.

```
> (char-downcase  #\M)        ; returns lowercase character
#\m

> (char-upcase  #\m)          ; returns uppercase character
#\M

> (char-upcase  #\4)          ; returns its argument if can't shift case
#\4

> (char-upcase  (char-downcase  #\M))
#\M

> (char->ascii #\A)           ; returns the ASCII code for the character
65

> (ascii->char 66)            ; returns the character for the ASCII code
#\B                           ; Note: The 66 used here is decimal.
```

These last two examples exhibit a naming convention in T. Procedures that convert their input argument to some other data type often have names with an embedded arrow, ->. They are called *coercion procedures*, and the arrow in the name is often pronounced *to*, as in *char-to-ascii* for char->ascii. We have already seen some numerical coercion procedures, such as ->integer (to-integer) and ->float (to-float).

6.3   String Operations

Many string operations are analogous to the list operations.

```
> (string-length  "short")   ; number of characters in given string
5

> (string-length  "a very long string with lots of characters")
42

> (string-head "a string")   ; returns the first character of given string
#\a                           ; analogous to CAR for lists

> (string-tail "a string")   ; returns the tail of given string
" string"                     ; analogous to CDR for lists

> (string-append "a " "string") ; joins copies of the given strings
"a string"                    ;   together; analogous to APPEND for lists
                              ; Note the space after #\a in "a string"
```

```
> (string-append "a " "big " "string")   ; string-append takes
"a big string"                           ;  any number of arguments

> (string-elt "J. S. Bach" 3)    ; (string-elt string n) returns the
#\S                              ; nth character (starting at 0) in string
                                 ; string-elt is short for string element

> (string-nthtail "J. S. Bach" 3)   ; (string-nthtail string n)
"S. Bach"                           ;  returns the nth tail in string

; (substring string start count)  returns a string of length count
;    starting at position start (zero-based) in string
> (substring "W. A. Mozart" 6 3)
"Moz"

; (string-posq character string)  returns the index of the first occurrence
;    of character in  string. If  character does not appear in
;   string  then returns ()
> (string-posq #\M "W. A. Mozart")
6

> (string-posq #\space "W. A. Mozart")
2

> (string-posq #\Z "W. A. Mozart")
()

> (string-upcase "united states")    ;  converts a copy of a string to
"UNITED STATES"                      ;  capital letters

> (string-downcase "Little MARGIE")  ;  converts a copy of the given
"little margie"                      ;  string to lowercase letters

; (map-string procedure string)  applies procedure  to each successive
;   character in  string and copies the results together as a string
> (map-string char-upcase "lisp")
"LISP"
```

The last example using map-string should make it apparent how one could define string-upcase. Here are some sample definitions of existing string procedures.

```
(define (string-downcase string)
   (map-string char-downcase string))

(define (string-length string)        ;  using STRING-TAIL recursion
   (cond ((string-empty? string) 0)
         (else (+ 1 (string-length (string-tail string)))))))

(define (string-equal? s-one s-two)
   (cond ((and (string-empty? s-one)
               (string-empty? s-two))
          t)                           ;  both strings are empty
         ((or  (string-empty? s-one)
               (string-empty? s-two))
          nil)                         ;  only one string is empty
         ((char= (string-head s-one)
                 (string-head s-two))  ;  if the two heads are equal
          (string-equal?              ;  then compare the tails
             (string-tail s-one)      ;  recursively
             (string-tail s-two)))
         (else nil)))                  ;  otherwise NIL
```

It is often useful to change other data types into strings, and vice versa. There are four coercion procedures to facilitate such changes.

```
> (list->string  '(#\h #\e #\l #\l #\o))   ;  converts a list of
"hello"                                     ;  characters into a string

> (string->list "hello")                    ;  converts a string into a
(#\h #\e #\l #\l #\o)                       ;  list of characters

> (symbol->string 'rubbish)                 ;  converts a symbol into
"RUBBISH"                                    ;  a string

> (string->symbol "GARBAGE")                ;  converts a string into
GARBAGE                                      ;  a symbol
```

6.4   Example: String Searching

One fairly common task in word processing is searching for an occurrence of a specific string in a lengthy text. For example, you may have several files in a directory and one of them contains the phrase 'list processing'. To find the file which contains that phrase, you can use a string searching routine such as the following.

```
> (string-search? "the" "now is the winter of our discontent")
#t

> (string-search? "The" "now is the winter of our discontent")
()                              ; Capital The is not in the string

; string-search?  first makes sure the input arguments are strings
;    If both strings are empty, they match.
;    If only one string is empty, they don't match.
;    If the first character of the pattern is not found in the text,
;       there is no match.  If the first character matches, see if the
;       remainder matches at that position.  Otherwise, start search
;       again at new position.

(define (string-search? pattern text)
  (cond ((null? (and (string? pattern)
                     (string? text)))
         (list 'error:non-strings: pattern text))
        ((and (string-empty? pattern)
              (string-empty? text))
         t)
        ((or (string-empty? pattern)
             (string-empty? text))
         nil)
        (else
         (let ((index (string-posq (string-head pattern) text)))
           (cond ((null? index) nil)
                 ((string-equal? pattern
                                 (substring text index
                                            (string-length pattern)))
                  t)
                 (else (string-search? pattern
                         (string-nthtail text (+ 1 index)))))))))
```

6.5   Example: Spelling Correction

We now present a program which is more complicated than anything given so far. Even though this program is a good bit larger, it has a clear and coherent structure which helps in understanding how the code works and simplifies the testing of the program by providing discrete modules to try out separately. It illustrates how large T programs are put together.

There are many programs now available as part of word processing packages that check and correct spelling. These programs usually consist of a large dictionary of common English words and a program to match words in the text with words in the dictionary. If a word in the text doesn't match a dictionary entry, then the word is probably misspelled.

Once you know that a word is misspelled, you need to find the *correct* spelling. Here is a method for proposing possible correct spellings by looking at minor variations of the misspelled word.

The procedure `spell-match` tries to correct the spelling of a word so that it matches one of the words from the dictionary. The procedure uses four methods for respelling a word:

1. *Letter deletion.* The procedure will sequentially delete each letter of the word and try to match the resulting word (which is one letter shorter) against the dictionary. For example, `commputer` would become `ommputer`, then `cmmputer`, and finally, `computer`, which would presumably match.

2. *Letter transposition.* Typists commonly transpose adjacent letters. The `spell-match` procedure should check for this condition by transposing each adjacent pair of letters in the word in sequence. For example, `copmuter` would become `ocpmuter`, then `cpomuter`, and finally, `computer`.

3. *Letter duplication.* The procedure doubles each letter in sequence to see if that results in a correct spelling. This is a special case of the next method.

4. *Letter insertion.* Often a single letter is left out. The `spell-match` procedure will go through the word sequentially and insert all possible letters at each position of the word. Note that there are many more combinations using this technique (`* 26 (+ 1 (string-length word)))`) than the previous three techniques combined. Therefore, for efficiency reasons, this method should be the last resort – only if the other three fail.

Here is how it works.

```
> (define (tag-word word)        ;  procedure to mark dictionary
    (put word 'ISA-WORD T)       ;    words as correctly spelled
    word)
#{Procedure 24 TAG-WORD}
```

```
;   Our demonstration dictionary will be quite small, just these six words.
```

```
> (map tag-word '(commuter computer computation computing compute
computers))
(COMMUTER COMPUTER COMPUTATION COMPUTING COMPUTE COMPUTERS)
```

```
> (spell-match 'computter)           ;  using letter deletion
COMPUTER
```

```
> (spell-match 'computtaion)           ;  using letter transposition
COMPUTATION

> (spell-match 'comuter)               ;  using letter duplication
COMMUTER

> (spell-match 'computin)              ;  using letter insertion
COMPUTING
```

Now we present the code for **spell-match**, except for two procedures, **string-insert** and **string-swap**, which you should define yourself (see exercise 6.6.6).

In these procedures, we assume that the words have all uppercase letters.

```
;;; spell-match  is the main procedure.  It first checks to see if its
;;;       argument is a symbol, in which case it is converted to a string.
;;;       It then checks for an empty string and a correctly spelled word.
;;;       If those tests both fail, it then tries its spelling correction
;;;       techniques.

(define (spell-match word)
  (cond ((symbol? word) (set word (symbol->string word))))
  (let ((word-length (string-length word)))
    (cond ((string-empty? word) nil)
          ((sm-check word))
          ((sm-deletion word word-length))
          ((sm-transposition word (- word-length 1)))
          ((sm-double word (- word-length 1)))
          ((sm-insertion word word-length))
          (else nil))))

;;; simple membership check
;;       Checks for the ISA-WORD property for the given word

(define (sm-check word)
  (cond ((string? word) (set word (string->symbol word))))
  (cond ((get word 'ISA-WORD) word)
        (else nil)))
```

```
;;;   delete letters case

(define (sm-deletion word-string index)
  (cond ((zero? index) nil)
        ((let ((new-word
                (string-append
                  (substring word-string 0 (- index 1))
                  (string-nthtail word-string index))))
           (sm-check new-word)))
        (else (sm-deletion word-string (- index 1)))))

;;;   transpose letters case
;;        uses the string-swap procedure

(define (sm-transposition word-string index)
  (cond ((zero? index) nil)
        ((sm-check (string-swap word-string index (- index 1))))
        (else (sm-transposition word-string (- index 1)))))

;;;   letter doubling case
;;        uses the string-insert procedure

(define (sm-double word-string index)
  (cond ((negative? index) nil)
        ((sm-check (string-insert word-string
                                   (string-elt word-string index)
                                   index)))
        (else (sm-double word-string (- index 1)))))

;;;   letter insertion case
;;        uses the string-insert procedure

(define (sm-insertion word-string index)
  (cond ((negative? index) nil)
        ((sm-insertion-check word-string index #\A))
        (else (sm-insertion word-string (- index 1)))))
```

```
;;; recursively goes through entire alphabet inserting characters at
;; index position checks each resulting word.

(define (sm-insertion-check word-string index new-char)
  (cond ((char> new-char #\Z) nil)
        ((sm-check (string-insert word-string new-char index) ))
        (else (sm-insertion-check word-string index
                                  (incr-char new-char)))))
```

```
; gets the next character, according to the ASCII code
(define (incr-char character)
   (ascii->char (+ 1 (char->ascii character)))))
```

6.6   Exercises

6.6.1   String Drill [3]

Evaluate the following expressions, first by hand, then with the help of the T interpreter.

```
(define x "the rain in Spain")
(define y "falls mainly on the plain.")
(string? x)
(alphabetic? (string-head y))
(uppercase? (string-elt x 13))
(char< (string-elt x 7) (string-elt y 7))
(string-empty? (string-tail
                (string-nthtail y (-1+ (string-length y)))))
(string-equal? x x)
(string-equal? x y)
(string-equal? x "x")
(char-downcase #\T)
(char-upcase #\T)
(char->ascii #\newline)
(char->ascii #\space)
(list->string '(#\A #\space #\l #\i #\s #\t #\bell))
(string->list "No Exit.")
(string->symbol (string-upcase "Hello"))
(symbol->string (car '(string-append "this" " and " "that")))
```

6.6.2   String Procedures [4*]

Write the following string procedures:

```
        lastchar
        capitalize
        case-string-equal?
        string-less?
```

> (lastchar "a string")   ; returns the last character in a string
#\g

> (capitalize "lisp")   ; converts the first character in a string
"Lisp"   ; to a capital.
                                 ; (This procedure already exists in T.)

> (case-string-equal? "LISP" "lisp")   ; compares two strings
#t   ; without regard to upper- or lowercase

> (case-string-equal? "LISP" "LISS")
()

> (string-less? "alpha" "beta") ; true if two strings are in
#t   ; alphabetic order

> (string-less? "beta" "alpha")
()

> (string-less? "alphabet" "alphabetize")
#t

> (string-less? "alphabetize" "alphabet")
()

6.6.3   Sorting Lists [6*]

One very common and important computer application is sorting. The subject of sorting is a well-established discipline in itself, and the details are far beyond the scope of this book. The reader is referred to [13] for a wealth of information.

In this exercise, we present a *merge sort* program for sorting lists of items. In our examples, we sort numbers, but this same method could be used to sort other objects, such as symbols, characters, and strings. The idea behind this algorithm is to break up the list to be sorted into smaller lists that are sorted, and then merge the small lists back together again, maintaining the proper ordering.

Below we present most of the procedures required, except the central **merge** procedure. The reader must provide this procedure. The reader should provide *two* versions: one for sorting numbers and one for sorting characters. We give examples of both **merge** and **msort**.

```
(define (msort l)
    (sort2 l nil))

(define (sort2 l tmplist)
    (cond ((null? l) (sort3 tmplist nil))
          (else (sort2 (cdr l)
                       (sort-add (list (car l)) tmplist)))))

(define (sort3 l tmplist)
    (cond ((null? l) tmplist)
          (else (sort3 (cdr l) (merge (car l) tmplist)))))

(define (sort-add x tmplist)
  (cond ((null? tmplist) (list x))
        ((null? (car tmplist)) (cons x (cdr tmplist)))
        (else
         (cons nil (sort-add (merge x (car tmplist))
                             (cdr tmplist))))))
```

```
> (merge '(2 7 9) '(1 8))
(1 2 7 8 9)

> (merge '(2 7 9) '())
(2 7 9)

> (merge '(9) '(5))
(5 9)

> (msort '(3 2 5 1))
(1 2 3 5)

> (msort '(4 3 6 5 7 8 9 1 2))
(1 2 3 4 5 6 7 8 9)
```

6.6.4   Roman Numeral Characters [4*]

Building on the roman->decimal procedure in section 4.3 above, write a procedure
which converts a Roman numeral string into a decimal number.

```
> (roman-char->decimal "MCXX")
1120

> (roman-char->decimal "mlxvi")
1066
```

6.6.5   String reverse [3*]

Write a procedure `string-reverse` which returns a backwards version of a given string.

```
> (string-reverse "hello")
"olleh"

> (string-reverse "a man a plan a canal panama")
"amanap lanac a nalp a nam a"

> (string-reverse "a fool a tool a pool loop a loot a loof a")
"a fool a tool a pool loop a loot a loof a"
```

6.6.6   Spelling Correction [4*]

Define `string-insert` and `string-swap` which are used in the `spell-match` program defined above. Note that `string-insert` should be able to insert a character in a string at any point, including the front and end of a string. If an index is out of bounds, then `string-insert` should return an error.

```
> (string-insert "hello" #\X 0)
"Xhello"

> (string-insert "hello" #\X 1)
"hXello"

> (string-insert "hello" #\X 4)
"hellXo"

> (string-insert "hello" #\X 5)
"helloX"

> (string-insert "hello" #\X 6)
ERROR-IN-STRING-INSERT

> (string-insert "hello" #\X -1)
ERROR-IN-STRING-INSERT

> (string-swap "hello there" 3 5)
"hel olthere"

> (string-swap "hello there" 5 3)
"hel olthere"
```

```
> (string-swap "hello there" 5 9)
"hellorthe e"

> (string-swap "hello there" 5 19)
ERROR-IN-STRING-SWAP
```

6.7 Chapter Summary

- Strings are composed of characters linked together, just as lists may be composed of objects linked together.

- Strings and characters are T objects.

- Strings in T are delimited by double quotes, e.g., **"a string"**.

- Characters in T are denoted by the character itself preceded by # and \, e.g., #\A.

- String and character predicates:

```
(char? object)
(string?  object)
(alphabetic? character)
(digit? character radix)
(uppercase? character)
(lowercase? character)
(char= character1 character2)
(char< character1 character2)
(char> character1 character2)
(charn= character1 character2)
(char>= character1 character2)
(char<= character1 character2)
(string-empty? string)
(string-equal? string1 string2)
```

- String and character operations:

```
(char-downcase character)
(char-upcase character)
(string-length string)
(string-head string)
(string-tail string)
(string-append . strings)
(string-elt string integer)
(string-nthtail string integer)
(substring string start count)
(string-posq character string)
(string-upcase string)
(string-downcase string)
(map-string procedure string)
```

- Conversion procedures:

```
(char->ascii character)
(ascii->char integer)
(list->string list)
(string->list string)
(symbol->string symbol)
(string->symbol string)
(char->string character)
```

Chapter 7

Ports: Output and Input

> *All places that the eye of heaven visits*
> *Are to a wise man ports and happy havens.*
> *Teach thy necessity to reason thus;*
> *There is no virtue like necessity.*

◇ WILLIAM SHAKESPEARE, *King Richard II (1595-1596)*

> *If you would not be forgotten,*
> *as soon as you are dead and rotten,*
> *either write things worth reading, or do things worth writing.*

◇ BENJAMIN FRANKLIN, *Poor Richard's Almanac (1738)*

T is very helpful. It always prints out the value of the last expression that it has evaluated. For example, when you type (+ 3 4), T will not only evaluate the expression, but will also print the resulting value **7**.

Often, though, you are interested in seeing some intermediate values or messages from your programs. You may also want to have some results printed to a file instead of to the terminal. Or, you may like your program to read in data that is stored in a file. T supports these types of *input* and *output* operations, both with your terminal and with files.

Files and terminals comprise the outside world for T and there is a very basic way of viewing this input and output relationship. To T, input, from either a file or a terminal, is a source of data. Output, to either a file or a terminal, is a receptacle for data. This source/receptacle idea is captured in the notion of a *port*, which is the abstraction T uses for the input/output.

A port is something from which data can be input, and to which data can be output. In some languages, including earlier versions of T, ports are referred to as *streams*. A port is both a source and a receptacle; a faucet and a drain. At the lowest level, a program's input and output generally comes one character at a time.

An input port is where the program gets characters, and an output port is where the program sends characters.

7.1   The Terminal Is a Port

When you perform an input or output operation, T has to know to which port you are referring. There are default ports which T uses for many operations. The primary ones are for terminal input and output. They are called standard input and output.

```
> (standard-input)               ; default port for input
#{Input-port "standard input"}

> (standard-output)              ; default port for output
#{Output-port "standard output"}

> (port? (standard-input))       ; port? is the predicate for ports
#t

> (port? 'standard-input)
()
```

These are T's generic ports.

7.2   Output: Writing to Ports

We can print to the terminal using a set of basic output commands. Here we define a procedure which takes a string, and prints it on the terminal using three separate methods.

```
(define (name-output name)
    (let ((term (standard-output)))
      (print name term)
      (write-spaces term 5)
      (write-string term name)
      (display name term)
      (newline term)
      nil))

> (name-output "Jesse James")
"Jesse James"     Jesse JamesJesse James
()
```

Here's what happened in **name-output:**

1. `term` is the local name given to the standard output port.

2. `(print object port)` simply prints out the given object on the given port. Note that the double quotes are included in the result.

3. `(write-spaces port count)` prints `count` spaces on the given port.

4. `(write-string port string)` prints the given string to the given port, but without the delimiting double quotes.

5. `(display object port)` like `write-string`, `display` prints an object to a port without delimiters.

6. `(newline port)` goes to the beginning of the next line of the output port.

7. `()` is the value printed as the result of evaluating the procedure.

We shall now explore some examples from the world of text formatting. One of the most widespread uses of computers today is word-processing, that is, editing and formatting text. This book has been prepared using computerized word-processing tools that make it very easy to specify where the text should appear on the page. For example,
text can be flush to the left margin,
                    or centered between the left and right margins,
                                        or flush to the right margin.
We can write some simple T procedures to perform these same functions.

The first procedure is `indent`, which prints a text string a given number of spaces from the left margin of the specified output port.

```
> (define (indent text indentation port)
    (newline port)
    (write-spaces port indentation)
    (write-string port text)
    repl-wont-print)
#{Procedure 142 INDENT}

> (indent "Good morning, Mr. Phelps." 10 (standard-output))

          Good morning, Mr. Phelps.
```

The reader should note the use of the global symbol `repl-wont-print` as the value returned by `indent`. This special T symbol has the obvious property that the READ-EVAL-PRINT loop does not print anything to the output port as its value. Thus, `repl-wont-print` is useful for those occasions when the programmer does not want the output cluttered up with miscellaneous values such as `T` or `()`.

Given the `indent` procedure, it is trivial to define the **flushleft** procedure.

```
> (define (flushleft text port)
    (indent text 0 port))
#{Procedure 153 FLUSHLEFT}

> (flushleft "Rive gauche" (standard-output))

Rive gauche
```

Printing text flush on the right margin requires knowing where the right margin is, or at least, the maximum width of an output line. The T procedure **line-length** returns the width (in characters) of the given output port.

```
> (line-length (standard-output))
79

> (define (flushright text port)
    (let ((indentation (- (line-length port)
                          (string-length text))))
      (indent text indentation port)))
#{Procedure 155 FLUSHRIGHT}

> (flushright "right makes might" (standard-output))

                                              right makes might
```

The **center** procedure is very similar to **flushright**.

```
> (define (center text port)
    (let ((indentation (quotient (- (line-length port)
                                    (string-length text))
                                 2)))
      (indent text indentation port)))
#{Procedure 158 CENTER}

> (center "*** T Party at 8 o'clock ***" (standard-output))

                  *** T Party at 8 o'clock ***
```

Now we can put them all together.

```
> (define (try-it)
    (let ((x (standard-output)))
      (flushleft "This is flushleft" x)
      (center "This Is Centered" x)
      (flushright "and this is flushright" x)
      (indent "Indented 5" 5 x)
      (indent "Indented 10" 10 x)))
#{Procedure 174 TRY-IT}

> (try-it)
```

```
This is flushleft
                        This Is Centered
                                        and this is flushright
        Indented 5
              Indented 10
```

Another text formatting example is the **split** procedure, which prints its first argument flush to the left margin, and the second argument flush to the right margin on the same line to the given output port – the third argument.

```
(define (split left-text right-text port)
    (flushleft left-text port)
    (write-spaces port
                  (- (line-length port)
                     (+ (hpos port)
                        (string-length right-text))))
    (write-string port right-text)
    repl-wont-print)
```

```
> (split "From here, ..." "... to eternity" (standard-output))

From here, ...                                    ... to eternity
```

The **split** procedure determines the number of spaces separating the left and right texts, which is the line width minus the sum of the right text length and the column position after printing the left text. This column position is given by the **hpos** procedure (horizontal position).

7.3   format

It should be apparent that a handful of output commands can be combined to format text in a variety of ways. Achieving these results can require a concerted programming effort. However, T provides a special procedure for formatting output: **format**. Here are some examples.

```
> (format (standard-output) "Hello, my name is ~s.~%" 'Joey)
Hello, my name is JOEY.
**VALUE-OF-FORMAT**

> (format T "How old are you, ~A?~%" "Joey")
How old are you, Joey?
**VALUE-OF-FORMAT**

> (define joey-age 12)
12

> (format nil "I am ~D year~P old." joey-age joey-age)
"I am 12 years old."

> (format T "My brothers are:
~5t~A: ~D year~P old and ~%~5t~A: ~D year~P old.~%"
"Paul" 5 5 "John" 1 1)
My brothers are:

     Paul: 5 years old and
     John: 1 year old.
**VALUE-OF-FORMAT**
```

The first argument to **format** is the destination of the output. The destination can be given as:

- a specific output port, such as **(standard-output)**. The value returned by **format** is then undefined.

- true (given as T). In this case, output is directed to the default **(standard-output)**. The value returned by **format** again is undefined.

- false (given as **nil**). In this case, the output is returned as a string as the value of **format**.

The second argument to format is a control string, which comprises both characters to be printed and control codes to give spacing information and the printing specifications for the remaining arguments, such as numbers, strings, and symbols. The control codes each begin with a *tilde* character (~). The control codes which don't match arguments include:

~**n**T: Tab to column number **n**.

~%: Begin a new line.

~~: Print a tilde.

The control codes which sequentially match the remaining arguments include:

~A: Display the next argument.

~S: Print the next argument.

~D: Print the next argument as a decimal number (base 10).

~B: Print the next argument as a binary number (base 2).

~O: Print the next argument as an octal number (base 8).

~X: Print the next argument as a hexadecimal number (base 16).

~P: Write an "s" if the next argument is greater than 1, else write nothing. This code can be used to control for simple plurals.

Here is another example of **format**.

```
(define (ascii-print character)
  (let ((code (char->ascii character)))
    (format t "The ASCII code for ~A (~S) is:"
        character character)
    (format t "~%~5tBinary: ~20t~b" code)
    (format t "~%~5tOctal: ~20t~o" code)
    (format t "~%~5tDecimal: ~20t~d" code)
    (format t "~%~5tHexadecimal: ~20t~x" code)
    repl-wont-print))
#{Procedure 37 ASCII-PRINT}

> (ascii-print #\A)
The ASCII code for A (#\A) is:
    Binary:        1000001
    Octal:         101
    Decimal:       65
    Hexadecimal:   41
```

7.4 Input: Reading from Ports

It is possible to use simple strings as input and output ports. Here is an example of a string as an input port. The procedure **string->input-port** converts a given string into an input port.

```
> (set x (string->input-port "one two three"))
#{String input-port "one two three"}
```

```
> x
#{String input-port "one two three"}

> (port? x)              ; x  is a port
#t

> (input-port? x)        ; x  is an input port
#t

> (output-port? x)       ; x  is not an output port
()

> (read-char x)          ;  reads a single character from given port
#\o

> (read-char x)          ;  note that it now returns the second character
#\n

> x                      ;  the  x port has had two characters removed
#{String input-port "e two three"}

> (unread-char x)        ;  this reverses the last read-char
#t

> (read-char x)          ;  read-char  now reads the previous character
#\n

> (read-char x)          ;  the third character is now read
#\e

> x                      ;  current value of port  x
#{String input-port " two three"}

; peek-char  reads next character but does not advance the port.
> (peek-char x)
#\SPACE

> x                      ;  note that #\space is still head character of x
#{String input-port " two three"}

> (read-line x)          ;  read an entire line from the given port
" two three"
```

```
> x                      ; the  x port is now empty
#{String input-port ""}

> (read-line x)          ; an empty port returns an End-Of-File token
#{Eof}                   ; when you try to read from the port. It is dry.

> (read-char x)
#{Eof}

> (eof? (read-char x))   ; eof?  predicate returns true for the Eof token.
#t

> (eq? EOF (read-char x))   ; EOF  is bound to the Eof token
#t

> (set y (string->input-port "three two one"))
#{String input-port "three two one"}

> (close y)              ; forces an end-of-file.  Closes port.
" "

> y                      ; the port is now empty
#{String input-port ""}
```

This simple example demonstrates the basic properties of input ports.

- The ports are a source of characters (in this case, from a string).

- The ports are often given names (that is, bound to variables, like **x** in this case).

- The predicates **port?** and **input-port?** will return true for input ports.

- Ports can be created (opened) and destroyed (closed).

- An empty port is indicated by the end-of-file token, which is tested by the **eof?** predicate.

- A simple one-character look-ahead scheme is afforded by the **peek-char** procedure.

- In addition to character-by-character input, one can read entire lines as strings using the **read-line** procedure.

It is also possible to read T objects from ports. The **load** command for reading T expressions from files relies on this facility. When you **load** a file, T performs the following actions:

1. Opens a port that reads characters from the given file.

2. Reads in the next T expression.

3. If end-of-file is encountered, then closes the port and quits.

4. Evaluates the current T expression, and returns to step 2.

The read operation from step 2 is demonstrated below.

```
> (set p (string->input-port "1 23 456 7890"))
#{String input-port "1 23 456 7890"}
```

```
> (read p)            ; note that  read returns a T number,
1                     ; not the character #\1
```

```
> (read p)            ; the next number is now returned
23
```

```
> p                   ; here is the current value of the port p
#{String input-port "456 7890"}
```

```
> (+ (read p) (read p)) ; the values of read can be used as arguments
8346                    ; for other procedures
```

```
> (read p)            ; the port  p is now empty
#{Eof}
```

```
> (set q (string->input-port "a bb (* 3 4)"))
#{String input-port "a bb (* 3 4)"}
```

```
> (read q)            ; read  returns the T symbol, not the
A                     ; character #\A
```

```
> (read q)
BB
```

```
> (read q)            ; read  returns a list expression
(* 3 4)
```

Note that **read** did not evaluate the expressions.

7.5   Files as Ports

The basic properties of string ports also apply to input and output to files.

The first step in reading or writing a file is to create a port by opening the file. The **open** command takes two arguments: the name of the file and a list of specifications of the types of access required. A file port may be opened for input (using the IN keyword), or output (using the keyword OUT), or for adding to the end of the file (using the APPEND keyword). Here is an example of an output file, and associated common output operations.

```
> (file-exists? "myfile.data")   ;  predicate to tell if a file has been
()                               ;  created

> (set p1 (open "myfile.data" '(out)))  ;  the output port is bound
#{Output-port "myfile.data"}            ;  to p1

> (file-exists? "myfile.data")          ;  now the file does exist
#t

> (write-char p1 #\A)         ;  write the given character on the port
#t

> (newline p1)                ;  begin a new line on output port
#t

> (write-spaces p1 1)         ;  write a blank character to output port
#t

> (display "This is a test" p1)  ;  print given object to port, without
#t                               ;  printing delimiting double quotes

> (define (fact n)            ;  define a simple procedure
      (cond ((zero? n) 1)
            (else (* n (fact (subtract1 n))))))
#{Procedure FACT}

> (print fact p1)             ;  prints object to given output port
**VALUE-OF-FORMAT**           ;  This value comes from format command
                              ;  explained above.

> (newline p1)                ;  another new line on output port
#t

> (pretty-print fact p1)      ;  nicer output style than print command
#t
```

```
> (close p1)                    ; end of output to port p1
#t
```

Now, let's look at the content of the file `myfile.data` to which we just wrote.

```
A
 This is a test#{Procedure FACT}
(NAMED-LAMBDA FACT
             (N)
             (COND ((ZERO? N) 1)
                   (ELSE (* N
                            (FACT (SUBTRACT1 N))))))
```

Here is a breakdown of where the characters came from.

1. The A in line 1 came from the `write-char` command.

2. The blank at the beginning of line 2 came from the `newline` command followed by the `write-spaces` command.

3. The string `This is a test` in line 2 is from the `display` command.

4. The object name `#{Procedure FACT}` in line 2 is from the `print` command.

5. The `NAMED-LAMBDA` expression which starts on line 3 is from the `newline` command followed by the `pretty-print` command.

We can now turn around and use that file for input.

```
> (set p2 (open "myfile.data" '(IN)))    ; open file for input
#{Input-port "myfile.data"}

> (list (read p2) (read p2) (read p2))   ; read the first three objects
(A THIS IS)

> (list (read p2) (read p2) (read p2))   ; read the next three objects
(A TEST# (**BRACED** PROCEDURE FACT))    ; note that the #{} notation
                                         ; is tricky to read back in

> (close p2)
()
```

7.6   Port Examples

We shall now define several procedures that do useful tasks with ports. The first one will simply copy one port (the input) to another (the output).

```
(define (port-copy p-input p-output)
    (cond ((or (not (input-port? p-input))   ;  error checking
               (not (output-port? p-output)))
           (write-string (error-output)
               "Foul port in PORT-COPY."))
          ((eof? (peek-char p-input))         ;  check for end-of-file
           '*END-OF-PORT-COPY*)
          (else                               ;  copy input to output
           (write-string p-output (read-line p-input))
           (newline p-output)
           (port-copy p-input p-output))))    ;  recursive call
```

The **port-copy** procedure does some error checking at first. If an error is found, a message is printed to the port given by **(error-output)**. This is usually defined to be the same as **standard-output**, that is, errors normally are printed to the terminal.

The procedure is recursive. The termination condition is end-of-file.

The following is a procedure which uses the **port-copy** procedure. The **type** procedure takes a file name (given as a string) and prints the contents of the file on the standard output.

```
(define (type file-name)
    (let ((file-port (open file-name '(IN))))
      (port-copy file-port (standard-output))
      (close file-port)))
```

The next example is a *filter*, that is, a program which reads an input and prints selected (and possibly changed) parts to its output. For example, you may wish to find all the three-letter words contained in a file.

```
(define (filter-file filter input-file output-file)
    (let ((in-port (open input-file '(in)))
          (out-port (open output-file '(out))))
      (filter-port filter in-port out-port)
      (close in-port)
      (close out-port)))
```

```
(define (filter-port filter in-port out-port)
   (cond ((eof? (peek-char in-port)) 'EOF)
         (else
          (let ((tmp (filter (read in-port))))
            (cond (tmp
                   (format out-port "~D~%" tmp)))
            (filter-port filter in-port out-port)))))

(define (3-letter-word? word)
   (cond ((symbol? word) (set word (symbol->string word))))
   (cond ((not (string? word)) NIL)
         ((= (string-length word) 3) word)
         (else nil)))
```

The first procedure, `filter-file`, opens the files to create the ports, calls the `filter-port` procedure, and finally closes the ports, forcing any pending output to be printed to the output port as it is closed.

The second procedure, `filter-port`, checks the the termination condition (end of the input port), and then proceeds to apply the filter procedure to the next object read from the input port. If the object passes through the filter, it is printed on the output port. The process continues with a recursive call to `filter-port`.

The third procedure, `3-letter-word?`, simply checks to see if its argument has three and only three letters.

Suppose that a file called `sample.in` contains a simple list of words: one two three four five six seven eight nine ten. We can use our filter program to extract the three-letter words.

```
> (filter-file 3-letter-word? "sample.in" "sample.out")
#t
```

Here are the contents of the file `sample.out`
```
"ONE"
"TWO"
"SIX"
"TEN"
```

Clearly, this is a pedestrian example. However, the author actually had occasion to get an exhaustive list of English three-letter words for use in a computer program to teach children how to read. The simple filter program given here, combined with an online English dictionary, provided such a list.

Filter programs, or file transducers, are very adaptable and useful *software tools*. They are discussed at length in Kernighan and Plauger's fine book [11].

7.7   Exercises

7.7.1   column-print [4*]

Write a procedure `column-print` which uses cdr recursion to print out string elements of a list indented in a column to the given output port.

```
> (column-print '("Go ahead" "make" "my" "  day") 5
    (standard-output))

  Go ahead
  make
  my
    day
```

7.7.2   split Command [4*]

This is a two-part question concerning the procedure `split`, which was given above on page 114. First, what's wrong with defining `split` as follows?

```
(define (split left-text right-text port)
    (flushleft left-text port)
    (flushright right-text port))
```

Second, redefine `split` without using the `hpos` procedure.

7.7.3   tab Command [4*]

Write a `tab` procedure which moves to a specified column in the given output port. If necessary, `tab` will move to the next line to arrive at the proper column.

Here is a sample program that shows how `tab` works.

```
> (define (sample-tab)
    (let ((s (standard-output)))
        (write-string s "This")
        (tab 10 s)
        (write-string s "is")
        (tab 30 s)
        (write-string s "a sample")
        (tab 5 s)
        (write-string s "of tab...")
        repl-wont-print))
#{Procedure 119 SAMPLE-TAB}

> (sample-tab)
This      is                    a sample
      of tab...
```

7.7.4 pinetree-print [5*]

Write a procedure `pinetree-print`, which prints a given string to the given output port in the shape of a tree (sort of).

```
> (pinetree-print "O Christmas tree, O Christmas tree..."
    (standard-output))

                        O
                        Ch
                     ristm
                    as tree
                    , O Chris
                   tmas tree..
                        .

(pinetree-print
"sprucesprucesprucesprucesprucesprucesprucesprucespruce"
            (standard-output))
                        s
                       pru
                      cespr
                     ucespru
                    cespruces
                   prucespruce
                  sprucespruces
                      pruce
```

7.7.5 peek-char Problem [3*]

What's wrong with this definition of peek-char?

```
(define (peek-char port)
  (read-char port)
  (unread-char port))
```

7.7.6 split-fill [4*]

Write a procedure `split-fill` which is similar to the `split` procedure defined in section 7.2, except that the new procedure will print a specified character repeatedly in the space between the left and right texts.

```
(split-fill "Birds, for the " #\. " pages 1-217" (standard-output))
Birds, for the ....................................... pages 1-217
```

7.7.7   Printing Recipes [4*]

Write a procedure `print-recipe` which takes a list of the form (**"name of recipe"** **(ingredient lists) (instruction steps)**). The ingredients would be sublists of quantity/item pairs, and the instructions would be sublists of ordered steps to be followed. The procedure `print-recipe` prints the recipe nicely on the specified port. For example,

```
(define recipe57
   '("Egg Salad"          ;  name of Recipe
     ((6 eggs)            ;  ingredients
      (3 TBS mayonnaise)
      (1 tsp curry)
      (1 dash tabasco sauce)
      (2 dill pickles)
      (1 tsp salt))
     ((Boil 2 quarts of water.)     ;  instructions
      (Add eggs to boiling water.)
      (After 13 minutes, remove eggs from boiling water.)
      (Rinse eggs in cold water and remove shells.)
      (Place eggs in large bowl, and chop finely with knife.)
      (Add mayonnaise, curry, tabasco, pickles, and salt.)
      (Serve on toast.))))

> (print-recipe recipe57 (standard-output))

                        Egg Salad
         6 EGGS
         3 TBS MAYONNAISE
         1 TSP CURRY
         1 DASH TABASCO SAUCE
         2 DILL PICKLES
         1 TSP SALT


    (1)   BOIL 2 QUARTS OF WATER.
    (2)   ADD EGGS TO BOILING WATER.
    (3)   AFTER 13 MINUTES, REMOVE EGGS FROM BOILING WATER.
    (4)   RINSE EGGS IN COLD WATER AND REMOVE SHELLS.
    (5)   PLACE EGGS IN LARGE BOWL, AND CHOP FINELY WITH KNIFE.
    (6)   ADD MAYONNAISE, CURRY, TABASCO, PICKLES, AND SALT.
    (7)   SERVE ON TOAST.
```

7.7.8   Defining format [6]

Write a simple version of the **format** procedure which takes exactly three arguments: an output port, a control string, and a single output argument.

    The control string can include any of the control codes of the real **format**, but a given control string may have only one occurrence of a control code which requires an argument. Thus, `"~A loves Mary."` is OK, but `"~A loves ~A"` is not. One exception is numeric control codes, such as `"~D"` and `"~P"`. A control string may have multiple numeric control codes, but they all match the same third argument, as in the following:

```
> (my-format (standard-output) "John ate ~D pizza~P.~%" 3)
John ate 3 pizzas.
**VALUE-OF-MY-FORMAT**

> (my-format (standard-output) "Mary ate ~D pizza~P.~%" 1)
Mary ate 1 pizza.
**VALUE-OF-MY-FORMAT**
```

7.7.9   File Revision [6]

One useful type of file filter is one that can change or correct parts of the file. For example, suppose you have a file containing a boilerplate paragraph with places for a name to be substituted. Here are the contents of `"gift.file"`, an example of a boilerplate text.

```
Thank you so much for the *GIFT*.
How did you know that Pat and I needed a
*GIFT*? Every time we look at the *GIFT*
we think of you.
```

    Write a procedure **revise-file**, which takes four arguments: an input file, an output file, a search pattern, and a replacement pattern. Here is a sample run on the above text.

```
> (revise-file "gift.file" "gift.out" "*GIFT*" "keyboard duster")

old: "Thank you so much for the *GIFT*."
new: "Thank you so much for the keyboard duster."

old: "*GIFT*? Every time we look at the *GIFT*"
new: "keyboard duster? Every time we look at the keyboard duster"
*END-OF-FILE-REVISION*
```

Note that the program prints out intermediate results when it makes a change, and that the program can handle multiple changes on one line. Here are the resulting contents of the output file.

```
Thank you so much for the keyboard duster.
How did you know that Pat and I needed a
keyboard duster?  Every time we look at the keyboard duster
we think of you.
```

7.7.10   File Comparison [5*]

Another useful software tool is a utility which compares files. That is, if you have two versions of a file, you can compare the two files to identify the precise ways in which they differ.

Write a procedure `compare-file`, which takes two filenames as arguments, and prints out lines that are different. Assume that both files are the same length – no deleted or inserted lines.

Here is an example, using the sample files from the preceding exercise.

```
> (compare-file "gift.file" "gift.out")

1: "Thank you so much for the *GIFT*."
2: "Thank you so much for the keyboard duster."

1: "*GIFT*?  Every time we look at the *GIFT*"
2: "keyboard duster?  Every time we look at the keyboard duster"
*END-OF-FILE-COMPARE*

> (compare-file "gift.file" "gift.file")
*END-OF-FILE-COMPARE*
```

In the second example, the files are identical, so no differences were found.

7.7.11   File Sorting [7]

Yet another common type of file transducer is a sort utility. We briefly looked at sorting in exercise 6.6.3.

In this exercise, we invite the reader to create a sort utility that will read in a file, sort each line of the file based a given set of key fields, lengths, and comparision predicates, and write the results to a given output file. Here is an example.

```
;;  Contents of file: names.txt
Mary        Jones       345-9090    123 Pine Street
Deborah     Smith       782-1245    456 Elm Street, 12-B
Susan       Brown       889-4321    789 Maple Street
Jane        Smith       345-7766    1212 Grove Terrace
Mary        White       889-3758    321 Avenue of Trees
Louise      Brown       782-3299    43 Oak Drive


;; filesort   takes three arguments:
;           input-file
;           output-file
;           list of key fields and comparison predicates
> (filesort "names.txt" "names.out" '((13 12 string-less?)
        (1 12 string-less?)))
*END-OF-FILESORT*


;;  Resulting contents of file: names.out
Louise      Brown       782-3299    43 Oak Drive
Susan       Brown       889-4321    789 Maple Street
Mary        Jones       345-9090    123 Pine Street
Deborah     Smith       782-1245    456 Elm Street, 12-B
Jane        Smith       345-7766    1212 Grove Terrace
Mary        White       889-3758    321 Avenue of Trees
```

The primary sort key is given first; in this case, it is the last names which start at the 13th character in each line and extend for 12 characters. The comparison predicate **string-less?** was given in the answer to exercise 6.6.2. The second sort key is the first names, which begin at the first position and extend for 12 characters.

7.8   Chapter Summary

- In T, *ports* are used both for input (a source for reading data) and output (a receptacle for writing data).

- Files and terminals are examples of ports; the default ports are (standard-input) and (standard-output).

- T provides a variety of basic procedures for writing data:

```
(print object port)
(write-spaces port count)
(write-string port string)
(newline port)
(write-char port character)
(pretty-print object port)
```

```
(display object port)
(format destination control-string . arguments)
```

as well as procedures and predicates for getting information about the output port:

```
(port? port)
(output-port? port)
(line-length port)
(hpos port)
```

- The special symbol **repl-wont-print** lives up to its name. It often is useful to return as a non-printing value of output routines.

- Strings can be used as input ports using **(string->input-port string)**.

- Files can be used for input and output as well. Useful predicates and operations include:

```
(file-exists? filename)
(open filename mode-list)
(close port)
```

- The end of file is designated by the value of **EOF**, which responds true to the predicate **(eof? object)**.

- T provides a variety of basic procedures for reading data:

```
(read-char port)
(unread-char port)
(peek-char port)
(read-line port)
(clear-input port)
(read port)
```

as well as procedures for getting information about the input port:

```
(input-port? port)
(eof? object)
```

Chapter 8

LAMBDA and LABELS

That best portion of a good man's life,
His little, nameless, unremembered acts
Of kindness and love.

◇ WILLIAM WORDSWORTH, *Lines Composed a Few Miles Above Tintern Abbey*
(1798)

In historical events great men – so called –
are but labels that serve to give a name to an event,
and like labels,
they have the least possible connection
with the event itself.

◇ LEO NIKOLAEVICH TOLSTOI, *War and Peace (1869)*

Objects in T can be created and assigned as values of variables. Thus, numbers, lists, characters, strings, ports, and procedures can be given names by binding them to symbols. If we define x to have the value of '(a-long-expression), we have in effect given '(a-long-expression) the name x. This technique provides a convenient shorthand or abbreviation, especially if we wish to refer to '(a-long-expression) more than once. For example, assume we have an ordered list of Presidents of the United States.

```
(define *us-presidents* '(washington adams jefferson ...))

(define (president? x)
    (memq? x *us-presidents*))

(define (first-president? x)
    (eq? x (car *us-presidents*)))
```

To use this list in different places, we need not duplicate the list. Instead, we simply use its name. This use of names to refer to frequently used data objects is the preferred method. In the above example, one can easily add new Presidents without having to change the existing code.

Often, however, the object is used in only one location, so there is no need to have a special name for it. We can simply use the explicit description of the object itself. For example, if we have a procedure which checks to see if its argument is the name of the first President of the United States, we can represent that name directly in the code.

```
(define (first-president? x)
   (eq? x 'washington))
```

When we use **define** to create a procedure, we are likewise assigning a name to the procedure. As with other named objects, the procedure's name makes it easier for us to reuse that object. In our examples so far, all of our procedures have been given names. We shall now see how to write nameless procedures.

8.1   lambda

The LISP language was derived in part from a mathematical formalism developed in the 1930's by Alonzo Church called the *lambda*-calculus or λ-calculus.[4] The use of the keyword lambda is one vestige of that early history. In T, one uses lambda at the beginning of a list to indicate the description of a procedure. The list element immediately following the *lambda* is a list of the variable names local to the procedure. Here are some examples.

```
> (lambda (n) (+ n 2))        ;  adds 2 to its argument
#{Procedure 29}

> (lambda (x) (* x 2))        ;  doubles its argument
#{Procedure 30}

> (procedure? car)            ;  procedure?  is a predicate for procedures
#t

> (procedure? 'car)
()

> (procedure? (lambda (x) (* x 2)))
#t
```

8.2   Procedural Arguments

In earlier chapters, we saw examples of procedures which had other procedures as
arguments. For example, the T procedures `map` and `map-string` take procedural
arguments. Previously, we used named procedures as the arguments, but it is also
possible to use lambda expressions. Here are examples of the use of `map` with named
procedures as well as lambda expressions.

```
> (map add1 '(1 2 3 4))
(2 3 4 5)

> (map (lambda (x) (+ x 2)) '(1 2 3 4))
(3 4 5 6)

> (map add '(1 2 3 4) '(5 6 7 8))
(6 8 10 12)

> (map (lambda (x) (format t "~A~%" (+ x 1))) '(1 2 3 4))
2
3
4
5
(**VALUE-OF-FORMAT** **VALUE-OF-FORMAT** **VALUE-OF-FORMAT**
**VALUE-OF-FORMAT**)

> (walk (lambda (x) (format t "~A~%" (+ x 1))) '(1 2 3 4))
2
3
4
5
*VALUE-OF-WALK*

> (map (lambda (x y) (+ x (* 2 y))) '(1 2 3 4) '(5 6 7 8))
(11 14 17 20)
```

We have introduced a new list procedure called `walk` which is similar to `map`, but
only for performing side-effects on lists. The value returned by `walk`, like the value
of `format`, is undefined.

It is important to recognize that lambda affords us a way to use procedures
without giving them explicit names. The last example could easily have been accomplished by defining another procedure that would add its first argument to twice
the value of its second argument. However, lambda lets us avoid that intermediate
step.

In fact, you can assign names to lambda expressions as an alternative way of
defining procedures.

```
> (define triple (lambda (x) (* 3 x)))
#{Procedure 38}

> (triple 5)
15
```

As opposed to the method used in previous chapters:

```
> (define (triple x) (* 3 x))
#{Procedure 40 TRIPLE}

> (triple 6)
18
```

Note that in the latter case, the printed value of the procedure includes its name.

Consider the following trivial cryptography example. We define a procedure **encode** which increments the ASCII value of a character by some given integer. The **decode** procedure reverses that operation. Then we define two additional procedures, **string-encode** and **string-decode**, to extend the operation to entire strings.

```
(define (encode char n)
        (ascii->char (+ (char->ascii char) n)))

(define decode (lambda (char n)
        (ascii->char (- (char->ascii char) n))))

(define (string-encode string n)
    (map-string (lambda (char) (encode char n)) string))

(define string-decode (lambda (string n)
    (map-string (lambda (char) (decode char n)) string)))

> (set x (string-encode "mary had a little lambda" 1))
"nbsz!ibe!b!mjuumf!mbnceb"

> (string-decode x 1)
"mary had a little lambda"
```

The reader should note that we have used lambda expressions in two distinct fashions. First, we have defined the procedures **decode** and **string-decode** with the explicit lambda syntax. Compare those definitions with the procedures **encode** and **string-encode**. They are equally acceptable.

Second, within the procedures **string-encode** and **string-decode**, we used lambda expressions as arguments to the procedure **map-string**. In each case, the lambda expression has one variable which gets bound to successive characters of the given string. Note that the increment variable, **n**, is simply embedded in the lambda expression, since it is the same for each character of the string.

8.3 apply

When we call a procedure, we have a number of ways in which we may specify the relationship between the procedure and its arguments. Here are three examples, which yield equivalent results.

```
> (+ 3 4)
7

> (car (map + '(3) '(4)))
7

> ((lambda (x y) (+ x y)) 3 4)
7
```

The second example may seem contorted, and the third example may seem mysterious. Actually, the third example is merely an expansion of the first example. Recall that when evaluating a procedural list expression, T expects the first element of the list to be a procedure which it then applies to the remaining elements of the list. In this third example, the first element of the list is a lambda expression, which of course has the value of a procedure. This particular lambda expression has two variables (x and y), which become bound to 3 and 4, respectively.

The T syntax provides this implicit interpretation. However, there is an explicit way of notating this process through the use of the procedure **apply**.

Here are two examples of **apply**.

```
> (apply + '(3 4))
7

> (apply (lambda (x y) (+ x y)) '(3 4))
7
```

The first argument to **apply** is the procedure that is being invoked. The remaining arguments comprise that procedure's arguments. Thus, + is applied to the list (3 4).

Multiple arguments may be separated, as long as the final argument given in **apply** is a proper list. The procedural argument to **apply** will use all of the remaining arguments.

```
> (apply + 3 '(4))
7
```

```
> (apply + 3 4 '())
7

> (apply + 3 4 5 6 7 '())
25

> (apply append '(1 2) '(3 4) '(5 6) '())
(1 2 3 4 5 6)

> (apply append '((1 2) (3 4) (5 6)))
(1 2 3 4 5 6)
```

Thus, **apply** provides an explicit way of indicating the process of procedural application. In T, the use of **apply** is particularly transparent, since procedures can be used freely as arguments themselves. Here are four examples of **apply** with equivalent expressions.

```
(apply car '((a b)))        ==>      (car '(a b))
(apply *  '(7 5))           ==>      (* 7 5)
(apply list 1 2 3 '())      ==>      (list 1 2 3)
(apply apply + 1 2 '() '()) ==>      (apply + 1 2 '())
```

The last example shows that **apply** can be given as a procedural argument to itself.

As promised in section 3.4, we shall give a recursive definition of **append**, using **apply**. Note that this definition requires a second procedure, **append2**, which takes exactly two arguments. The regular **append** procedure takes any number of arguments.

```
(define (append . lists)
    (cond ((null? lists) '())
          ((null? (cdr lists)) (car lists))
          ((null? (cddr lists)) (append2 (car lists) (cadr lists)))
          (else (append (car lists) (apply append (cdr lists))))))

(define (append2 list1 list2)
    (cond ((null? list1) list2)
          (else (cons (car list1) (append2 (cdr list1) list2)))))
```

In chapter 17, we will see that **apply** is an important underlying component of the T interpreter.

8.4   Special cond Syntax

While we are examining instances of using procedures as arguments, we should mention a special feature of **cond** which can invoke a one-argument procedure.

As the reader should recall, the **cond** form comprises a series of test-action pairs. The tests are checked in order, and if a test returns a non-NIL result, the corresponding action expressions are evaluated and no more tests are checked. There are many times when the test may involve a significant calculation, the result of which is needed by the action clause.

For example, here is a program which calculates a person's bonus pay based on three different categories of compensation. Employees on commission get 30 percent of their accumulated commission; salaried employees get 10 percent of their annual salary; and stockholders get a 25 percent stock dividend.

```
;;    data base of annual employee compensation
(put 'joe 'sales-commission 20000)
(put 'mary 'salary 25000)
(put 'john 'stock-holdings 500)

(define (calculate-bonus person)
    (cond ((get person 'sales-commission)
           (* (get person 'sales-commission) .30))
          ((get person 'salary)
           (* (get person 'salary) .10))
          ((get person 'stock-holdings)
           (* (get person 'stock-holdings) .25))
          (else
           'warmest-personal-regards)))

> (calculate-bonus 'mary)
2500.0

> (calculate-bonus 'john)
125.0
```

Note that the test to determine which category of bonus applies also determines the base amount for calculating the bonus. Thus, the above code has to perform exactly the same calculation twice.

One way to get around the redundant calculation is by using a temporary variable to hold the result, as shown in the following code.

```
(define (calculate-bonus person)
  (let ((temp nil))
    (cond ((set temp (get person 'sales-commission))
           (* temp .30))
          ((set temp (get person 'salary))
           (* temp .10))
          ((set temp (get person 'stock-holdings))
           (* temp .25))
          (else
           'warmest-personal-regards))))
```

This method helps a little bit, but it is awkward and introduces its own inefficiencies.

T affords us a better way. The use of the result of a non-NIL test in **cond** by the respective action clause is provided for in T through a special symbol: **=>**. When placed directly after the test clause within **cond**, the **=>** symbol indicates that the result of the test should be passed as the argument to the action clause. Of course, this use requires that the action clause have one and only one argument.

We can use this technique to revise our **calculate-bonus** procedure.

```
(define (calculate-bonus person)
   (cond ((get person 'sales-commission)
          =>
          (lambda (val) (* val .30)))
         ((get person 'salary)
          =>
          (lambda (val) (* val .10)))
         ((get person 'stock-holdings)
          =>
          (lambda (val) (* val .25)))
         (else
          'warmest-personal-regards)))
```

This special syntax for **cond** is not limited to lambda expressions. The only requirement is that the procedure in the action clause take a single argument. A named procedure could do as well, as the following example shows.

```
(define (smallnumber->word num)
   (cond ((assq num '((1 . one) (2 . two) (3 . three)))
          =>
          cdr)
         (else 'not-a-small-number)))
```

```
> (smallnumber->word 3)
THREE
```

```
> (smallnumber->word 10)
NOT-A-SMALL-NUMBER
```

8.5 Naming Local Procedures: labels

We have seen how lambda expressions can be used anonymously within other procedures. The cryptography procedure **string-encode** given on page 134 uses both a lambda expression and a call to another named procedure: **encode**. If there are no other procedures that call **encode**, then it is not really useful or necessary to define it on its own. It could be incorporated directly into the definition of **string-encode**.

```
(define (string-encode string n)
    (map-string
        (lambda (char)
            (ascii->char (+ (char->ascii char) n)))
        string))
```

Alternatively, we could actually give a *local* name to **encode** that could only be referenced from within the **string-encode** procedure.

```
(define (string-encode string n)
    (let ((encode (lambda (ch num)
                    (ascii->char (+ (char->ascii ch) num)))))
        (map-string (lambda (char) (encode char n)) string)))
```

We saw in chapter 5 how to use **let** to create variables that are local to a given procedure. The use of local variables is especially helpful in avoiding name conflicts when a program is large and complex. By using local variables, a programmer generally makes certain that the variable to which he is referring is in fact the one he intended.

Similarly, naming conflicts can occur with procedure names as well as with variable names. If a programmer is developing a very large program, possibly as part of a group effort involving a team of programmers, it is extremely important that the programmer avoid creating global objects — either variables or procedures — that might collide with other objects.

In the present example, we have made **encode** a local procedure within **string-encode**. Thus, even if another **encode** procedure has been defined elsewhere, the code for **string-encode** will still perform as expected.

Just as T provides a special syntax for defining global procedures, there is also a special form in T for defining local procedures, namely **labels**. The use of **labels** can be viewed as a cross between **define** and **let**. Here are two definitions of **string-encode** using **labels**.

```
(define (string-encode string n)
   (labels ((encode
              (lambda (ch num)
                (ascii->char (+ (char->ascii ch) num))))))
      (map-string
         (lambda (char) (encode char n)) string)))

(define (string-encode string n)
   (labels (((encode ch num)
                (ascii->char (+ (char->ascii ch) num)))))
      (map-string
         (lambda (char) (encode char n)) string)))
```

The first example is almost identical to the use of **let** given above. The second example does not use an explicit lambda expression, but rather adopts the implicit syntax of **define**. In addition to this variant syntax, **labels** differs from **let** in one other major way: variables defined with **labels** can themselves refer to other variables defined in the same expression, including references to themselves. Thus, **labels** allows the programmer to create local recursive procedures.

For example, here is a simple definition of the **length** procedure which is implemented using a local recursive procedure.

```
(define (length l)
  (labels (((count-length l n)
              (cond ((null? l) n)
                    (else (count-length (cdr l) (+ 1 n)))))))
     (count-length l 0)))
```

The **count-length** procedure keeps an accumulator variable, **n**, which it increments at each recursive call.

This use of an accumulator is similar to the **above-average** and **below-average** procedures defined earlier (see page 71). We can easily incorporate the recursive subfunction **below-average** as a local procedure using **labels**.

```
(define (above-average num-list)
  (labels (((below-average num-list count total)
              (cond ((null? num-list) (/ total count))
                    (else (below-average (cdr num-list)
                                         (+ count 1)
                                         (+ (car num-list)
                                            total)))))))
     (below-average num-list 0 0)))
```

In addition to this facility of recursive reference, a programmer may sometimes wish to cross-reference local variables – that is, have one local variable defined in terms of another. Here is a variation on the **son-of-zeller** exercise given on page 31, but with the argument given as a list of the form **(day month year)**.

```
(define (bad-zeller date)
    (let ((day    (car date))
          (month (cadr date))
          (year  (caddr date))
          (century (quotient year 100))
          (decades (- year (* 100 century)))
          (leap  (cond ((leap-year? year) 1)
                       (else 0))))
        (zeller day month century decades leap)))
```

In this example, several of the local variables are defined in terms of other local variables: **century** refers to **year**, **decades** refers to both **year** and **century**, and **leap** refers to **year**. As might be inferred from the procedure's name, this use of **let** does not work. This limitation of **let** becomes apparent when you understand that **let** is defined in terms of lambda in the following fashion.

```
(let ((variable-1 value-1)
      (variable-2 value-2)
        . . .
      (variable-n value-n))
    body-of-procedure )
```

is translated into

```
((lambda (variable-1 variable-2 ... variable-n)
    body-of-procedure)
  value-1 value-2 ... value-n)
```

Thus, our definition of **bad-zeller** is translated into the following.

```
(define (bad-zeller date)
    ((lambda (day month year century decades leap)
       (zeller day month century decades leap))
     (car date)
     (cadr date)
     (caddr date)
     (quotient year 100)       ; year  is undefined here and below
     (- year (* 100 century))  ; century  is undefined here
     (cond ((leap-year? year) 1)
           (else 0))))
```

The problem arises when the value of the variable **year** is referred to by the other local variables, **century**, **decades**, and **leap**. Also, the value of the variable **decades** refers to the value of another local variable, **century**. One method to solve the problem would be to replace references to the variable **year** with its value (caddr date) and to define **decades** in another fashion, for example, as (remainder (caddr date) 100). A second way would be to use nested **let** expressions, as follows.

```
(define (good-zeller date)
    (let ((day (car date))
          (month (cadr date))
          (year (caddr date)))
      (let ((century (quotient year 100))
            (leap (cond ((leap-year? year) 1)
                        (else 0))))
        (let ((decades (- year (* 100 century))))
          (zeller day month century decades leap)))))
```

which is translated into

```
(define (good-zeller date)
    ((lambda (day month year)
       ((lambda (century leap)
          ((lambda (decades)
             (zeller day month century decades leap))
           (- year (* 100 century))))
        (quotient year 100)
        (cond ((leap-year? year) 1)
              (else 0))))
     (car date)
     (cadr date)
     (caddr date)))
```

The **good-zeller** procedure solves the problem of cross-reference by defining the local variables **century** and **leap** nested within the scope of the **year** variable, and by defining **decades** nested within the scope of the **century** variable. This nesting method is effective in these cases, but there is a third alternative which is cleaner and clearer: **let***, which behaves like **let** except it allows local variables to refer to earlier local variables. Here is an example.

```
> (set a 5)
5

> (let ((a 10) (b a)) b)
5

> (let* ((a 10) (b a)) b)
10
```

In the **let** expression, the variable **b** gets its value from the global value of **a**, which is 5. In the **let*** expression, **b** gets its value from the local value of **a**, which is 10.

We can apply **let*** to our **zeller** problem.

```
(define (better-zeller date)
    (let* ((day    (car date))
           (month (cadr date))
           (year   (caddr date))
           (century (quotient year 100))
           (decades (- year (* 100 century)))
           (leap   (cond ((leap-year? year) 1)
                         (else 0))))
        (zeller day month century decades leap)))

> (better-zeller '(1 7 1983))     ;     1 September 1983
4                                 ;     was a Thursday.
```

This definition works. The reason is that **let*** provides sequential binding of variables. Thus, **better-zeller** is equivalent to the following definition using **let**.

```
(define (better-zeller date)
    (let ((day    (car date)))
     (let ((month (cadr date)))
      (let ((year   (caddr date)))
       (let ((century (quotient year 100)))
        (let ((decades (- year (* 100 century))))
         (let ((leap   (cond ((leap-year? year) 1)
                             (else 0))))
          (zeller day month century decades leap)))))))))
```

On the other hand, **labels** appears to do the right thing as well. The explicit effect of **labels** is equivalent to the following transformation.

```
(labels ((variable-1 value-1)
         (variable-2 value-2)
          . . .
         (variable-n value-n))
    body-of-expression)
```

can be described in terms of **let** and **set**.

```
(let ((variable-1 undefined-value)
      (variable-2 undefined-value)
      ...
      (variable-n undefined-value))
  (set variable-1 value-1)
  (set variable-2 value-2)
  ...
  (set variable-n value-n)
  body-of-expression)
```

The **undefined-value** indicates that the programmer cannot (and need not) know what value may have initially been given to the variables, since the variables are presently bound to their specified values. This definition of **labels** appears to have the same effect as **let***. However, T does not actually specify **labels** this way, and the order in which the variables are assigned values is itself undefined in T. Thus, the programmer should use **let*** when such functionality is required.

8.6   Mutually Recursive Procedures

In the preceding section, we argued for the use of **labels** on grounds of clarity and conciseness. These are important criteria. However, there are situations that require **labels** out of necessity — cases which **let** cannot handle directly. These cases involve recursion. The locally recursive definition of **length** given on page 140 would be much trickier with **let**. (See exercise 8.7.5.)

An extension of recursion is *mutual recursion*. That is, multiple procedures that are each defined in terms of the other.

In the answer to exercise 7.7.6, we defined a simple procedure **repeat-char** which prints a given character repeatedly to a port.

```
(define (repeat-char port char count)
   (cond ((zero? count) repl-wont-print)
         (else (write-char port char)
               (repeat-char port char (- count 1)))))
```

```
> (repeat-char (standard-output) #\* 10)
**********
```

Consider an extended version of **repeat-char** which prints a series of three characters, instead of just one. However, the number of characters in the resulting string might not be an even multiple of three. One way to handle this is with three subprocedures which call each other in sequence. These procedures can be created using **labels**.

```
(define (repeat-trio port ch1 ch2 ch3 count)
   (labels (((pr-ch1 count)
              (cond ((zero? count) repl-wont-print)
                    (else (write-char port ch1)
                          (pr-ch2 (- count 1))))))
            ((pr-ch2 count)
              (cond ((zero? count) repl-wont-print)
                    (else (write-char port ch2)
                          (pr-ch3 (- count 1))))))
            ((pr-ch3 count)
              (cond ((zero? count) repl-wont-print)
                    (else (write-char port ch3)
                          (pr-ch1 (- count 1)))))))
      (pr-ch1 count)))
```

```
> (repeat-trio (standard-output) #\* #\. #\- 10)
*.-*.-*.-*
```

The procedure **repeat-trio** comprises three subprocedures, **pr-ch1**, **pr-ch2**, and **pr-ch3**, each of which checks for the termination condition (if **count** is zero), and then writes its respective character to the port, and calls the next subprocedure. Following these three definitions, the body of the **labels** is simply a call to the first procedure, **pr-ch1**, which starts the ball rolling.

The reader might have noticed that the three subprocedures in **repeat-trio** have virtually identical definitions. It is possible to take advantage of this similarity and define all three procedures in terms of the underlying operations. Here is another definition of **repeat-trio**.

```
(define (repeat-trio port ch1 ch2 ch3 count)
   (labels (((pr-char char count next)
              (cond ((zero? count) repl-wont-print)
                    (else (write-char port char)
                          (next (- count 1)))))
            ((pr-ch1 count)
             (pr-char ch1 count pr-ch2))
            ((pr-ch2 count)
             (pr-char ch2 count pr-ch3))
            ((pr-ch3 count)
             (pr-char ch3 count pr-ch1)))
      (pr-ch1 count)))
```

In this example, the procedure **pr-char** is used to define each of the other subprocedures. Note that the arguments to **pr-char** include not only the specific character to be printed and the number of characters left to be printed, but also the name of the next procedure to be called. That is, the procedures themselves are used as arguments to `pr-char`.

8.7   Exercises

8.7.1   Expression Drill [4]

Evaluate the following expressions, first by hand, then with the help of the T interpreter.

```
(lambda (y z) (+ y z 3))
((lambda (y z) (+ y z 3)) 4 5)
(set x (lambda (y z) (+ y z 3)))
(x 6 7)
(map x '(1 2 3 4) '(5 6 7 8))
(set y (lambda (n m) (n 3 m)))
(y x 5)
(apply y x 5 '())
(apply apply y x 5 '() '())
(apply list (list '(y x 7) '(y x 8)))
(apply list (list (y x 7) (y x 8)))
(apply x (list (y x 7) (y x 8)))
(apply x (apply list (list (y x 7) (y x 8))))
(apply append (apply list (list '(y x 7) '(y x 8))))
(let ((x 5) (y x)) y)
(let* ((x 5) (y x)) y)
```

8.7.2   More Cryptography [6]

The simple cryptography system given in this chapter is fairly easy to crack. One way of making it more difficult is to use a more complex key. That is, instead of incrementing each letter the same amount, change the increment amount with every letter using a prearranged key.

Write two procedures, **new-string-encode** and **new-string-decode**, that each take three arguments: the text to be encoded (or decoded), a key text, and an integer. Each character of the key text is converted to its ASCII code and then divided by the integer. The resulting remainder is added to the respective character in the target text. If the key text is longer than the target text, then it is appropriately truncated. If the key text is shorter, then it is repeated as necessary.

Here is an example.

```
(define *key-text* "He who hesitates is last.")

> (set x (new-string-encode "Mary had a little lambda" *key-text*
```

```
7))
""Odvy&nej#d poxwoi oephge"

> (new-string-decode x *key-text* 7)
"Mary had a little lambda"
```

The reader should note that `map-string` does not allow multiple string arguments, but that `map` can have multiple list arguments.

8.7.3 Deck of Cards [5*]

Write a procedure `make-deck` which takes two arguments, a list of ranks and a list of suits, and produces a list of individual pairs.

```
> (define *suits* '(clubs diamonds hearts spades))
(CLUBS DIAMONDS HEARTS SPADES)

> (define *ranks* '(ten jack queen king ace))
(TEN JACK QUEEN KING ACE)

> (make-deck *ranks* *suits*)
((TEN . CLUBS) (JACK . CLUBS) (QUEEN . CLUBS) (KING . CLUBS)
(ACE . CLUBS) (TEN . DIAMONDS) (JACK . DIAMONDS) (QUEEN . DIAMONDS)
(KING . DIAMONDS) (ACE . DIAMONDS) (TEN . HEARTS) (JACK . HEARTS)
(QUEEN . HEARTS) (KING . HEARTS) (ACE . HEARTS) (TEN . SPADES)
(JACK . SPADES) (QUEEN . SPADES) (KING . SPADES) (ACE . SPADES))
```

This procedure can be written using `map` twice with lambda expressions, as well as `apply`. Exercise 14.7.13 discusses how to shuffle the cards.

8.7.4 reverse with labels [5*]

Rewrite the procedure `reverse` using `labels` to create a local recursive procedure.

8.7.5 Length Problems [5*]

There are two problems with the following definition of `length`. The first is its name. The second is that it does not work.

```
(define (bad-length l)
  (let ((count-length
         (lambda (l n)
            (cond ((null? l) n)
                  (else (count-length (cdr l) (+ 1 n)))))))
    (count-length l 0)))
```

The local procedure `count-length` is defined using `let`, which does not permit recursive reference. Thus, when the code is executed, T will complain that `count-length` is unbound.

Rewrite this procedure using `let` in a way that overcomes this limitation.

8.8   Chapter Summary

- Lambda expressions provide a means of creating unnamed procedures.

- `procedure?` is a predicate for procedures.

- The procedure `walk` is similar to `map`, but does not return a significant result. `walk` is used for performing side-effects.

- A lambda expression may be used as a procedural argument in T expressions, such as `map` and `walk`.

- Lambda expressions may be given names through assignment to variables via `define`.

- `apply` is a procedure which invokes a given procedure explicitly on a list of objects.

- `cond` uses `=>` between test and action clauses to indicate that the result of the successful evaluation of the test clause should be passed as the single argument to the action clause.

- T allows the creation of local procedures with either `let` or `labels`.

- Local variables created with `let*` can refer to earlier local variables within the `let*` scope.

- `labels` provides a convenient way to create mutually recursive procedures.

Chapter 9

Control

In our apprenticeship in the T program building trade, we have thus far encountered a variety of building materials and techniques. We have seen many kinds of objects, including numbers, symbols, lists, procedures, characters, strings, and ports. We have learned a number of ways of writing programs to manipulate those objects, primarily through conditional evaluation, procedure calls, and particularly recursion.

In this chapter we shall examine a variety of control techniques — methods for specifying the order of evaluation within a program.

9.1   block and block0

The order of evaluation of *arguments* to a procedure is undefined in T. That is, if you have an expression (f (g x) (h y)), the arguments to f may or may not be evaluated in left-to-right order. Thus, **h** might be evaluated before **g**, due to efficiency considerations decided by the compiler (see chapter 17). Usually, this undefined order of evaluation is not a problem. However, if the evaluation of arguments results in side-effects, then incorrect code could result. Consider the following expression.

```
    (put (pop lst) (pop lst) (pop lst))
;  where lst is: (john father-of jack)
```

Depending on the order of evaluation of arguments, any of the following expressions could result:

```
    (put john father-of jack)      ;  The intended result.
    (put john jack father-of)
    (put father-of john jack)
    (put father-of jack john)
    (put jack father-of john)
    (put jack john father-of)
```

Programmers should be aware of this hazard, and plan accordingly.

Fortunately, the order of evaluation of *expressions* within a lambda body is predictable. Given a T procedure with a list of expressions to be evaluated, there is an implicit order of evaluation, namely, left to right, and top to bottom. Furthermore, the value returned by the procedure is the value of the last expression evaluated.

Here is a trivial example.

```
> ((lambda () 1 2 3 4 5))
5
```

In this case, the integers – themselves T expressions – are evaluated from left to right, and the value of the final expression, 5, is returned as the result. Thus, the fact that the last value is returned is simply a consequence of the order of evaluation.

There are times when the programmer may prefer to return some value other than the value of the last expression. For example, the programmer may wish to calculate some value, then perform some operation (usually one with side-effects), and then return the value calculated.

It should be apparent how to accomplish this with local variables, but T provides a simple sequencing mechanism, the **block0** form, which evaluates a sequence of one or more expressions, and returns the value of the *first*, not the last. The opposite effect is achieved with **block**, which is equivalent to T's normal actions. Here are examples.

```
> (block 1 2 3 4)
4
```

```
> (block0 1 2 3 4)
1

> (block (set x '(a b c d)) 'x)
X

> (block0 (set x '(a b c d)) 'x)
(A B C D)

> (block (block0 1 2) (block 3 4) (block0 5 6))
5
```

In exercise 7.7.5, we presented the following definition of the procedure peek-char:

```
(define (old-peek-char port)
  (read-char port)
  (unread-char port))
```

We pointed out that this procedure does not return the desired result, namely, a character. With the use of block0, we can rectify our error.

```
(define (new-peek-char port)
  (block0
    (read-char port)
    (unread-char port)))

> (set s (string->input-port "blocks, stones, senseless things"))
#{String-input-port 189}

> (new-peek-char s)
#\b

> (old-peek-char s)
#t
```

This example demonstrates the utility of block0. The programmer will find less need to use block, since it mirrors T's default sequencing behavior. However, in contexts that expect a single argument, block can provide a convenient way to package multiple expressions into one sequence of expressions.

9.2   case and select

In sections 3.8 and 3.9, we saw how to use a key to retrieve data from a table, represented either as association lists or as property lists. It is also possible for a key to control the execution of a program, using T's **case** and **select** forms.

The **case** form can be viewed as a hybrid between association lists and **cond**. Here is an example:

```
(define (classify x)
  (case x
    ((whale bear cat dog horse) 'mammal)
    ((penguin sparrow eagle ostrich) 'bird)
    ((lawyer accountant programmer stock-broker) 'yuppie)
    ((trout whale bass catfish cod) 'fish)
    (else 'plant)))

> (classify 'cat)
MAMMAL

> (classify 'programmer)
YUPPIE

> (classify 'tulip)
PLANT
```

The structure of **case** should be apparent. There are two arguments: a key and a set of clauses. The **car** of each clause is a list of keys, and the **cdr** is a set of expressions. The last clause may simply have **else** as its **car**. If the given key matches one of keys in a given clause (using **eq?**), then, as in **cond**, the **cdr** of that clause is evaluated and the rest of the **case** clauses are skipped. If none of the keys of the clauses match the given key, and the last clause contains **else** as its **car**, then the **cdr** of the last clause is evaluated. Note that the keys in the **case** clauses are not evaluated; they are constants. They should not be quoted.

The **select** form is similar to **case**, except its keys are evaluated.

```
(define (find-grocery food)
  (select food
    (('milk 'eggs 'cheese *dairy-special*)      'dairy-case)
    (('vanilla 'chocolate *flavor-of-the-week*) 'frozen-foods)
    (('lamb 'beef 'chicken *butchers-choice*)   'meat-counter)
    (('lettuce 'tomatoes 'apples *fresh-pick*)  'produce)
    (else (push *not-in-stock* food )
          'not-in-stock)))
```

```
(define *not-in-stock* '())
(define *dairy-special* 'egg-nog)
(define *flavor-of-the-week* 'rocky-road)
(define *butchers-choice* 'turkey)
(define *fresh-pick* 'strawberries)

> (find-grocery 'eggs)
DAIRY-CASE

> (find-grocery 'turkey)
MEAT-COUNTER

> (find-grocery 'ham)
NOT-IN-STOCK

> *not-in-stock*
(HAM)
```

The **find-grocery** procedure directs a shopper to the location of the requested item. The procedure takes advantage of the fact that **select** evaluates its keys. The items which are always kept in stock are encoded as quoted values, but the seasonal items are left as global variables. Thus, when the turkey is all gone and replaced with ham next week, the procedure **grocery** can still work, merely by setting *butchers-choice* to the new value. The global variable *not-in-stock* keeps track of those items requested by customers that are not available.

9.3   Iteration and do

In most programming languages, the usual method for performing some repetitive process is a loop. Looping constructs in programming languages take various forms, including do/while, do/until, repeat loops, for loops, and the notorious goto loops. A loop, be it in FORTRAN, BASIC, or Pascal, has several key components.

- initial conditions: the state of the variables when beginning the loop.

- termination condition: the state required for ending the loop.

- transition specifications: how the state changes from one cycle to the next.

- body: code to be executed each cycle through the loop.

The looping control method is also called *iteration*. Up until now, we have not used iteration in T. We have used recursion. The same basic phenomena underlie both. In principal, anything you can do with recursion, you can accomplish with iteration, and vice versa.

T provides two principal iterative constructs: **do** and **iterate**. We shall first examine **do**. Here is an iterative procedure to find the average of a list of numbers using **do**.

```
(define (i-average lst)
    (do ((nlist lst (cdr nlist))
         (count 0 (+ 1 count))
         (total 0 (+ (car nlist) total)))
        ((null? nlist) (/ total count))))

> (i-average '(1 2 3 4 5 6 7))
4
```

The procedure **i-average** demonstrates the basic structure of **do**. The first argument to **do** is a list of three-part variable specifications. The **do** variables in **i-average** are nlist, count, and **total**.

The first part of each specification is the name of the variable. The second part is that variable's initial value, and the third part is the transition specification for that variable. During each iteration, the variables are given new values according to these transition functions. For example, the **count** variable is given an initial value of 0, and each time through the loop, the value of **count** is incremented by 1.

The second argument to **do** is the termination clause. The **do** termination clause in **i-average** is `((null? nlist) (/ total count))`. The **car** of the clause is the exit test, and the **cdr** contains expressions which are evaluated upon termination. The value returned by **do** is the value of the last of these expressions — or the value of the exit test itself if there are no exit expressions. So, **i-average** stops when **nlist** becomes empty, and then returns the final **total** divided by the final **count** as the value of **i-average**.

Here is a step-by-step account of **i-average**.

```
1.  (set nlist nlist)          ; Initialize variables.
    (set count 0)
    (set total 0)

2.  (null? nlist)              ; Termination test.
    if true, goto step 5
    else, continue to next step.

3.  (set nlist (cdr nlist))    ; Update values of variables.
    (set count (+ 1 count))
    (set total (+ total (car nlist)))

4.  goto step 2                ; Resume loop.
```

```
5.  Terminate loop.              ;  End of loop.
    Return value: (/ total count)
```

Actually, T is smarter than the above detail would suggest. In particular, there is a problem with the order of assignment statements in step 3. As shown here, the algorithm would not add the first element into the total.

Note that **trace** will be of little value in debugging a faulty **do** expression. There are no recursive calls for one to trace. Instead, the programmer can take advantage of the optional third argument to **do**, which allows zero or more arbitrary T expressions. These expressions are evaluated if the exit test fails. They would appear between steps 2 and 3 in our diagram above. Thus, **i-average** could be rewritten to produce intermediate output.

```
(define (i-average nlist)
    (do ((nlist nlist (cdr nlist))
         (count 0 (+ 1 count))
         (total 0 (+ (car nlist) total)))
        ((null? nlist) (/ total count))
      (format t "count: ~d" count)
      (format t "~15T total: ~d ~%" total)))
```

```
(i-average '(1 2 3 4 5))
count: 0        total: 0
count: 1        total: 1
count: 2        total: 3
count: 3        total: 6
count: 4        total: 10
3
```

Note that the final case, where **count** becomes 5, is not printed. The **format** statements are not evaluated on the last element of the list, since the termination test has been triggered.

9.4 Iteration versus Recursion

To give the reader a feel for the differences between iteration and recursion, we now present examples of problems treated both ways. First, the reader might review the recursive definitions for average given earlier. (See page 70 and following.)

Next, here are two definitions of **length**. The first is recursive, and the second is iterative.

```
;  Recursive implementation of length
(define (r-length lst)
    (cond ((null? lst) 0)
          (else (+ 1 (r-length (cdr lst))))))
```

```
; Iterative implementation of length
(define (i-length lst)
    (do ((l lst (cdr l))
         (result 0 (+ 1 result)))
        ((null? l) result)))
```

Which is better? Which is clearer? *De gustibus non disputandum est.* There can be differences in efficiency. These are discussed in chapter 16.

We give one more set of examples for comparison, slightly more involved. The task of **remove-pairs** is to reduce all adjacent duplicate letters in a string to a single letter. For example, "moon" becomes "mon"; "BAAA" becomes "BA"; and "remove" remains "remove". The first implementation is recursive, and the next is iterative.

```
(define (r-remove-pairs word)
    (cond ((string-empty? word) word)
          ((string-empty? (string-tail word)) word)
          ((char= (string-head word)
                  (string-head (string-tail word)))
           (r-remove-pairs (string-tail word)))
          (else
           (string-append (substring word 0 1)
                          (r-remove-pairs (string-tail word)))))))

(define (i-remove-pairs word)
    (do ((word word (string-tail word))
         (result "" (cond ((char= (string-head word)
                                  (string-head (string-tail word)))
                           result)
                          (else
                           (string-append result
                                          (substring word 0 1))))))
        ((cond ((string-empty? word) result)
               ((string-empty? (string-tail word))
                (string-append result
                               (substring word 0 1)))
               (else nil)))))
```

The reader who is not yet convinced that recursion and iteration can achieve the same results should review the examples in this section. The obdurately incredulous reader may still proceed to the next section for further evidence.

9.5   iterate

T provides another form of iterative control with the straightforward name: **iterate**. The **iterate** form takes three arguments: an identifier, a list of variable-value pairs (as in **let**), and a body of expressions to be evaluated. The identifier may be called within the expressions, in which case control resumes at the beginning of the body. When the body of expressions have been evaluated, **iterate** concludes, and returns the value of the last expression in the body. The variables given in the second argument to **iterate** act as arguments for any call to the identifier.

Here are some examples. The first, **repeat-char**, is taken from the answer to exercise 7.7.6.

```
(define (repeat-char ch count port)
   (iterate again ((count count))
      (cond ((zero? count) repl-wont-print)
            (else (write-char port ch)
                  (again (- count 1))))))

> (repeat-char #\+ 9 (standard-output))
+++++++++
```

The iteration identifier is **again**. There are no iteration arguments in this example. The iteration body in **repeat-char** is a simple **cond** clause. This clause executes repeatedly due to the call to **again**. The execution terminates when the **count** reaches zero.

We can implement the familiar **length** procedure using **iterate**.

```
(define (it-length lst)
   (iterate looptag
      ((l lst)
       (result 0))
      (cond ((null? l) result)
            (else (looptag (cdr l) (+ result 1))))))

> (it-length '(a b c d e))
5
```

In **it-length**, the iteration identifier is **looptag**, which takes two iteration arguments: **l** and **result**. The body is a **cond** clause, as in **repeat-char**.

The **iterate** form in T is deceptively named, as it is implemented recursively with **labels**, as follows.

```
(iterate name
          ((argument-1 value-1)
           (argument-2 value-2)
           ...
           (argument-n value-n))
          body-of-expression)
```

is expanded into

```
(labels
   (((name argument-1 argument-2 ... argument-n)
     body-of-expression))
   (name value-1 value-2 ... value-n))
```

Thus, the difference between iteration and recursion is automatically eliminated through use of the `iterate` form.

9.6   catch

Another type of control structure is afforded by the **catch** form, which provides a very general mechanism for returning values from computations. The structure of **catch** comprises two arguments: an identifier and a body of expressions to be evaluated. The identifier becomes an exit procedure from the body of expressions which returns its own single argument as its value. In a sense, **catch** is the opposite of **iterate**. Within **iterate**, a call to the identifier continues the computation, while within **catch**, a call to the identifier stops the computation. In neither case can the identifier be invoked outside the scope of the originating expression, that is, outside the **catch** or **iterate**.

Here is a simple example in which the identifier **finish** becomes the name of the escape procedure, also called a *throw*, which ends the **catch** expression. The **finish** procedure has one argument, **result**, which is returned as the value of **catch**.

```
(define (fact n)
    (catch finish
        (labels (((sub-fact n result)
                     (cond ((zero? n) (finish result))
                           (else (sub-fact (- n 1)
                                           (* n result)))))))
            (sub-fact n 1))))
```

```
;     Another definition of fact
(define (fact n)
    (catch finish
        (labels (((sub-fact n result)
                    (cond ((zero? n) result)
                          (else (sub-fact (- n 1)
                                          (* n result)))))))
        (sub-fact n 1))))
```

The second definition above of **fact** also uses **catch**, but the escape procedure **finish** is never invoked. In this case, the value returned by **catch** is simply the value returned by the body expression, **labels**. This merely shows that **catch** does not have to exit with a throw.

Here is a more compelling example of **catch** using an iterative version of **mem?**.

```
(define (it-mem? predicate obj lst)
    (catch throw
        (do ((lst lst (cdr lst)))
            ((null? lst) nil)
            (if (predicate obj (car lst)) (throw t)))))
```

Here are some trivial examples in which the use of the escape procedure makes a difference in the value of the **catch** expression.

```
> (catch f (reverse (append (cons 1 '(2)) (cons 3 '(4)))))
(4 3 2 1)

> (catch f (reverse (append (cons (f 1) '(2)) (cons 3 '(4)))))
1
```

The latter example shows how the programmer can use **catch** precipitously to interrupt the normal execution of an expression.

The short examples of **catch** given in this section illustrate how it works. However, in each case, it would be very easy to get rid of **catch** and achieve the same results. In fact, it would preferable. In short code segments, **catch** is rarely needed. The utility of **catch** becomes apparent in larger code segments in which the flow of control can be complex, and **catch** provides a convenient escape mechanism.

The following section focuses on such a program, and provides a good example of **catch**.

9.7 Example: Binary Guessing Game

A common computer game is one that attempts to guess an animal that the player has thought of. The program asks a number of yes or no questions, and finally makes a guess, based on the player's responses to the questions. If the computer guesses incorrectly, the program asks the player to tell it the name of the animal and a yes/no question that can be used to differentiate between the new animal and the program's previous guess. This new information then becomes part of the program's knowledge base.

Here is output from a sample session for the animal guessing game.

```
> (binary)

Think of an animal.              ;  the player responds to
Have you got one yet? y          ;  the program's questions

Does it purr? n

Is it gray? n

Is it bigger than a person? y

Does it have stripes? n

Are you thinking of a GORILLA? n

What animal were you thinking of? horse

Type a yes/no question that can distinguish
between a GORILLA and a HORSE.
=> Is it a domestic animal?        ;  the player types this question

And how would you answer that question for a HORSE? y

Do you want to play again? y

Think of an animal.
Have you got one yet? y

Does it purr? n

Is it gray? y

Are you thinking of an ELEPHANT? y

Hot tomatoes!  I guessed it!

Do you want to play again? n
```

```
Do you wish to save the current animal database? y
Backing up data to file: binary.animal

Backup complete.
To restore data, type (load "binary.animal")

 So long, animal lover.
```

As the final lines show, the program allows the player to save the current information in a file. If the player subsequently loads the file and invokes **(binary)**, the program will start again, including the new information about horses.

The structure of the program itself is actually independent of any knowledge about animals. In fact, the program can be used for virtually any domain of knowledge, including one close to the author's heart, as shown below. The **binary-init** procedure sets up the program for a new session.

```
> (binary-init 'reverse "T procedure" nil)
()
> (binary)

Think of a T procedure.
Have you got one yet? y

Are you thinking of REVERSE? n

What T procedure were you thinking of? length

Type a yes/no question that can distinguish
between REVERSE and LENGTH.
=> Does this procedure return a list?

And how would you answer that question for LENGTH? n

Do you want to play again? y

Think of a T procedure.
Have you got one yet? y

Does this procedure return a list? n

Are you thinking of LENGTH? n

What T procedure were you thinking of? string-upcase
```

162 CHAPTER 9. CONTROL

```
Type a yes/no question that can distinguish
between LENGTH and STRING-UPCASE.
=> Does this procedure take a string as its only argument?

And how would you answer that question for STRING-UPCASE? y

Do you want to play again? y

Think of a T procedure.
Have you got one yet? ?         ; the player types a ?

Type Yes, No, or Quit.         ; the program gives directions

Think of a T procedure.
Have you got one yet? quit
*END-OF-BINARY*
```

As this session demonstrates, the program can operate in diverse domains.

The reader should notice that this second session ended abruptly, at the request of the player, who typed **quit** in response to a yes/no question. The program allows the player to end a session at any time through this means. This facility is implemented with **catch**.

We shall now look at the code itself. There are only two procedures: **binary-init** and **binary**. The former is far shorter. It initializes the global variables used by **binary**.

```
(define (binary-init item category flag)
    (set *category* category)
    (set *determiner-flag* flag)
    (put '*binary-tree* 'answer item)
    (put '*binary-tree* 'question nil)
    (put '*binary-tree* 'yes     nil)
    (put '*binary-tree* 'no      nil))
```

The variable *category* contains a string, such as **"animal"**, and is used in several messages to the player. The variable *determiner-flag* is set to true to indicate that items should be preceded by a determiner ("a" or "an") when printed, otherwise, false.

The information about the items themselves, be they animals or T procedures or plays by Shakespeare, is kept on a network of property lists. There are four possible data elements for each node.

1. **answer.** The value of a terminal node. For example, ELEPHANT or REVERSE.

2. **question.** A yes/no question represented as a string. For example, "Does this animal have webbed feet?"

3. **yes.** The name of another node in the network, in this case, the one to visit if the answer to **question** is yes.

4. **no.** The name of another node in the network, in this case, the one to visit if the answer to **question** is no.

Using **binary-init**, the player sets up a root node to the question tree with an **answer** item, and empty values for **question**, **yes**, and **no**.

We now turn our attention to the program itself. However, even though **binary** is only one procedure, it is made up of several secondary procedures that are defined with **labels**. We shall therefore look at **binary** in stages, rather than present it in one whole piece.

```
(define (binary)
 (catch quit-action
  (labels
   (((query yes-action no-action else-action)
     (case (read (standard-input))
           ((y yes t)    (yes-action))
           ((n no nil)   (no-action))
           ((q quit)     (quit-action '*end-of-binary*))
           (else
            (format t "~%Type Yes, No, or Quit.~%")
            (else-action))))

    ((start)
     (format t "~%Think of ~A~A."
         (sub-determ *category*) *category*)
     (format t "~%Have you got one yet? ")
     (query
         (lambda () (process-node '*binary-tree*))
         start
         start))
```

The first element of the procedure definition is the **catch** form. The rest of the procedure is contained as the body of the **catch**, which allows the **quit-action** identifier to be called from anywhere within the procedure.

The **labels** form opens the body of the **catch** clause, and we then begin to define local procedures. In this code segment we get **query** and **start**. We shall use the **query** procedure throughout the program to prompt the user for yes/no responses. The three arguments to **query** are the procedures to invoke based on the player's input: yes, no, or other. The fourth alternative, quit, is handled directly within **query** as a call, or throw, to the **catch** identifier **quit-action**.

The second local procedure, **start**, is the first to get called. It prompts the player to select an item of the given category. If the player is not ready, the **start** procedure is called again. Otherwise, the first **query** argument is invoked.

The output routines often check to see what kind of determiner is appropriate, using the following two procedures.

```
((determiner word)
 (cond ((null? *determiner-flag*) "")
       (else   (sub-determ word))))

((sub-determ word)
 (let ((str (cond ((string? word) word)
                  (else (symbol->string word)))))
   (case (string-head str)
     ((#\a #\e #\i #\o #\u #\y
       #\A #\E #\I #\O #\U #\Y)  "an ")
     (else                       "a ")))))
```

If the next word starts with a vowel, use **"an"**, otherwise, use **"a"**.

The **start** procedure began the traversal of the question tree with the call (**process-node '*binary-tree***), which invokes the following procedure.

```
((process-node tree-node)
 (cond ((get tree-node 'question)
        =>
        (lambda (q) (process-question q tree-node)))
       ((get tree-node 'answer)
        =>
        (lambda (a) (process-answer a tree-node)))
       (else 'error-in-sub-binary))))
```

If the current node has a question, then the program processes that question. If there is no question, then the current node is a terminal node, so there must be an answer to process.

```
((process-question ques node)
 (format t "~%~A " ques)
 (query
  (lambda () (process-node (get node 'yes)))
  (lambda () (process-node (get node 'no)))
  (lambda () (process-question ques node))))
```

```
((process-answer ans node)
  (format t "~%Are you thinking of ~A~S? "
            (determiner ans) ans)
  (query
   (lambda () (format t "~%Hot tomatoes!  I guessed it!~%")
              (play-again?))
   (lambda () (add-item node ans)
              (play-again?))
   (lambda () (process-answer ans node)))))
```

To process a question, the program asks the question and prompts for a response. The program then either processes the appropriate yes or no node, or it asks the question again.

When there are no questions to ask at the current node, the **process-answer** procedure makes a guess. If it is correct, the program displays unbounded excitement. In the event of failure, the program resolutely tries to learn from its mistakes, and become a better program.

```
((add-item old-node old-item)
  (let ((yes-node (generate-symbol 'node))
        (no-node  (generate-symbol 'node))
        (new-item nil)
        (new-question nil))
    (format t "~%What ~A were you thinking of? " *category*)
    (set new-item (read (standard-input)))
    (format t "~%Type a yes/no question that can distinguish")
    (format t "~%between ~A~S and ~A~S.~%=> "
              (determiner old-item) old-item
              (determiner new-item) new-item)
    (clear-input (standard-input))
    (set new-question (read-line (standard-input)))
    (set-up-old-node old-node new-question yes-node no-node)
    (set back-up-flag T)
    (format t
       "~%And how would you answer that question for ~A~S? "
       (determiner new-item) new-item)
```

```
(iterate looptag ()
  (query
   (lambda ()
          (set-up-new-node yes-node new-item)
          (set-up-new-node no-node  old-item))
   (lambda ()
          (set-up-new-node no-node  new-item)
          (set-up-new-node yes-node old-item))
   looptag))))
```

The **generate-symbol** procedure creates unique identifiers, such as NODE.55, for naming new nodes.

The reader should note the use of **iterate** at the end of **add-item** to provide a default repetition if the player types an inappropriate response.

The **add-item** procedure does some bookkeeping with the old and new nodes, setting and resetting property list values.

```
((set-up-old-node old-node new-question yes-node no-node)
   (put old-node 'question new-question)
   (put old-node 'answer nil)
   (put old-node 'yes yes-node)
   (put old-node 'no  no-node))

((set-up-new-node node item)
   (put node 'answer item))
```

That completes the main portion of the program. The remainder of the code is concerned with replaying the game, and saving the new information in a file.

```
((play-again?)
 (format t "~%Do you want to play again? ")
 (query
  start
  (lambda ()
    (save-data?)
    (format t "~% So long, ~A lover.~%~%" *category*)
   repl-wont-print)
  play-again?))
```

Once again, the **query** procedure appears as the backbone of this program.

```
((save-data?)
 (cond ((null? back-up-flag) nil)
       (else
         (format t
           "~%Do you wish to save the current ~A data base? "
           *category*)
         (query
           back-up-data
           (lambda () nil)
           save-data?))))

(back-up-flag nil)
```

The local variable **back-up-flag** is initially false, which indicates that no changes have been made to the data base. The procedure **add-item**, which adds information, sets **back-up-flag** to true. So, if the player tries to exit the program after changes have been made, the program gives the player the opportunity to save the changes.

```
((back-up-data)
 (let ((filename (string-append "binary." *category* ))
       (port nil))
   (format t "Backing up data to file: ~A~%" filename)
   (set port (open filename '(out)))
   (format port "(herald ~A)~%" *category*)
   (format port "(set *category* ~S)~%" *category*)
   (format port "(set *determiner-flag* ~A)~%"
                *determiner-flag*)
   (back-up-node '*binary-tree* port)
   (close port)
   (format t "~%Backup complete.")
   (format t "~%To restore data, type (load ~S)~%"
              filename)))
```

The program saves the data in a file, in a way that can be loaded back in conveniently. The procedure **back-up-data** first opens the file and writes out the global variable information, then it calls the procedure **back-up-node**, which recursively traverses the question tree, writing out the information at each node.

```
 ((back-up-node node port)
  (let ((question (get node 'question))
        (answer   (get node 'answer)))
    (cond ((and (null? question)
                (null? answer))
           nil)
          (question
           (format port "(put '~A 'question ~S)~%"
                        node question)
           (let ((yes-node  (get node 'yes))
                 (no-node   (get node 'no)))
             (format port "(put '~A 'yes '~A)~%"
                          node yes-node)
             (back-up-node yes-node port)
             (format port "(put '~A 'no '~A)~%"
                          node no-node)
             (back-up-node no-node port)))
          (answer
           (format port "(put '~A 'answer '~A)~%" node answer))
          (else nil)))))
;;  -----    ** end of labels definitions ** -----
   (start)))))
```

As the comment indicates, **back-up-node** is the last local procedure definition. It is followed by the body of the **labels** expression, which is a simple call to **start**.

Here are the contents of the file **"binary.animal"** which resulted from the first example run above.

```
(herald animal)
(set *category* "animal")
(set *determiner-flag* T)
(put '*BINARY-TREE* 'question "Does it purr?")
(put '*BINARY-TREE* 'yes 'NODE.99)
(put 'NODE.99 'question "Does it run on regular gas?")
(put 'NODE.99 'yes 'NODE.101)
(put 'NODE.101 'answer 'FERRARI)
(put 'NODE.99 'no 'NODE.102)
(put 'NODE.102 'answer 'CAT)
(put '*BINARY-TREE* 'no 'NODE.100)
(put 'NODE.100 'question "Is it gray?")
(put 'NODE.100 'yes 'NODE.103)
(put 'NODE.103 'answer 'ELEPHANT)
(put 'NODE.100 'no 'NODE.104)
(put 'NODE.104 'question "Is it bigger than a person?")
(put 'NODE.104 'yes 'NODE.107)
```

```
(put 'NODE.107 'question "Does it have stripes?")
(put 'NODE.107 'yes 'NODE.109)
(put 'NODE.109 'answer 'TIGER)
(put 'NODE.107 'no 'NODE.110)
(put 'NODE.110 'question "Is it a domestic animal?")
(put 'NODE.110 'yes 'NODE.105)
(put 'NODE.105 'answer 'HORSE)
(put 'NODE.110 'no 'NODE.106)
(put 'NODE.106 'answer 'GORILLA)
(put 'NODE.104 'no 'NODE.108)
(put 'NODE.108 'answer 'MONKEY)
```

This program was intended to demonstrate the utility of **catch** in the context of a complex control setting. (See exercise 9.8.5.)

Useful though **catch** may be in these circumstances, it may also introduce a new of source of problems. Consider the following code segment for a program which interactively interrogates the user based on questions it reads from a file.

```
(catch finish
  (open-a-file-and-ask-questions-of-user finish)
  (close-file))
```

If the **(open-a-file-and-ask-questions-of-user)** segment ends with a throw to the **catch** via **finish**, then the **(close-file)** code is never executed. Chances are, this is not the effect intended by the programmer.

What the programmer most likely wanted was to provide a way to end the session early, but still wanted to close the file. T provides a way for the programmer to have his cake and eat it too with **unwind-protect**.

```
(catch finish
  (unwind-protect
    (open-a-file-and-ask-questions-of-user finish)
    (close-file)))
```

Here, **unwind-protect** acts as a barrier, of sorts, between the **catch** and the expressions. If any throw occurs inside **(open-a-file-and-ask-questions-of-user)**, the **unwind-protect** intervenes, and does not let control pass back to the respective **catch** until the **(close-file)** has been evaluated. In general, **unwind-protect** is triggered only by a throw from its first argument, in which case the remaining zero or more arguments are evaluated.

The situation of recovering from errors with open ports is so common that T has a special form just for the occasion: **with-open-ports**.

```
    (with-open-ports (port-specs) . body)
;   where each port-spec is of the form
    (identifier port-expression)
```

The `port-expression` is normally a call to `open`, which then returns a port bound to its respective identifier. After the `body` is evaluated, all the local ports are closed – even if there was a non-standard exit from `body`, as with `catch` or even `reset`. Thus, `unwind-protect` is built into `with-open-ports`.

Here is our earlier example, now `with-open-ports`.

```
(catch finish
  (with-open-ports
    ((port-id (open-a-file)))
    (ask-questions-of-user finish)))
```

9.8   Exercises

9.8.1   Bottles of Beer [2*]

Why does this chapter have one of the same epigraphs as the recursion chapter?

9.8.2   Iterative Average [5*]

Rewrite the `i-average` procedure using the `iterate` form instead of `do`.

9.8.3   More Spelling Correction: Soundex [7*]

In section 6.5, we developed one way to detect and correct spelling errors. Another method, which depends on detecting words spelled the way they sound, is the Soundex algorithm, which is described by Knuth in [13].

The idea behind Soundex is psychologically appealing, namely, that people can detect misspelled words that *sound* like actual words. Thus, a person would not be at a loss when confronted with *Misisipy*, or *Road Island*, or *Dellawear*. Note that the spelling corrector in section 6.5 would not have corrected any of those errors. Soundex could fix them all.

Here is how it works. To see how a word should be spelled, Soundex first creates a phonetic code for that word, consisting of a letter followed by one to three digits. It then retrieves the correctly spelled word corresponding to that code. If there are more than one correct word for that code, or no correct words, then Soundex fails.

The codes themselves are based on the sounds of the words, according to the following method.

1. All double letters are removed from the word, as with our `remove-pairs` procedure given above.

2. The first letter of the word is used as the first letter of the code.

3. Each subsequent letter of the word is examined, until either the end of the word is reached, or the code length is four characters.

4. The digit corresponding to the given letter is added to the code. The following table gives the digit-letter groupings. Note that vowels are not coded.

1:	B F P V
2:	C G J K Q X
3:	D T
4:	L
5:	M N
6:	R
7:	S Z

The algorithm presented in Knuth does not have a category 7; "S" and "Z" had been included in category 2. However, that resulted in a duplicate Soundex code (A625) for "Arizona" and "Arkansas." Under the revised scheme, "Arizona" becomes A675.

Here are examples of Soundex at work.

```
> (soundex 'harry)
H6

> (soundex 'hairy)
H6

> (soundex 'Missouri)
M76

> (soundex 'misery)
M76

> (soundex 'Arizona)
A675

> (soundex 'Arkansas)
A625
```

Simply generating a code for a word is not intrinsically useful. However, the code can be used as an index to the correct spelling of the word. In the example below, the **tag-word** procedure enters the code-word pair in a table (such as a property list or association list). The **isa-word** procedure retrieves the correctly spelled word, and compares it with the given word.

```
> (map tag-word '("Georgia" "Mississippi" "Delaware" "Rhode
Island"))
("GEORGIA" "MISSISSIPPI" "DELAWARE" "RHODE ISLAND")
```

```
> (isa-word "Road Island")
"No. How about RHODE ISLAND ?"

> (isa-word 'misisipy)
"No. How about MISSISSIPPI ?"

> (isa-word "dellawear")
"No. How about DELAWARE ?"

> (isa-word 'georgia)
#t

> (isa-word 'quebec)
"No match at all."
```

Write the three procedures **soundex**, **tag-word**, and **isa-word**. Then load all fifty states and try it out.

9.8.4   Unwind protection [4*]

unwind-protect protects only its first argument. Suppose you have the following code.

```
(catch finish
   (unwind-protect
      (step-one)
      (step-two)
      (step-three)))
```

As it stands, if a throw occurs in **(step-one)**, then **unwind-protect** will ensure that **(step-two)** and **(step-three)** will be executed. However, if the throw occurs in **(step-two)**, **unwind-protect** will not guarantee execution of **(step-three)**. In fact, it will generate an error.

How could you rewrite the code so that both **(step-one)** and **(step-two)** will be protected, and guarantee execution of **(step-three)** if there is a throw in the two earlier steps?

9.8.5   Binary Game Catch [5*]

What would happen if within the **query** local procedure given on page 163 the line of code is altered as follows?

```
      ((q quit)      (quit-action '*end-of-binary*))
;  is changed to:
      ((q quit)       '*end-of-binary*)
```

9.9   Chapter Summary

- The order of evaluation of arguments to a procedure is undefined in T.

- The `block` and `block0` forms are sequencing constructs. `block` returns the value of the last expression, mirroring T's normal evaluation, and `block0` returns the value of its *first* expression.

- `case` and `select` allow a programmer to use key values to control program execution.

- Iteration and recursion are the two fundamental control techniques.

- T provides two basic iterative control forms: `do` and `iterate`.

- The T form `catch` can be viewed as the opposite of `iterate`: calls to a `catch` identifier end execution, while calls to an `iterate` identifier repeat execution.

- `catch` is best used in programs with large, complex flow of control.

- `unwind-protect` can guard against dangerous `catch` side-effects. The special form `with-open-ports` uses `unwind-protect` to ensure that ports get closed in the event of non-standard exits.

Chapter 10

Debugging

Programmers make errors. Ineluctably, computers make errors. It is the job of the
programmer to

- prevent errors.

- detect errors.

- elucidate errors.

- recover from errors.

These activities are aspects of the debugging enterprise. The term *debugging*, with
its underlying connotations of pestilence and epidemics, is most apt. Programmers
soon realize that the most benign error – a typing mistake or a faulty assumption
– can result in a computer wreaking havoc at the speed of light.

Continuing the health/disease metaphor, the four aspects of debugging can
be viewed as immunization, presentation of symptoms, diagnosis of the disease, and
finally, treatment and cure.

10.1 Preventing Errors

A pound of prevention is worth an ounce of cure. Contrary to folk advice, it is preeminent to safeguard good health. Preventing computer errors can be much more important than recognizing and correcting them after the fact. Knowing how to repair the tiny bug in your electronic funds transfer program is of little solace once the error has moved all the bank's assets to the KGB's Swiss bank account.

Clearly, the best way to handle errors is not to create them in the first place. One of the major sources of errors in T programs is improper or unbalanced parentheses. The best solution for this problem is a good text editor that can automatically balance parentheses.

However, even if a definition has the right number of parentheses, they may not always be in the right places. Here is an example in which T does not complain when the procedure is defined, just when it is called.

```
(define (fact n             ;  fatal misplaced right paren
    (cond ((zero? n) 1)
          (else
           (fact (* n (fact (- n 1)))))))))
#{Procedure 29 FACT}

> (fact 4)

** Error: wrong number of arguments to interpreted procedure
   (FACT 4)

>> (argspectrum fact)
(2)

>> (fact 3 4)
()
```

The problem is that the initial argument list did not get closed. The programmer indented the code properly and added enough parentheses at the end to allow the procedure to be defined, but the definition is faulty. The call to **argspectrum** indicates that **fact** expects two arguments, not one. Thus, we got an error because T wanted another argument. T could not figure out what we really meant to do. All T knew was that we had promised to deliver two arguments every time we called **fact**. Notice that the call of **(fact 3 4)** does not generate a T error. Notice that it does not generate a useful answer either. It merely has the right number of arguments – in a manner of speaking.

The **argspectrum** form used above can help the programmer find out how many arguments a procedure requires. Here are some examples.

```
> (argspectrum subst)
(4)                          ; subst  takes four arguments
```

```
> (argspectrum +)
(0 . T)                        ; + takes any number of arguments

> (argspectrum map)
(2 . T)                        ; map  takes two or more arguments

> (argspectrum argspectrum)
(1)                            ; argspectrum  takes one argument
```

The basic advice for error prevention is probably as useful as it is profound: *be careful*. Typing errors (typo's) can be prevented by the attentive programmer. Conceptual errors (thinko's) can be avoided by similar diligence and energy.

Throughout this book, we describe techniques for designing and developing programs. These techniques – such as the use of local variables instead of global variables, modular program design, and proper indentation and commenting styles – are meant to make it easier for the programmer to write correct code. However, these techniques do not make it impossible to write incorrect code.

The hope is that the suggestions presented in this chapter, and throughout this book, will enable the programmer not only to make fewer errors, but also to limit the scope and damage of those errors that do occur.

10.2   Detecting Errors

Murphy's Law states that if anything can go wrong, it will. The programmer's corollary is: Murphy was an optimist.

Here is a partial list of the types of errors that T can detect and complain about.

- Wrong number of arguments to a procedure (see above).

- Unbound variable reference.

- Calling a non-procedure.

- Wrong object type as argument to a procedure.

- Index out of range.

And here are examples of each of these errors. In this case, the programmer wishes to find the absolute value of 3.1.

```
> (abs 3. 1)            ; typed space before 1

** Error: wrong number of arguments to procedure
  (ABS 3 1)
>> (abbs 3.1)          ; spelling error
```

```
** Error: variable ABBS is unbound
>>> ('abs 3.1)        ;  quoted abs by mistake

** Error: attempt to call a symbol
   (ABS 3.1)
>>>> (abs "3.1")      ;  should not use string

** Error: non-numeric argument
   (LESS? ... "3.1" ...)
>>>>> (abs (nth '(2.1 3.1) 2))  ; nth  is 0-based

** Error: illegal index into list
   (NTH (2.1 3.1) 2)
>>>>>>
```

In these simple examples, it is not too difficult to identify what's wrong and how to correct it. The error messages are fairly helpful, even though they don't really get at the underlying cause of the error. The messages reveal the symptoms, which usually lead to the diagnosis of the disease.

However, imagine that you have written a large program comprising dozens of files and thousands of lines of code. In the course of execution, the program hits one of these errors and T spits out one of these messages. These error messages are generated by calls to T's own procedures. However, it is the procedures that you defined that made the mistake of too many arguments or an unbound variable. How do you find the error in your code?

Furthermore, imagine that you execute your enormous program and it does not produce any error messages. However, it does not produce the expected answer either. How do you find the error in your code?

The answer is to do what T does. If T's procedures can detect errors and signal them, so can your code. Here is an example of error checking.

```
(define (salary-of person dept)
    (cond ((not (isa-person? person))
           (error "SALARY-OF. non-person: ~A" person))
          ((not (isa-department? dept))
           (error "SALARY-OF. non-department: ~A" dept)))
    (get-salary person dept))


> (salary-of 'fido 'security)

** Error: SALARY-OF. non-person: FIDO
>>
```

One of the greatest sources of errors is bad data. Therefore, it is important to check any data to make sure that it is what you expect. The procedure **salary-of** is little more than a call to the **get-salary** procedure. However, it first checks its arguments to make sure that they are of proper types. When we call **salary-of** with a first argument of **fido**, who is not a person, we trigger the **error** clause.

The **error** procedure is very similar to **format**. It prints out its arguments in the same fashion as **format**, with several exceptions. First, the errors are always printed to the port **(error-output)**, which is usually the same as **(standard-output)**. Second, **error** prepends the the string "** **Error:** " to the format control string. Finally, **error** stops execution and places T at the next command level in another read-eval-print loop.

If the reader takes a moment to review T's regular error messages, it should be apparent that they too are based on the **error** procedure.

This use of **error** to check the validity of arguments is so common or worthwhile, or both, that T provides a special procedure, **check-arg**, which directly implements the entire process, as shown here.

```
(define (salary-of person dept)
    (get-salary (check-arg isa-person? person salary-of)
                (check-arg isa-department? dept salary-of)))

> (salary-of 'fido)

** Error: some argument didn't answer true to ISA-PERSON?
   (SALARY-OF ... FIDO ...)
>>
```

The **check-arg** procedure takes three arguments: the predicate used for type-checking, the object to be checked, and the name of the procedure to be printed as context in the error message. In the above example, the predicate is **isa-person?**, the object is **person**, and the procedure name is **salary-of**. Note that this name does not have to be the name of the procedure in the immediate context, though that would be the normal choice. If the predicate applied to the object returns true, then **check-arg** returns the object as its value. Otherwise, **check-arg** signals an error.

As the programmer should be aware, error checking is not without cost. Most computers can do only one thing at a time. The time that the computer spends checking arguments is time *not* spent executing the other instructions. That is to say, error checking slows down the code. Also, adding special error checking routines to programs slows down the programmer. The assumption is that the time invested by both programmer and computer in checking for errors will be offset by the time not spent by both man and machine later due to errors. The programmer will find it easier and quicker to fix mistakes, and the computer will devote its energies to productive execution, not infinite loops.

Still, there are times when the programmer feels certain that his program is free of errors, and is concerned about speeding up the execution of the code. The programmer can improve the performance of his program by turning off the error checking. T provides three levels of error checking, given as three settings of the (recklessness) object: low, medium, and high.

```
> (recklessness)               ;  normal (and sensible) setting
LOW

> (set (recklessness) 'high)
HIGH

> (recklessness)
HIGH
```

With the high setting, recklessness turns off much of the error checking built into T. If you have used some code for a long time without any errors, and thus, have high confidence in the correctness of that code, then you may be tempted to run with a medium or high setting to recklessness. This may improve your code's efficiency. However, if the recklessness setting is elevated and your code does in fact generate an error, your program may have traveled through hyperspace by the time you find out that it was headed off course.

In detecting errors, we are identifying symptoms. We are looking for indications of trouble. The programmer should freely use **error** and **check-arg** to find the problem before it spreads.

10.3   Elucidating Errors

Even if we know we have an error, we still may not know what caused the error. A message like "wrong number of arguments to procedure" is about as helpful as telling the doctor that you have a stomach pain. Neither piece of information, by itself, provides a diagnosis. However, each may suggest alternatives to explore.

How can the T programmer clarify and explain errors? There are several techniques available. The first method is one introduced in section 4.1, **trace**. When the programmer traces a procedure, particularly a recursive procedure, T prints out helpful information indicating every time that procedure was called, the values of the arguments, and the values of the result.

Here is a definition of factorial with a subtle error.

```
(define (fact n)
    (cond ((<= n 1) 1)
          (else (+ n (fact (- n 1))))))

> (fact 0)
1
```

```
> (fact 1)
1

> (fact 3)
6                              ;  no errors so far.  must be correct.

> (fact 4)
10                             ;  hmmm.  Answer should be 24.

> (trace fact)
[Assigning FACT]
FACT traced.

> (fact 4)

;0 Calling FACT with arguments (4)
; 1 Calling FACT with arguments (3)
;  2 Calling FACT with arguments (2)
;   3 Calling FACT with arguments (1)
;   3 Returned from FACT with value 1
;  2 Returned from FACT with value 3     ;  expected 2.
; 1 Returned from FACT with value 6
;0 Returned from FACT with value 10
10

> (untrace)

#{Procedure 28 FACT} untraced.
```

This example demonstrates one of the most insidious and beguiling types of errors: a program that is sometimes correct. We almost cannot believe that the program is making a mistake. After all, it gave the right answer on three test cases in a row; it must be correct. We become like a mother defending her child. "How can you accuse my son of stealing apples? Little Joey is an angel. He always helps me wash the dishes."

Yet, we know in our heart of hearts that a program that makes mistakes is a bad program. It must be repaired. The fact that it sometimes works properly may make it even harder to locate the error.

A practical problem using **trace** can be that it produces too much output to view on the screen. That is, some of the information printed from **trace** may scroll off the top of the screen before everything is completed. Also, it is sometimes useful to be able to review an entire T session at the terminal, to track down where the programmer may have made a mistake.

T allows the programmer to copy the terminal session to an output file using the `transcript-on` procedure. Given a filename as its only argument, `transcript-on` writes everything that appears on the terminal – entered by either the programmer or T itself – to the specified file. A call to the `transcript-off` procedure terminates the copying and closes the file, which can then be viewed in an editor, printed, or whatever. Here is an expurgated example.

```
> (transcript-on "fact.output")
OK

> (trace fact)
[Assigning FACT]
FACT traced.

> (fact 100)

  ...       ;     lots of output here...

> (transcript-off)
OK
```

A copy of the terminal session now appears in the file `fact.output`, an edited copy of which is presented below.

```
;;; T transcript file fact.output

> (trace fact)
[Assigning FACT]
FACT traced.

> (fact 100)

  ...       ;     lots of output here...

;;; End of transcript file
```

On workstations such as the Apollo, transcripts are provided automatically in T process windows, so there is no need for their explicit definition. However, with most terminals, the use of transcript files can be quite useful.

While we are talking about files, it is common to encounter errors when reading procedure definitions in from a file. The T interpreter will display its error message, and programmer has to go back to the file to find out where in the file the error occurred. One way to help identify the specific procedure responsible for the error is through the values printed by T when loading files. The object `(load-noisily?)` can be set to true or false, to indicate whether the programmer wants these values to be printed or not. Here is an example.

```
> (set (load-noisily?) nil)  ;  The programmer turns off printing.
()
> (load "~t/cd.t")

;Loading "~t/cd.t" into USER-ENV

** Read error: end of file inside list (missing right bracket)
   (port = #{Input-port 37 #[Filename () () "~t/cd.t"]})
>> (reset)

Top level
> (set (load-noisily?) t)    ;  The programmer turns on printing.
#t
> (load "~t/cd.t")

;Loading "~t/cd.t" into USER-ENV
[Redefining CD] CD [Redefining D] D [Redefining PWD] PWD

** Read error: end of file inside list (missing right bracket)
   (port = #{Input-port 38 #[Filename () () "~t/cd.t"]})
>>
```

With (load-noisily?) turned off, the programmer has little information to help him identify where in the file the error occurred. As usual, T's error message says a lot less than desired. However, when we turn (load-noisily?) back on, T prints out the names of the procedures that are defined in the file – along with the message that these procedures had been previously defined. Thus, when the error occurs this second time, it is after T has read and executed the definitions of cd, d, and pwd. Therefore, we know that the error appears in the procedure definition immediately following the pwd procedure.

As the T programmer should be aware by now, a misplaced parenthesis can cause no end of trouble. In addition to using a smart text editor, the programmer can take advantage of T's built in "pretty printer." Here is an example.

```
(define (bad-length lst)
    (cond ((null? lst) 0))
          (else (+ 1 (bad-length (cdr lst))))))
```

This definition of the length procedure looks pretty good. However, it will result in an infinite loop. The reason behind this problem can be seen better with T's PP form.

```
> (pp bad-length)

(LAMBDA (LST)
        (COND ((NULL? LST) 0))
        (ELSE (+ 1 (BAD-LENGTH (CDR LST)))))

> (pp good-length)

(LAMBDA (LST)
        (COND ((NULL? LST) 0)
              (ELSE (+ 1 (GOOD-LENGTH (CDR LST))))))
```

There is an extra right parenthesis following the 0 in the **bad-length** definition.
The **pp** or pretty print form displays a procedure definition with proper indentation
to indicate the level of nesting at each line. **pp** provides a good way to check
procedures that you suspect of having improperly balanced parentheses.

Sometimes, in the course of tracking down an error, the programmer may
wish to examine the definition of a procedure, along with any comments that may
accompany the definition. Thus, **pp** may not be enough.

Furthermore, once the programmer has identified an error, and knows how to
correct it, he probably wants to post the correction to the disk file in which the error
originated. In large programs that comprise dozens of files, it is sometimes difficult
to keep track of which procedure came from which file. T helps the programmer
out in this regard by doing the necessary bookkeeping. The programmer can query
T with **where-defined**, as follows.

```
> (where-defined cd)
#[Filename () () "~t/cd.t"]

> (where-defined where-defined)
#[Filename YALE-RING TSYS DEBUG T]
```

The procedure **cd** was defined in the file **cd.t** in the **t** subdirectory of the user's
home directory ~. **where-defined** was itself defined on Yale's Apollo ring computer
network, in the T system directory (TSYS), in the file **debug.t**.

10.4 Error Recovery

As the reader must have noticed by now, when T signals an error, or when the
error or **check-arg** procedures signal an error, T prints out a message, prints
a slightly different prompt, and waits for input from the user. T is then at a
nested command level, with a read-eval-print loop. These nested command levels
are called "breakpoints" – they are points where there is a break in the execution
of the program.

Until now, we have encountered breakpoints only when T detected errors, or our own code signaled an error. It is also possible for the programmer to place an explicit breakpoint in his code using the **breakpoint** procedure, shown here.

```
(define (print-name)
    (format t "~%My name is ~A.~%"
            (breakpoint "What is your name?"))
    repl-wont-pint)

> (print-name)

What is your name?
>> (ret 'mabel)                    ;  typed by programmer

My name is MABEL.

** Error: variable REPL-WONT-PINT is unbound
>> (ret repl-wont-print)      ;  typed by programmer

>
```

There are several things to note, starting with the behavior of **breakpoint**. The argument to **breakpoint** is a message to be printed before entering the breakpoint. At the breakpoint itself, the programmer uses the special **ret** procedure to return a value which will then be the result of the original call to **breakpoint**.

The procedure **print-name** continues, but there is trouble. This time, we have a typo – we left out the second **r** in **repl-wont-print** – so T complains. Again, we use **ret** to pass back the required result.

This example shows that it is often possible to catch and patch errors on the fly. Both **error** and **check-arg** call **breakpoint**, and **ret** provides a way to pass back corrected values and continue the computation.

We should emphasize that the breakpoint is a read-eval-print loop, and the programmer can use it in much the same way he would the normal top command level loop. The programmer can define, redefine, or invoke procedures, or virtually anything else he chooses. Usually though, the programmer simply wants to get back to the previous level.

Thus far, we have seen two ways to exit a breakpoint. The first was with **reset**, which returned us to the top command level. The second is **ret**, which returns us to the previous command level, and allows us to pass a result back as well, continuing the previous computation. **ret** with no arguments is equivalent to **(ret nil)**.

We can also return to the previous level and cancel the current computation by typing the end-of-file character at the breakpoint prompt, as shown below.

```
> (print-name)

What is your name?
>> (+ 3 4)                ; The breakpoint loop is still
7                         ; a read-eval-print loop.

>> (car (cdr '(a b c d)))
B

>> (print-name)

What is your name?       ; the programmer types the eof character,
>>> *** EOF ***          ; which T echos as *** EOF ***

>> *** EOF ***

> (print-name)

What is your name?
>> (print-name)

What is your name?
>>> (ret)

My name is ().

** Error: variable REPL-WONT-PINT is unbound
>>> *** EOF ***

>> *** EOF ***

> *** EOF ***
** Use (EXIT) to exit.   ; eof does not work at the top command level
```

We see here that the end-of-file character simply pops the programmer back a level, without trying to continue the previous computation at that level.

In addition to calls to **error** and **breakpoint**, the programmer can usually cause T to stop what it is doing and enter a breakpoint by typing the interrupt character. The interrupt and end-of-file characters vary according to the machine's operating system. The three primary operating systems for which T has been implemented are UNIX, VMS, and Apollo Aegis. Their character assignments for interrupt and end-of-file are as follows:

Operating system	interrupt	end-of-file
UNIX	^C or DEL	^D

```
VMS              ^C          ^Z
Aegis            ^Q          ^Z
```

When the programmer types end-of-file at a breakpoint, he is telling T to forget about continuing the original computation. Implicit in this action is the fact that T keeps track of *how* to continue the computation, should it be necessary. That is, when T hits a breakpoint, for whatever reason, it has to retain the state of the computation necessary for it to resume execution where it left off. It can sometimes be helpful for the programmer to examine the state information that T retains. One way to do this is through the procedure **backtrace**, shown below.

```
> (print-name)

What is your name?
>> (backtrace)
 Continue into        Module  Code
 PRINT-NAME           ()      (FORMAT T "~%My name is ~A.~%" ---
 PRINT-NAME           ()      (BLOCK (FORMAT T ---
 READ-EVAL-PRINT-LOOP REPL
 **BREAKPOINT         REPL
 BIND-INTERNAL        THROW
 **BREAKPOINT         REPL
 TOP-LEVEL            BOOT
>> *** EOF ***
> (backtrace)
 Continue into        Module  Code
 TOP-LEVEL            BOOT
> (bad-length '(1 2 3))
** Interrupt
>> (backtrace)
 Continue into        Module  Code
 *AEGIS-FAULT*        AEFAULT
 (anonymous)          AEXENO
 BAD-LENGTH           ()      (BAD-LENGTH (CDR LST))
 BAD-LENGTH           ()      (+ 1 (BAD-LENGTH (CDR LST)))
 BAD-LENGTH           ()      (ELSE (+ 1 (BAD-LENGTH (CDR LST))))
 BAD-LENGTH           ()      (+ 1 (BAD-LENGTH (CDR LST)))
 BAD-LENGTH           ()      (ELSE (+ 1 (BAD-LENGTH (CDR LST))))
** Interrupt
>>> (reset)
```

In this example, the programmer typed the interrupt character twice, at the points indicated by ** Interrupt. The first time, he stopped the infinite recursive calls to **bad-length**. The second time, he interrupted the finite, but lengthy, control stack listing of the calls to **bad-length**.

`backtrace` prints out data about the control stack. There are three columns of information provided by `backtrace`. The first column gives the name of the procedure to which control will pass upon completion of the current call. If the procedure does not have a name, which means it was a lambda expression, the first column entry is "anonymous."

The second column gives the name of the source file where the first column procedure was defined. A () in column two indicates that the procedure was typed in at the terminal, not loaded in from a file.

The third column is the source code for the procedure, if T can provide it. Sometimes that source code is abbreviated if there is not enough room on the line to print it all.

The programmer who avails himself of `backtrace` will encounter procedure names that are unfamiliar and mysterious. Where did they come from? To put it briefly, T rewrites your code for you. When you define a procedure, T transforms that code to make it more efficient and easier to execute. Many of these transformations are performed with macros, the fundamentals of which are discussed in the next chapter.

Finally, for the programmer who wants to explore the control stack in greater detail, T has the (debug) procedure. debug provides an interactive mechanism for climbing up and down the stack, examining its contents, and returning values to the previous computations. Here is a brief example.

```
> (print-name)

What is your name?
>> (debug)
#{Continuation 59}
  PRINT-NAME            ()        (FORMAT T "~%My name is ~A.~%" ---

debug: ?           ; debug  prompts for input.  user types ?
  ?  Print summary of inspector commands.
  A  Apply a procedure to the current object.
  B  Enter a read-eval-print loop in an appropriate environment.
  C  Inspect another object.
  D  Go to next deeper continuation (i.e. stack frame).
  E  Evaluate an expression in current object's environment.
  L  List values of lexical variables out to nearest locale.
  M  Macro-expand current object, and pretty-print the expansion.
  P  Pretty-print current object.
  Q  Exit the inspector.
  R  Return a value to a continuation, continuing execution there.
  U  Go back to inspecting previous object.
  V  Inspect current object's unit (compiled module).
```

W Give file name of current object's definition.
X Display object's contents or other relevant information.
= Print object, its hash, and its address.
The A, C, and E commands will prompt for an expression.

```
debug: 1
No local variables.

debug: p

(FORMAT T "~%My name is ~A.~%" (BREAKPOINT "What is your name?"))

debug: d          ; move down the stack
#{Continuation 60}
 PRINT-NAME            ()        (BLOCK (FORMAT T ---

debug: p

(BLOCK (FORMAT T "~%My name is ~A.~%"
               (BREAKPOINT "What is your name?"))
       REPL-WONT-PINT)

debug: u          ; move up the stack
#{Continuation 59}
 PRINT-NAME            ()        (FORMAT T "~%My name is ~A.~%" ---

debug: r 'mabel ; return the value 'mabel

My name is MABEL.

** Error: variable REPL-WONT-PINT is unbound
>> (debug)
#{Continuation 59}
 BIND-INTERNAL         THROW

debug: q          ; quit debug

>> *** EOF ***
```

For most programmers, crawling up and down the control stack is a technique
of last resort. Still some programmers embrace this particular type of exercise.
Those hardy souls are reminiscent of the reformers described by New York City
Mayor Jimmy Walker, as people who would enjoy riding through the sewer in a
glass-bottom boat.

10.5   Exercises

10.5.1   my-error [5*]

The **error** procedure is useful for signaling errors in a programmer's own code. Write a customized version called **my-error**, which performs the same tasks as **error** but prepends a slightly different message, as shown below.

```
> (my-error "~A is not a person" 'fido)

** My error: FIDO is not a person
>> (my-error "I need a number less than 10. ~D is not." 99)

** My error: I need a number less than 10. 99 is not.
>>>
```

10.5.2   Buggy fact [3*]

There was a problem with the **fact** procedure given on page 179. What was the bug?

10.5.3   bad-length Problem [4*]

The **bad-length** procedure described in this chapter results in an infinite loop. The text points out the misplaced parenthesis, which thus undermines the termination test, and is therefore the fundamental cause of the error. However, that does not completely explain why **bad-length** never terminates. What exactly is **bad-length** trying to do as it burns up computer cycles from here to eternity?

10.5.4   Pretty Printer [7]

Write your own pretty printer. It should take two arguments: an output port and an object. The procedure should take the arbitrary object and print it out with clear indentation. We offer no examples, except to say that the indentation rules provided in section 2.7 should be a guide. Furthermore, the programmer may find it useful for the pretty printer to be recursive, to allow it to call itself on embedded objects.

10.5.5   Argument Checking [5]

Add argument error checking to each of the exercises listed below. Try to make the error detection code as specific as possible without undermining the purpose of the original program.

    1. **leap-year?** – Exercise 2.11.10, page 31.

2. `make-person` – Exercise 3.10.4, page 56.

3. `make-person2` – Exercise 3.10.5, page 56.

4. `daughter-of-zeller` – Exercise 3.10.7, page 57.

5. `make-change` – Exercise 4.7.3, page 73.

6. `check-book` – Exercise 4.7.10, page 74.

7. `now-account` – Exercise 4.7.11, page 75.

8. `make-change` – Exercise 5.4.3, page 90.

9. `case-string-equal?` – Exercise 6.6.2, page 105.

10. `roman-char->decimal` – Exercise 6.6.4, page 106.

11. `string-swap` – Exercise 6.6.6, page 107.

12. `string-insert` – Exercise 6.6.6, page 107.

13. `split` – Exercise 7.7.2, page 124.

14. `print-recipe` – Exercise 7.7.7, page 126.

15. `soundex` – Exercise 9.8.3, page 170.

10.6   Chapter Summary

- Errors are a fact of programming life. Programmers need techniques to prevent, detect, clarify, and correct errors.

- T checks for and signals errors in most of its procedures.

- T provides the programmer with a number of useful tools for debugging, including the following:

```
(argspectrum procedure)
(error . error-message)
(check-arg predicate object procedure)
(recklessness)
(trace procedure)
(untrace)
(transcript-on filename)
(transcript-off)
(load-noisily?)
(pp procedure)
(where-defined object)
(breakpoint . message)
(debug)
```

- Breakpoints are nested command levels that occur where the previous command level has been interrupted. Here are several ways to trigger a breakpoint:

```
(error . error-message)
(check-arg predicate object procedure)
(breakpoint . message)
interrupt character
```

- A breakpoint is a read-eval-print loop, but the programmer can exit the breakpoint and return to a higher command level using these methods:

```
(ret . object)
(reset)
end-of-file character
```

Chapter 11

Macros

The T language is extensible. It is possible for the programmer to redefine or expand the T programming language.

Clearly, one way to change T is through procedure definitions. When we create a new procedure, we have, in a sense, enlarged the language. We can also define synonyms for existing procedures. For instance, we could create two new (and more perspicuous) names for T's basic accessor primitives.

```
> (define head car)
#{Accessor 27 CAR}

> (define tail cdr)
#{Accessor 28 CDR}

> (head (tail '(a b c d)))
B
```

There are two other ways to modify the T language: creating new special forms with *macros*, and creating new interpretations for individual characters with *read macros*. These methods affect the syntax of the language. In this chapter we shall examine each method.

11.1   Defining Macros

We have seen a number of different control mechanisms in T, including recursion, **do**, **iterate**, and **catch**. However, readers familiar with other programming languages will realize that other control structures are possible, including repeat loops, do/while loops, do/until loops, and for loops. Some programmers may prefer to implement these control structures in T, especially when translating code to T from some language which uses these forms.

In the answer to exercise 7.7.6, we defined a procedure **repeat-char**, which printed a given character a specified number of times. Here is a revised definition of **repeat-char** using the, as yet undefined, **repeat** loop.

```
(define (repeat-char port char count)
    (repeat count
            (write-char port char)))

> (repeat-char (standard-output) #\x 5)
xxxxx()
```

This definition of **repeat-char** is arguably cleaner than the previous recursive definition. The **repeat** special form consists of two arguments: the number of times to execute the given code, and the body of the code. We might consider writing **repeat** as a procedure, **p-repeat**.

```
(define (p-repeat n body)
    (do ((count n (- count 1)))
        ((<= count 0) nil)
        (body)))
```

However, this does not behave exactly the way we intended.

```
> (p-repeat 5 (write-char (standard-output) #\x))
x
    ** Error: attempt to call a non-procedure
    (1)
>>
```

The problem is that the code gets evaluated too soon. Then the **p-repeat** procedure ends up trying to evaluate (1), which is the value returned by the initial call to **write-char**.

One way around this is to pass an actual procedure, instead of the list expression. The easiest way to do this is with a lambda expression.

```
> (p-repeat 5 (lambda () (write-char (standard-output) #\x)))
xxxxx()
```

This method works, but it does not really match our initial desire to create a new syntactic control structure. The underlying problem is to avoid the initial evaluation of the arguments.

In procedures, the order of evaluation is as follows:

1. Evaluate each of the procedure's arguments.

2. Evaluate the body of the procedure.

In special forms, or macros, the order of evaluation is:

1. Evaluate the body of the macro.

2. Evaluate the resulting body of the expanded macro.

The evaluation of a procedure's arguments is occasionally delayed until step 2 by using the **quote** (') special form.

Here is one way to define a synonym for **quote**.

```
> (define-syntax (qu x)
    (list (quote quote) x))
#{Syntax 22 QU}


> (qu a)          ;  expands into:  (quote A)
A
```

The **qu** macro goes through two stages of evaluation. When it is called, as in **(qu a)**, the expression **(list (quote quote) x)**, with x bound to **A**, is evaluated in the first state, which results in **(quote A)**. Then, the latter expression is evaluated, resulting in simply **A**.

Thus, macros must build a list structure which can then be evaluated. Note that macros are created with the **define-syntax** special form, which is quite similar in style to the **define** special form used for creating procedures.

We now return to our **repeat** form, which we can define as a macro.

```
(define-syntax  (repeat n . body)
    (append '(do)
        (list (list (list 'count n (list '- 'count 1))))
        (list (list (list '<= 'count 0) nil))
        body))
```

```
(repeat 5 (write-char (standard-output) #\x))
```

expands into:

```
(do ((count 5 (- count 1)))
    ((<= count 0) ())
    (write-char (standard-output) #\x))
```

which gives a final result of:

```
xxxxx()
```

Note that the definition of **repeat** allows for multiple expressions in the body of the code. The dot which separates the variable names **n** and **body** indicates that more than one expression may appear following the repetition count. The resulting list of expressions are bound together to the **body** variable. Here are examples showing this feature.

```
> (let ((x 0)
        (y 1))
    (repeat 4 (set x (+ x 1))           ;  two expressions in body
              (set y (* x (* y y))))
    y)
576

> (repeat 4)                            ;  empty body
()
```

As defined above, **repeat** always returns (). However, you might wish to define it to return a specific value. (See exercise 11.6.2.)

11.2 Backquote

As discussed in the chapter on debugging, parentheses are the bane of the T programmer. Proper indentation, pretty printers, and clever text editors which know how to balance parentheses go a long way towards preventing problems caused by mismatched parentheses.

But just when we might think that the problem of balancing parentheses is under control, we encounter macros where the parentheses lay hidden until the first-stage evaluation. The programmer may never see this level of parentheses at all, but still have to specify it with complete accuracy in terms of **list**, **append**, **cons**, and friends.

It would be much easier if the programmer could merely describe what the first-stage result should look like, rather than having to give directions for how to build it.

A solution is at hand — the backquote. The backquote character (`` ` ``) acts similarly to the regular single quote (`'`). They both inhibit evaluation.

```
> 'atom
ATOM

> `atom
ATOM
```

```
> '(a b c d)
(A B C D)

> `(a b c d)
(A B C D)

> '(set x (* 3 7))
(SET X (* 3 7))

> `(set x (* 3 7))
(SET X (* 3 7))
```

The difference is that backquote can be used to specify *partial evaluation* of its constituents, by use of a preceding comma.

```
> `(set x ,(* 3 7))
(SET X 21)

> `(set x ,(car '((+ 3 4) (- 7 3) (* 2 6))))
(SET X (+ 3 4))

> `(set x ,(car `(,(+ 3 4) (- 7 3) (* 2 6))))
(SET X 7)
```

The effect of the comma should be apparent. It causes the following expression to be evaluated. All other expressions within the backquoted expression are not immediately evaluated.

One additional feature of the backquote facility is the ability to *splice* in lists, that is, interpolating a list structure without its outside layer of parentheses. The splice operation is specified with a comma followed by an at-sign (,@). Here are examples.

```
> `(set x (* ,(cdr '((+ 3 4) (- 7 3) (* 2 6)))))     ;  not quite right
(SET X (* ((- 7 3) (* 2 6))))

> `(set x (* ,@(cdr '((+ 3 4) (- 7 3) (* 2 6)))))    ;  ,@ does the trick
(SET X (* (- 7 3) (* 2 6)))

> `(set y (list ,@(cdr '('(j jones) '(m smith) '(d white)))))
(SET Y (LIST (QUOTE (M SMITH)) (QUOTE (D WHITE))))
```

The most common use of backquote is in macro definitions. The backquote allows the programmer to specify the result of the first-stage evaluation. Here are our earlier definitions of qu and repeat given with the backquote facility.

```
(define-syntax (qu x)
   `(quote ,x))

;    or even shorter!
(define-syntax (qu x)
   `',x)

(define-syntax  (repeat n . body)
   `(do ((count ,n (- count 1)))
        ((<= count 0) nil)
      ,@body))
```

Even though **repeat** seems to behave just the way we specified, there is a problem with both of our definitions. Consider the following code.

```
> (let ((count 1)) (repeat 5 (format t "~A" count)))
54321()
```

What happened? We expected this code to print five 1's. Here is the expanded version of that last expression.

```
(let ((count 1))
    (do ((count 5 (- count 1)))
        ((<= count 0) ())
      (format t "~A" count)))
```

We have a serious collision of identifiers. The **count** within the **format** statement was intended to refer to the **let count**, but it actually refers to the **do count**, which is the name of the variable within **repeat**.

There are several ways around this dilemma. One common way, which is not guaranteed, is to pick unusual names for macro variables. So instead of **count**, we might use **%%??count??%%** or some other ridiculous-looking name, on the assumption that no programmer would ever call our macro with another variable of the same name.

A better way is to bind the arguments of the macro outside the scope of the local macro variables. Here is **repeat** with safety bindings.

```
(define-syntax  (repeat n . body)
  `(let ((code (lambda () ,@body))
         (n ,n))
     (do ((count n (- count 1)))
         ((<= count 0) nil)
       (code))))

> (let ((count 1)) (repeat 5 (format t "~A" count)))
11111()
```

Now the code runs properly.

One of the widely held tenets of software engineering is that of "minimizing keystrokes" (or simply "mk"). The thought is that the less one has to type, the less the chance for error, and the less time required. (However, short identifiers can be harder for people to read and understand.)

In the spirit of this mk principle, the programmer can create a useful abbreviation for `lambda` using the macro facility. We pick an infrequently used ASCII character: `^`. Below we give the macro definition and some examples of its use.

```
(define-syntax (^ . rest)
   `(lambda . ,rest))

> ((^ (x) (+ x 5)) 3)
8

> (map (^ (y) (* y 2)) '(1 2 3 4))
(2 4 6 8)
```

The use of this abbreviation can be made more meaningful and appealing when combined with a bit-mapped display screen that allows the programmer to edit the display's fonts. Specifically, a programmer can redefine `^` to be the actual Greek character λ.

```
> ((λ (z) (* z 9)) 7)
63

> (map (λ (n) (- n 1)) '(10 11 12 13))
(9 10 11 12)
```

Some programmers find great psychic rewards in such symbolic achievements.

11.3 Macros versus Procedures

Many of T's special forms are implemented as macros. Examples include `define`, `set`, `push`, and `pop`. Here are simple macro definitions of the latter two. The actual definitions of `push` and `pop` are more involved, to ensure that their arguments do not get evaluated twice.

```
(define-syntax (my-pop stack)
   `(block0
      (car ,stack)
      (set ,stack (cdr ,stack))))

(define-syntax (my-push stack obj)
   `(set ,stack
         (cons ,obj ,stack)))
```

```
> (set x '(1 2 3 4))
(1 2 3 4)

> (my-pop x)
1

> (my-push x 5)
(5 2 3 4)

> x
(5 2 3 4)

> (my-push (car (my-push x '(7 8))) 9)
(9 7 8)
```

; The second **my-push** was evaluated twice by the first one.
; This resulted in an extra push.
```
> x
((9 7 8) (7 8) 5 2 3 4)

> (set y '(5 2 3 4))
(5 2 3 4)
```

; The real **push** works correctly, with no second evaluation.
```
> (push (car (push y '(7 8))) 9)
(9 7 8)

> y
((9 7 8) 5 2 3 4)
```

These examples should be fairly easy to grasp. However, the reader may wonder why **push** and **pop** were not defined as procedures. Wouldn't that have been even simpler?

Let's try defining **pop** as a procedure.

```
(define (bad-pop stack)
    (block0
        (car stack)
        (set stack (cdr stack))))

> (set x '(1 2 3 4))
(1 2 3 4)
```

```
> (bad-pop x)
1                           ;  so far, so good

> x
(1 2 3 4)                   ;  oops — something went wrong

> (bad-pop x)
1
```

The problem with **bad-pop** is that the **set** form does not evaluate its first argument. Thus, the expression **(set stack (cdr stack))** changes the value of the local variable **stack**, but not the global variable **x**. Macros provide a way to get at the difference between a variable's name and its value. Problems can sometimes arise, as discussed earlier with the variable **count** in the **repeat** macro and in exercise 11.6.7.

If macros provide such flexibility, why not use them exclusively, instead of procedures? Good question. Let's try a simple case – a macro which increments its argument.

```
(define-syntax (madd1 x)
    `(+ 1 ,x))

> (madd1 5)
6

> (madd1 (* 7 8))
57
```

Our **madd1** macro appears to work fine. However, there are other uses for procedures.

```
> (map add1 '(1 2 3 4 5))    ; add1  is a procedure
(2 3 4 5 6)

> (apply add1 '(8))
9

> (map madd1 '(1 2 3 4 5))

** Warning: reference or assignment to reserved word MADD1 as a
variable

** Error: variable MADD1 is unbound
>> (reset)
```

```
Top level
> (apply madd1 '(8))

** Warning: reference or assignment to reserved word MADD1 as a
variable

** Error: variable MADD1 is unbound
>>
```

T seems to get mad when the programmer uses the **madd1** macro as a named
argument.

Procedures in T are full-fledged data objects. They can be passed as arguments. Macros, on the other hand, are ephemeral. A macro is expanded and the
resulting list structure is inserted directly into the given context. This means that
macros cannot be passed as objects. The above example with **apply** would be like
writing the following.

```
> (apply '(+ 1 x) '(8))

** Error: attempt to call a non-procedure
  ((+ 1 X) 8)
>>
```

One further ramification of the order of evaluation of macros concerns define-
time dependencies of code that includes macros. Suppose you create the following
simple procedures **foo**, which calls **baz**, defined in sequence.

```
(define (foo x)
    (baz x))

(define (baz z) (+ 5 z))

> (foo 3)
8
```

Everything is copacetic. However, if we try the same trick, but make **baz** a macro
instead of a procedure, we lose.

```
(define (foo2 x)
    (baz2 x))

(define-syntax (baz2 z)
    `(+ 5 ,z))
```

```
> (foo2 3)
```

```
** Error: variable BAZ2 is unbound
>>
```

Why the error? At the time **foo2** was defined, the reference to **baz2** was assumed to be to an identifier whose value would be a procedure. At this point, though, we have defined **baz2** as a macro, so there is no variable name associated with it. However, if we were now to redefine **foo2**, the **baz2** macro would get properly expanded inside of the procedure definition and the code should run without a hitch.

```
(define (foo2 x)
    (baz2 x))
```

```
> (foo2 3)
8
```

The moral of this lesson is that macros should be defined and loaded before defining any code that calls the macros. Furthermore, when the definition of a macro is changed, the programmer needs to redefine all definitions that called the macro. These order-of-definition rules do not apply to procedure calls.

11.4   Syntax Tables

A macro can be viewed as a source-to-source transformation of code. For each T special form or macro symbol, there is a corresponding transformation. T indexes these associations between symbols and transformations in *syntax tables*.

Syntax tables are related to environments, which are discussed in chapter 15. The **define-syntax** form enters new macros in the current syntax table. Here are some of the other basic commands relating to syntax tables.

```
> standard-syntax-table
#{Syntax-table 61 STANDARD-ENV}
```

```
> (env-syntax-table (repl-env))
#{Syntax-table 60 USER-ENV}
```

```
> (syntax-table-entry standard-syntax-table 'define)
#[Syntax DEFINE]
```

```
> (syntax-table-entry standard-syntax-table 'repeat)
()
```

```
> (syntax-table-entry (env-syntax-table (repl-env)) 'repeat)
#{Syntax 39 REPEAT}

> (set (syntax-table-entry
              (env-syntax-table (repl-env)) 'repeat) nil)
[Redefining syntax REPEAT] ()

> (syntax-table-entry (env-syntax-table (repl-env)) 'repeat)
()

> (repeat 5 (format t "X"))
X

** Error: variable REPEAT is unbound
>>
```

T starts off with a standard syntax table in a standard environment, and copies this into a programmer work area or scratch environment. This is the read-eval-print loop environment or **repl-env**. Again, see chapter 15 for environment details. The two main syntax table operations are the following.

- **(env-syntax-table environment)** returns the syntax table associated with the given environment.

- **(syntax-table-entry syntax-table symbol)** returns the special form object associated with the given symbol in the syntax table. If there is no entry, the procedure returns false. In this case, we have defined the **repeat** macro in the read-eval-print loop environment, but it is not a part of T's standard environment. Note that this procedure is settable. We remove the entry for **repeat** by setting it to false.

In debugging macro definitions, it is often useful to examine their expansion. This can be done with the **macro-expand** procedure which takes two arguments: the expression to be expanded and the associated syntax table. We define a convenient procedure, **ma**, which will expand its argument using the read-eval-print loop environment's syntax table. Note that the expression is not actually evaluated.

```
> (define (ma exp)
     (macro-expand exp (env-syntax-table (repl-env))))
#{Procedure 66 MA}

> (ma '(define (fact x)
              (cond ((zero? x) 1)
                    (else (* x (fact (- x 1)))))))
(DEFINE-VAR FACT (NAMED-LAMBDA FACT (X) (COND ((ZERO? X) 1)
(ELSE (* X (FACT (- X 1)))))))
```

```
> (ma '(cond ((zero? x) 1) (else (* x (fact (- x 1)))))))
(IF (ZERO? X) 1 (IF ELSE (* X (FACT (- X 1)))
**NO-MORE-COND-CLAUSES**))

> (ma '(repeat 5 (format t "a")))
(DO ((COUNT 5 (- COUNT 1))) ((<= COUNT 0) ()) (FORMAT T "a"))

> (ma '(my-push x 9))
(SET X (CONS 9 X))

> (ma '(push x 9))
(MODIFY-LOCATION X (LAMBDA (FETCH.296 STORE.297)
(STORE.297 (CONS 9 (FETCH.296)))))
```

These examples begin to expose some of the internals of T. We shall not here endeavor to explain what all these creatures do, but merely acknowledge their existence. We first expand a **define** form, which becomes something called **DEFINE-VAR**. We then expand the **cond** form, which turns into a series of embedded **if**'s. Our old friend **repeat** expands in the expected way, as does **my-push**. T's **push**, on the other hand, is more complex, as earlier advertised.

The programmer will find macro expansion to be quite helpful when writing macros on his own. Macro expansion also provides an instructive means to explore the way in which T is implemented. See chapter **17** for a discussion of source-to-source transformations in T's implementation.

11.5   Read Macros

T's macro facility allows the programmer to tailor the language to his own requirements, extending the language with new constructs, and even altering the way in which old constructs are interpreted.

T also allows the programmer to change the way individual characters are interpreted. The programmer has no way of creating new characters — of enlarging the size of T's alphabet. However, the programmer can provide a new meaning for an old character using read macros.

T interprets the meaning of characters as it reads them from an input port, usually the terminal or a file. Characters fall into several categories:

- Whitespace. Characters like space, tab, or newline. T's reader ignores these.

- Read macros. Characters that have a mind of their own, as it were. These each invoke special reading routines, discussed below.

- Escape. The backslash character (\) is used to turn off any extra interpretation of the next character. For example, a\;b produces the symbol A;B, including the embedded semicolon.

- Others. These characters, such as letters and digits, are read sequentially until some other category of character is encountered, e.g., whitespace or read-macros. At that point, accumulated characters are converted into a symbol or number, as appropriate. Lowercase letters are converted to uppercase.

Standard read macro characters in T include the following:

;   Comment character. Ignores the remaining input on the current line.

"   Doublequote character. Delimits a string.

'   Quote character. Converts `'foo` to `(quote foo)`.

`   Backquote character. Discussed above.

,   Comma character. Used with backquote.

(Left parenthesis. Begins a list.

)   Right parenthesis. Ends a list.

T uses tables to keep track of what characters are in which categories, and which ones are exceptions. These tables are called *read tables*.

Just as T has standard ports for input and output, T has a default read table, namely `standard-read-table`. It would be possible to change this read table directly, but it is safer and wiser to make changes to a copy, rather than to `standard-read-table` itself. Here is how to make your own read table, and associate it with an input port.

```
> (define my-read-table
    (make-read-table standard-read-table 'my-read-table))
#{Read-table 22 MY-READ-TABLE}

> (port-read-table (standard-input))
#{Read-table 21 STANDARD-READ-TABLE}

> (set (port-read-table (standard-input)) my-read-table)
#{Read-table 22 MY-READ-TABLE}

> (port-read-table (standard-input))
#{Read-table 22 MY-READ-TABLE}
```

`make-read-table` returns as its value a new read table, which is a copy of the first argument. The second argument, which appears redundant, is used by T for debugging. The `port-read-table` procedure tells what read table is used for the given input port. We can use `set` to change that table.

The programmer who manipulates read tables will often want to associate a particular read table with a file, to indicate that the file requires special interpretation of certain characters. For example, a programmer may have special comment characters or data abbreviation read macros for certain files. T allows the programmer to include this information with the **herald** form at the beginning of the file.

```
(herald myfile (read-table my-read-table))
```

In this example, the **read-table** declaration inside the **herald** form instructs T to use **my-read-table** when reading in the expression contained in this file. This assumes, of course, that the programmer has already created **my-read-table**.

The programmer can also associate a specific syntax table with a file in the herald form, in a similar fashion.

```
(herald myfile (syntax-table my-syntax-table))
```

Now that we know how to tell T which read table to use when, we can start examining and changing the contents of the table. We use the procedure **read-table-entry**, which takes two arguments, a read table and a character.

```
> (read-table-entry my-read-table #\space)
0

> (read-table-entry my-read-table #\%)
2

> (read-table-entry my-read-table #\M)
2

> (read-table-entry my-read-table #\7)
2

> (read-table-entry my-read-table #\;)
#{Procedure 28 READ-COMMENT}

> (read-table-entry my-read-table #\()
#{List-reader 25}

> (set (read-table-entry my-read-table #\%)
       (read-table-entry my-read-table #\;))
#{Procedure 28 READ-COMMENT}

> (read-table-entry my-read-table #\%)
#{Procedure 28 READ-COMMENT}
```

```
> (set (read-table-entry my-read-table #\;) 2)
2

> (define (x;2 x) (* 2 x))    % This is a comment
#{Procedure 58 X\;2}

> (x;2 8)
16
```

In the current implementation, whitespace characters have read table entries of
0. Regular graphics characters have entries of 2, and read macro characters have
entries which are procedures to be executed. The standard entries for all the ASCII
characters are given in appendix B.

In the above example, we made **%** a comment character, and **;** a regular
character. We can also define new procedures for read macros. For example, in
some artificial intelligence pattern matchers, such as described in [3], a symbol
preceded by a question mark, such as **?person**, is a variable which can match any
token in the input. So the pattern "**?person went to the store**" would match
the input sentence "**John went to the store**," and the variable **?person** would be
bound to **John**. We can create a read macro for **?** which will convert **?person** into
(***var* person**), so that the pattern matcher will have an easier time recognizing
variables in the pattern lists. Namely, a variable will be any list whose **car** is ***var***.

Here is a read macro definition for **?**.

```
(set (read-table-entry my-read-table #\?)
     (lambda (port ch read-table)
       (ignore ch)
       (ignore read-table)
       (list '*var* (read-refusing-eof port))))
#{Procedure 68}

> (set x '?person)
(*VAR* PERSON)

> '?(one two three)
(*VAR* (ONE TWO THREE))
```

A read macro procedure takes three arguments, a port, a character, and a
read table. In this case, the character argument, which is bound to the character
being assigned, and the read table argument, which may reference a particular read
table, are not used, and the **ignore** form tells the compiler not to worry about that
fact. The procedure then creates a list, with a **car** of ***var*** and a **cdr** comprising
the next object read from the port. Instead of **read**, read macros typically call

read-refusing-eof, which is simply a version of **read** which does not expect an end of file.

11.6   Exercises

11.6.1   Expression Drill [3]

Evaluate the following expressions, first by hand, then with the help of the T interpreter.

```
(set x (* (+ 5 4) (+ 7 3)))
`(set x (* (+ 5 4) (+ 7 3)))
`(set x (* ,(+ 5 4) (+ 7 3)))
`(set x (* ,(+ 5 4) ,(+ 7 3)))
`(set x ,(* (+ 5 4) (+ 7 3)))
(car (cdr (cdr '(a (b c (d)) (e)))))
`(car (cdr (cdr '(a (b c (d)) (e)))))
`(car (cdr ,(cdr '(a (b c (d)) (e)))))
`(car (cdr ,@(cdr '(a (b c (d)) (e)))))
`(car ,(cdr (cdr '(a (b c (d)) (e)))))
`(car ,@(cdr (cdr '(a (b c (d)) (e)))))
```

11.6.2   repeat Macro with a Value [5*]

Redefine the **repeat** macro, but add an argument that will be returned as the value upon completion. For example,

```
(define (repeat-char port char count)
    (repeat count repl-wont-print
            (write-char port char)))

(repeat-char (standard-output) #\! 10)
!!!!!!!!!!
```

Assume that the returned value is affected by side-effects in the body **of repeat**.

11.6.3   repeat with iterate [5*]

Rewrite **repeat** one more time, but use **iterate** instead of **do**. Have this **repeat** take a result argument, as in the preceding exercise.

11.6.4   Changing the T Prompt [6*]

T's Read-Eval-Print loop prompts the programmer for input with some number of
>'s indicating the number of current command level. This prompt is printed by
a procedure given as the value of (repl-prompt). Furthermore, the programmer
can provide his own procedure, but it must take a single argument — a number
indicating the level of nesting. The procedure returns a string. Here is an example.

```
> (my-prompt 1)
"Yes, Master>"

> (my-prompt 5)
"Yes, Master>>>>>"

> (set (repl-prompt) my-prompt)
#{Procedure 101 MY-PROMPT}

Yes, Master>
```

Write the my-prompt procedure, using the repeat macro just defined. Then,
write a second procedure new-prompt which returns a prompt procedure. There
are two arguments to new-prompt, the initial text string and the string to
be repeated. With this new procedure, you could create my-prompt with
(new-prompt "Yes, Master" ">"). Here are other examples.

```
> (set hello-prompt (new-prompt "hello" "."))
#{Procedure 112}

> (hello-prompt 3)
"hello..."

> (set goodbye-prompt (new-prompt "good" "-bye"))
#{Procedure 113}

> (goodbye-prompt 8)
"good-bye-bye-bye-bye-bye-bye-bye-bye"
```

This exercise is hazardous. If you replace the repl-prompt procedure with
one that causes an error, you can bid your T process good-bye-bye-bye.

Also, you may have to redefine the preceding repeat macro to allow you to
modify the result value in the body of the repeat.

11.6.5   while Macro [5*]

Write a while macro which takes two or more arguments. The first argument
is a test expression, and the second argument is the result to be returned. The

remaining expressions are the body of the calculation. As long as the first expression
is non-NIL, then the remaining expressions are repeatedly evaluated. Here is an
example with `repeat-char` defined using `while`.

```
(define (repeat-char port char count)
    (while
        (> count 0)              ;  test clause
        repl-wont-print          ;  result clause
        (write-char port char)
        (set count (- count 1))))
```

```
> (repeat-char (standard-output) #\! 10)
!!!!!!!!!!!
```

11.6.6   until Macro [5*]

Based on the previous exercise, write an `until` macro which takes two or more
arguments. `until` has the same form as `while`, except the polarity of the test
is reversed: as long as the test is false, the remaining expressions are repeatedly
evaluated. Here is an example with `repeat-char` defined using `until`.

```
(define (repeat-char port char count)
    (until
        (= count 0)              ;  test clause
        repl-wont-print          ;  result clause
        (write-char port char)
        (set count (- count 1))))
```

```
(repeat-char (standard-output) #\^ 10)
^^^^^^^^^^
```

11.6.7   block0 Macro [7*]

There is a problem with the following macro definition for `block0`.

```
(define-syntax (block0 first . rest)
   `((lambda (x) ,@rest x) ,first))
```

There are certain cases in which it will not work properly.

Write another macro definition of `block0` that works correctly. The local
variable `x` used in the definition of `block0` may conflict with an occurrence of a
variable in the `rest` expressions, as below.

```
> (block0 1 (set x 2) 3)
2
```

The solution given before to this problem was to bind the executable body as a local procedure outside the scope of the other local variables, as below.

```
(define-syntax (my-block0 first . rest)
  `(let ((rest (lambda () ,@rest)))
     ((lambda (x) (rest) x) ,first)))
```

There are other solutions which are variations on this method. Rewrite **block0** in another way that eliminates the variable name conflict.

11.6.8 dpsq Macro [6*]

One common use of macros is for situations in which the programmer does not want the arguments evaluated. Here is such a case: the Define PropertieS-Quoted, or **dpsq** macro.

We shall first describe the procedure **dps**, which takes one or more arguments of the form: node-name property value property value, etc. It returns nil, and as a side-effect, puts the given values on the property list of the node. **dpsq** is a macro version of **dps** which does not evaluate its arguments. Here are examples of both.

```
> (dps 'john 'age 23 'mother 'mary 'father 'jack)
()

> (get 'john 'age)
23

> (get 'john 'father)
JACK

> (dpsq jack age 53 wife mary son john)
()

> (get 'jack 'son)
JOHN
```

Here is one definition of the **dps** procedure, albeit a faulty one.

```
(define (dps . l)
  (let ((node (pop l)))
    (cond ((null? l) nil)
          (else
           (put node (pop l) (pop l))
           (apply dps (cons node l))))))
```

Identify and correct the problem in this definition, and then define the **dpsq** macro in terms of **dps**.

11.6.9   ISA Inheritance Hierarchy [4*]

In artificial intelligence programs, programmers often represent knowledge with inheritance hierarchies. That is, if an item is an instance of a particular class, then that item assumes the properties of that class unless otherwise indicated. One simple way of implementing property inheritance is with "ISA" links in a property list database. Here is an example.

```
(walk (lambda (l) (apply dps l))
     '((jane isa programmer sex female income forty-k)
       (john isa programmer sex male ingests junk-food)
       (programmer isa person income thirty-k)
       (person isa mammal)
       (mammal isa organism)
       (organism ingests (food air)))))
*VALUE-OF-WALK*

> (isa-get 'jane 'sex)
FEMALE

> (isa-get 'jane 'income)
FORTY-K

> (isa-get 'john 'income)
THIRTY-K

> (isa-get 'jane 'ingests)
(FOOD AIR)

> (isa-get 'john 'ingests)
JUNK-FOOD
```

We created a simple class hierarchy of organisms, including two individuals, Jane and John. The procedure `isa-get` checks the local node for the given property. If it is not found, then `isa-get` recursively climbs the inheritance hierarchy.

Write the `isa-get` procedure.

11.6.10   Data-Driven dpsq Macro [8*]

Data has structure. Knowledge has content. We can begin to add content to our data structures by making them behave differently according to the content of the input. For example, we know that a person may have only one spouse at a time, but may have several children and several siblings concurrently. We know that if X is the spouse of Y, then Y is the spouse of X. We know that if X is the sibling of Y, then Y is the sibling of X, and so forth.

Just as we used the `isa` property in the preceding exercise to model inheritance, we can create a data-drive version of `put` – `ddput` – which reacts in specific ways to other properties. We can then use `ddput` instead of `put` inside `dps`.

Here is an example of this revised version of `dps` and `dpsq` which is triggered by a set of special properties, marked with a ! prefix.

```
(walk (lambda (1) (apply dps 1))
      '((isa !invert-onto instances)
        (instances !multiple-values t)
        (*relationship !multiple-values t)
        (relationship !save-property t)
        (children isa *relationship)
        (sibling isa *relationship !invert-value t)
        (father isa relationship)
        (spouse isa relationship !invert-value t)
        (joe-jr father joe-sr spouse mary children pat children
sue)))
*VALUE-OF-WALK*

> (pppq joe-jr)

JOE-JR
    CHILDREN          (SUE PAT)
    SPOUSE            MARY
    FATHER            JOE-SR

> (pppq relationship)

RELATIONSHIP
    INSTANCES         (SPOUSE FATHER)
    !SAVE-PROPERTY    T

> (pppq *relationship)

*RELATIONSHIP
    INSTANCES         (SIBLING CHILDREN)
    !MULTIPLE-VALUES  T

>  (dpsq mary sibling dorothy sibling arthur)
()
```

```
> (pppq mary)

MARY
    SIBLING            (ARTHUR DOROTHY)
    SPOUSE            JOE-JR

> (pppq arthur)

ARTHUR
    SIBLING            MARY
```

There is a lot going on beneath the surface in this example. Here is a list of the properties that **ddput** must deal with.

- **!invert-onto** When **ddput** encounters a property that itself has an **!invert-onto** property, **ddput** calls itself recursively, reversing the current node and value on the property specified by the flag. In this example, the **isa** property automatically inverts its arguments via an **instances** property.

- **!multiple-values** This property flag tells **ddput** that the value should be added to any existing values on this node's given property, but without duplication. Here, the properties of **instances** and *****relationship** may have multiple values. Also, **children** and **sibling** properties may have multiple values, as inherited via the **isa** hierarchy from *****relationship**.

- **!save-property** This flag is one alternative to the **!multiple-values** flag. If **ddput** encounters a property flagged as **!save-property**, and there is an existing value, this old value is moved to a backup node, which is given as the value to a **save-node** property on the main node. We shall see an example below.

- **!invert-value** Some properties, like spouse and sibling, are commutative. These values may be automatically inverted. In this example, entering the fact that Joe's spouse is Mary results in the automatic entry of Mary's spouse being Joe.

- **(pppq node)** This is a special form which calls the procedure **(ppp node)**, just as **dpsq** calls **dps**. The procedure **ppp** prints out the properties and values associated with the node. This procedure requires that **ddput** keep a list of the properties assigned in the first place. The most convenient place for such a list is on the node itself under some special property, such as **!ddprops**.

- **!invert-property** This is similar to the **!invert-value**, with the value and property reversed. That is, the additional entry is made on the property list of the property. This is demonstrated below with the **job** property.

- !lambda-property The idea here is to allow complete flexibility to the programmer. The value of a !lambda-property is a procedure which takes the three **put** variables: node, property, and value. This procedure is invoked when its property is asserted. We demonstrate this feature below.

Continuing this example, we have Joe remarry, have another child, and go to work at two jobs to support his growing family.

```
> (dpsq joe-jr spouse louise children jackie)
()

> (pppq joe-jr)

JOE-JR
     SAVE-NODE            SAVE.4
     CHILDREN            (JACKIE SUE PAT)
     SPOUSE              LOUISE
     FATHER              JOE-SR

> (ppp (get 'joe-jr 'save-node))

SAVE.4
     SPOUSE              MARY

> (dpsq job !invert-property t !multiple-values t)
()

> (dpsq plumber isa job)
()

> (dpsq carpenter isa job)
()

> (dpsq joe-jr job plumber job carpenter)
()

> (pppq joe-jr)

JOE-JR
     JOB                 (CARPENTER PLUMBER)
     SAVE-NODE           SAVE.4
     CHILDREN            (JACKIE SUE PAT)
     SPOUSE              LOUISE
     FATHER              JOE-SR
```

```
> (pppq job)

JOB
     CARPENTER          (JOE-JR)
     PLUMBER            (JOE-JR)
     INSTANCES          (CARPENTER PLUMBER)
     !MULTIPLE-VALUES   T
     !INVERT-PROPERTY   T
```

The !save-property flag under relationship resulted in saving Joe's previous spouse under a separate node. We then defined job to allow multiple values, and to be inverted under the job node. Thus, we can keep track of all the plumbers and carpenters automatically.

We close with an example of the !lambda-property. We decide to treat sons as male children, with a specified father.

```
> (dps 'son '!lambda-property
     (lambda (node prop val)
        (ddput node 'children val)
        (ddput val 'sex 'male)
        (ddput val 'father node)))
()

> (dpsq joe-jr son lester)
()

> (pppq joe-jr)

JOE-JR
     JOB                (CARPENTER PLUMBER)
     SAVE-NODE          SAVE.4
     CHILDREN           (LESTER JACKIE SUE PAT)
     SPOUSE             LOUISE
     FATHER             JOE-SR

> (pppq lester)

LESTER
     FATHER             JOE-JR
     SEX                MALE
```

Modify dpq to use ddput, and write ddput, ppp, and pppq.

11.6.11   msg Macro [8]

The `format` procedure in T is convenient and helpful. However, it is sometimes difficult to manage to get all the control string options associated with their respective arguments. It would be preferable to be able to give the formatting information side by side with the arguments. The `msg` macro, which is found in some other dialects of LISP, provides just this capability.

Here is an example of `msg` at work.

```
> (msg "Hello" t)
Hello
**VALUE-OF-MSG**

> (msg t "Hello" t "there" t)

Hello
there
**VALUE-OF-MSG**

> (set x 5)
5

> (msg "John is" 1 x 1 "year" (plur x) 1 "old" t)
John is 5 years old
**VALUE-OF-MSG**

> (msg (bin x) " + " (bin x) " = " (bin (+ x x)) t)
101 + 101 = 1010
```

`msg` takes a variable number of arguments, each of which may be one of over a dozen types listed below.

- *string*   Display the string.

- t   Start a new line.

- *number*   Move that number of spaces.

- *-number*   Skip that number of lines.

- (TO port)   Redirect output to the given port. The default output port is (standard-output).

- (TAB number)   Tab to the specified column number.

- (RIGHT string)   Display the given text flush right. Use the current output line if possible. Otherwise, start on the next line.

- (CENTER string) Display the given text centered on the line. Move to the next line if necessary.

- (HEX number) Print the given number in hexadecimal.

- (OCT number) Print the given number in octal.

- (BIN number) Print the given number in binary.

- (PLUR number) If the number is greater than 1, then display an 's', otherwise, nothing. This is used for simple plurals, as given in the above example.

11.6.12 Comment Read Macro [7]

The normal comment character (;) allows the programmer to specify single line comments. Often, a programmer finds it more convenient to have multiline comments, without having to place a special character at the beginning of each line. This facility can be achieved with a read macro.

Define a read macro character, !, which introduces a multiline comment. When the T reader encounters !, it should ignore all characters until it comes across a left parenthesis in the first column of a line. Here is an example.

```
(herald myfile (read-table *my-read-table*))

!   The comment read macro has been defined in
    *my-read-table*.  T is ignoring these lines.

    It is waiting for a left paren in column 1.
    Here it comes now.

(define the-answer-to-the-problems-of-the-world nil)
;   The define on the previous line was executed by T.
```

11.7 Chapter Summary

- The syntax of T can be modified with macros.

- Macros are created using the **define-syntax** special form.

- Macros are useful for creating new control mechanisms, since they allow for selective evaluation of their arguments.

- The backquote read-macro allows for selective evaluation of list expressions through the use of its comma and comma-at-sign syntax.

- Macros and procedures are not interchangeable. In particular, macros cannot be passed as arguments, whereas procedures can. Also, macros are expanded at the time they are read, whereas procedures are evaluated at the time they are called.

- T stores macros definitions in syntax tables, which are associated with environments. The `standard-syntax-table` is copied into a scratch syntax table in the read-eval-print loop environment. These tables are accessed with the following procedures.

    ```
    (env-syntax-table environment)
    (syntax-table-entry syntax-table symbol)      ; settable
    ```

- For debugging and exploratory purposes, it is often useful to expand macro expressions using the `macro-expand` procedure.

    ```
    (macro-expand expression syntax-table)
    ```

- T uses read tables to the record the method of interpretation for characters. The default is `standard-read-table`.

- Read macros allow the programmer to change T's interpretation of individual characters. Read tables are manipulated with the following procedures.

    ```
    (make-read-table read-table identifier)
    (port-read-table port)                   ; can be set
    (read-table-entry read-table character) ; can be set
    ```

- The `herald` form can be used to specify a file's read table and syntax table.

- The `ignore` special form advises the compiler not to pay attention to variables that are created but not referenced.

- The programmer can redefine the prompt issued by T's Read-Eval-Print loop by resetting (`repl-prompt`).

Chapter 12

Structures

It is easy to lose sight of the fact that computers don't really manipulate lists or objects or strings or numbers or symbols or even binary digits. The computer only sees one kind of data: voltages. Electricity is the computer's primal world.

Not only is that fact easy to forget, it is absolutely necessary to forget when thinking about writing computer programs. T's objects are abstractions, built in a principled way from more primitive elements. These abstractions allow the programmer to specify actions in a clear and concise fashion.

Furthermore, T allows the programmer to make his own data abstractions, to create and manipulate new types of data objects. Why would the programmer wish to create an abstraction? For the same reason that the programmer would not want to specify programs in terms of voltage manipulations – for power and clarity of expression.

12.1 Structures

In section 8.5, we defined the `better-zeller` procedure, which took one argument, a list of the form `(day month year)`.

```
(define (better-zeller date)
   (let* ((day    (car date))
          (month  (cadr date))
          (year   (caddr date))
          (century (quotient year 100))
          (decades (- year century))
          (leap    (cond ((leap-year? year) 1)
                         (else 0))))
      (zeller day month century decades leap)))
```

This program depends on the fact that the date is represented precisely as that three-element list. However, the *reference* to a piece of data, and the *representation* of that data should be separate whenever possible. One simple way to do this is by defining accessor procedures that are specific to the `date` data structure, as below.

```
(define (better-zeller date)
   (let* ((day    (date-day date))
          (month  (date-month date))
          (year   (date-year date))
          (century (quotient year 100))
          (decades (- year (* 100 century)))
          (leap    (cond ((leap-year? year) 1)
                         (else 0))))
      (zeller day month century decades leap)))

(define date-day car)
(define date-month cadr)
(define date-year caddr)
```

All we have done is to define synonyms for the accessor functions used in the previous example. The code should execute exactly as it did before. However, a person looking at the code should find it easier to understand the code. In fact, the clarity of the names of the new accessor procedures make it reasonable to do away with the `day` and `month` variables in the `let*` form all together:

```
(define (better-zeller date)
   (let* ((year  (date-year date))
          (century (quotient year 100))
          (decades (- year (* 100 century)))
          (leap  (cond ((leap-year? year) 1)
                       (else 0))))
      (zeller (date-day date)
              (date-month date)
              century decades leap)))
```

We keep the other variables, **year**, **century**, and **decades**, for purposes of clarity and economy.

T provides a method to implement new data structures, like **date**, directly, with the **define-structure-type** form, demonstrated below.

```
> (define-structure-type date day month year day-of-week)
#{Structure-type DATE}

> (set x (make-date))
#{Structure DATE 83}

> (structure? x)
#t

> (date? x)
#t

> (date-day x)

** Error: attempt to access uninitialized DAY component of
#{Structure DATE 83}
>> *** EOF ***

> (set (date-day x) 1)
1

> (set (date-month x) 7)
7

> (set (date-year x) 1983)
1983

> (date-day x)
1
```

```
> (date-month x)
7

> (date-year x)
1983

> (better-zeller x)
4

> (set (date-day-of-week x) 4)
4
```

The reader should note that the arguments to **define-structure-type** are not evaluated. Thus, **define-structure-type** is not a procedure, but a special form.

The first argument to **define-structure-type** is the name of the new data structure, and the remaining arguments are the names of the components. Defining a structure type has several effects, which are apparent in the above example.

- It creates a data structure constructor, **make-date**, which forms its name by adding the data structure name, **date**, to the end of **make-**.

- It creates a data structure predicate, **date?**. Structures created with the constructor will answer true to the predicate. They will also answer true to the more general predicate **structure?**. The name of the predicate is simply the data structure name with a question mark suffix.

- It creates selector procedures for accessing the data, **date-day**, **date-month**, **date-year**, and **date-day-of-week**.

- The data structure values are not initialized. Referencing a value that has not been set generates an error.

- Data structure values can be specified using the indirect **set** described in chapter 5.

The call to **better-zeller** works fine with the revised **date** data structure. The reader should realize that we selected the names of the new accessor functions in **better-zeller** with premeditation. It is important to realize that the order of component names in the call to **define-structure-type** does not affect the programmer's use of the resulting procedures. For example, we could have used the following.

```
> (define-structure-type date year month
                    day day-of-week zodiac-sign)
#{Structure-type DATE}
```

```
> (set y (make-date))
#{Structure DATE 93}

> (set (date-day y) 1)
1

> (set (date-month y) 12)
12

> (set (date-year y) 1986)
1986

> (better-zeller y)
6
```

We have changed the order of arguments and even added one, `zodiac-sign`. The accuracy of **better-zeller** is unaffected for dates with the new definition.

The programmer should appreciate the utility of the abstraction of these data structures. Imagine trying to alter the original explicit list data structure for **date** in the manner we just did for the abstract data structure. The programmer would have been forced to rummage through his code to identify all references to days, months, and years. In fact, the programmer who did not use such mnemonic terms might be forced to examine every occurrence of **car**, **cadr**, and **caddr**.

12.2   Structures: More Details and Examples

Structures can contain other structures as components. In fact, they can have recursive components. Here is an example from the domain of baseball.

We shall define a data structure to keep track of baseball games for a league. The pieces of information to record for each game include the following.

- date of the game.

- name of the home team.

- name of the visiting team.

- the final score.

- the next home game.

Here are the relevant T data structures, and examples of operations for manipulating structure types. Note that **define-structure-type** creates a symbol of the form **name-stype** which is bound to the structure type created.

```
> (define-structure-type game date home visitor score next)
#{Structure-type GAME}

> (define-structure-type score home visitor)
#{Structure-type SCORE}

> (stype-id score-stype)
SCORE

> (stype-constructor game-stype)
#{Structure-constructor GAME}

> (eq? make-game (stype-constructor game-stype))
T

> (stype-predicator score-stype)
#{Structure-predicator SCORE}

> (eq? score? (stype-predicator score-stype))
T

> (stype-selector game-stype 'next)
#{Selector GAME NEXT}

> (eq? game-next (stype-selector game-stype 'next))
T

> (selector-id (stype-selector game-stype 'next))
NEXT

> (stype-selectors score-stype)
(#{Selector SCORE HOME} #{Selector SCORE VISITOR})
```

define-structure-type returns an object which, not too surprisingly, is called a structure type. In the example above, we create two new structures, whose types are bound to game-stype and score-stype, respectively. Using these names, we demonstrate the effects of various structure operations:

- stype-id returns the name associated with the given structure type.

- stype-constructor returns the constructor for the given structure type.

- stype-predicator returns the predicate for the given structure type.

- stype-selector returns the accessor procedure for the component specified for the given structure type.

- **selector-id** returns the name of the component for the given selector procedure.

- **stype-selectors** returns a list comprising all the accessor procedures for the given structure type.

These operations provide a convenient way to manipulate structures. One final operation, **stype-master**, allows the programmer to specify default values for components in structures. Here is an example.

```
> (set (score-home (stype-master score-stype)) 0)
0

> (set (score-visitor (stype-master score-stype)) 0)
0

> (set (game-home (stype-master game-stype)) 'bulldogs)
BULLDOGS

> (set game1 (make-game))
[Binding GAME1] #{Structure GAME 96}

> (set (game-date game1) (make-date))
#{Structure DATE 97}

> (set (game-score game1) (make-score))
#{Structure SCORE 99}

> (set (game-next game1) (make-game))
#{Structure GAME 98}

> (set (game-visitor game1) 'crimson)
CRIMSON

> (score-home (game-score game1))
0

> (score-visitor (game-score game1))
0

> (game-home game1)
BULLDOGS
```

```
> (map (lambda (x) (x game1)) (stype-selectors game-stype))
(#{Structure DATE 97} BULLDOGS CRIMSON
#{Structure SCORE 99} #{Structure GAME 98})
```

Using **stype-master**, we specify default values for the scores and home team. We then create an instance of the game data structure, which itself contains instances of the date structure, the score structure, and the game structure itself.

With one more operation, **structure-type**, we can write a general procedure for listing the contents of an instance of a structure. **structure-type** takes one argument, an object which is a structure, and returns the type of that structure. If its argument is not a structure, **structure-type** returns false.

```
(define (reveal-struct struct)
  (let ((stype (structure-type struct)))
    (map (lambda (selector)
           (let ((component (selector struct)))
             (cond ((structure? component)
                    (reveal-struct component))
                   (else component))))
         (stype-selectors stype))))

> (set (date-day (game-date game1)) 1)
1

> (set (date-month (game-date game1)) 3)
3

> (set (date-year (game-date game1)) 1986)
1986

> (set (date-day-of-week (game-date game1))
          (better-zeller (game-date game1)))
4

> (set (date-zodiac-sign (game-date game1)) nil)
()

> (reveal-struct game1)

** Error: attempt to access uninitialized DATE component
of #{Structure GAME 98}

> (set (game-next game1) nil)
()
```

```
> (reveal-struct game1)
((1986 3 1 4 ()) BULLDOGS CRIMSON (0 0) ())
```

In this example, we set the date of the big game, and then attempt to print out the information. However, we hit an error when we try to reference the **date** field of the game structure refered to by the **next** field in the current game structure. We then reset this **next** field to nil, and try again, this time with success.

We can now expand on this example to show how various data structures can be combined in programs. We shall use the game data structure as a component for a system which keeps statistics and calculates league standings.

For each team in the league, we will keep track of the number of games won and lost, the winning percentage, and the number of "games behind." The games behind statistic is the standard way of comparing the performance of two baseball teams, based on their respective won and lost records. Here are examples.

```
(define (games-behind a b)
    (/ (+  (- (team-won b)
              (team-won a))
           (- (team-lost a)
              (team-lost b)))
       2))

(define (game-average team)
  (->float
    (/ (team-won team)
       (+ (team-won team)
          (team-lost team)))))
```

```
> (define-structure-type team name won lost average behind)
#{Structure-type TEAM}

> (set bulldogs (make-team))
#{Structure TEAM 104}

> (set (team-name bulldogs) 'bulldogs)
BULLDOGS

> (set (team-won bulldogs) 12)
12

> (set (team-lost bulldogs) 4)
4
```

```
> (set crimson (make-team))
#{Structure TEAM 105}

> (set (team-name crimson) 'crimson)
CRIMSON

> (set (team-won crimson) 8)
8

> (set (team-lost crimson) 8)
8

> (game-average bulldogs)
0.75

> (game-average crimson)
0.5

> (games-behind crimson bulldogs)
4

> (games-behind bulldogs crimson)
-4

> (games-behind crimson crimson)
0
```

Thus, **games-behind** is a comparison predicate. As such, we can use it to rank the teams. Here is a ranking program, which uses the merge sort routine introduced in exercise 6.6.3 on page 105.

```
(define (print-standings teams)
 (let ((ranking (msort teams)))
  (labels ((top-team (car ranking))

          ((post-stats team)
           (set (team-average team)
                (game-average team))
           (set (team-behind team)
                (games-behind team top-team)))

          ((print-head)
           (format t "~%Team ~12TWon Lost Average Games Behind"))
```

```
((print-stats team)
 (format t "~%~A ~12T~A ~16T~A ~21T~A ~29T~A"
     (team-name team)
     (team-won team)
     (team-lost team)
     (round-off (team-average team))
     (team-behind team))) )

(walk post-stats teams)
(print-head)
(walk print-stats ranking)
repl-wont-print)))
```

```
;; round-off  converts repeating decimals to standard
;;    three-digit W/L numbers.
(define (round-off x)
    (->integer (* x 1000)))
```

```
;;  We have entered data for other teams in the league.
> (set *league* (list bears lions tigers bulldogs crimson))
(#{Structure TEAM 121} #{Structure TEAM 119} #{Structure
TEAM 120} #{Structure TEAM 104} #{Structure TEAM 105})
```

```
>  (print-standings *league*)
```

Team	Won	Lost	Average	Games Behind
BULLDOGS	12	4	750	0
TIGERS	9	6	600	5/2
CRIMSON	8	8	500	4
BEARS	7	12	368	13/2
LIONS	4	14	222	9

12.3 Anonymous Structures

The special form define-structure-type did not evaluate any of its arguments, and furthermore gave names to the constructor, selector, and predicator operations.

T provides another way to create structures that both evaluates its arguments, and creates anonymous operations: make-stype. This procedure could be useful for the programmer to create structures on the fly, and have the program itself manipulate them. Here is a simple example.

```
> (set task-stype (make-stype 'task '(name resources status)))
#{Structure-type TASK}
```

```
> (stype-id task-stype)
TASK

> (stype-constructor task-stype)
#{Structure-constructor TASK}

> (set task1 ((stype-constructor task-stype)))
#{Structure TASK 68}

> (set ((stype-selector task-stype 'name) task1)
       "Clean up my room")
"Clean up my room"

> (set ((stype-selector task-stype 'resources) task1) '(3 weeks))
(3 WEEKS)

> (set ((stype-selector task-stype 'status) task1) 'pending)
PENDING

> (reveal-struct task1)
("Clean up my room" (3 WEEKS) PENDING)
```

The make-stype procedures allows the programmer to write programs which themselves create and manipulate structures.

12.4 Exercises

12.4.1 Sorting Teams [4*]

Modify the msort routine from exercise 6.6.3 so that it will sort the baseball teams appropriately in the print-standings procedure defined above.

12.4.2 Score Updates [5*]

Write a procedure final-score, which takes three arguments: a game structure, the final home team score, and the final score for the visitor. The procedure then posts the scores in the game structure and also updates the team standings as appropriate. Here is an example.

```
> (reveal-struct game1)
((1986 3 1 4 ()) BULLDOGS CRIMSON (15 3) ())

> (set (game-home game1) bulldogs)
#{Structure TEAM 104}
```

```
> (set (game-visitor game1) crimson)
#{Structure TEAM 105}

> (final-score game1 15 3)
END-OF-UPDATE

> (print-standings *league*)
```

Team	Won	Lost	Average	Games Behind
BULLDOGS	13	4	764	0
TIGERS	9	6	600	3
CRIMSON	8	9	470	5
BEARS	7	12	368	7
LIONS	4	14	222	19/2

Note that we first alter the contents of the game structure node to include **team** structures for the **home** and **visitor** components, instead of simply the names of the teams.

The programmer may find it useful to use T's **increment** special form, which adds one to its argument and sets the argument with that new value, as shown here with the companion **decrement** special form.

```
> (set x 8)
8

> (increment x)
9

> x
9

> (decrement x)
8

> x
8
```

12.4.3 Person Structures [4]

Exercises 3.10.4 and 3.10.5 used association lists and property lists to implement a simple data base of facts about people. Write the **make-person** procedures again, but use structures.

12.4.4 Structured Guessing Game [7]

In section 9.7, we created a general program for binary guessing games. The underlying data representation for the tree of information was property lists.

Rewrite the entire program, using structures instead of property lists throughout. Note that this will require developing a method for writing structures to a file in a way that can be loaded back into the T interpreter.

12.4.5 Database Management [8]

Write an interactive database management system, comprising the following procedures:

- **(create-db)** A procedure which prompts the user for the name of the database, and the name and default values of the data elements of each record. If an existing structure type is entered as a component name, then the program further prompts for a name to identify that element. It then creates a new structure with the given name and components, and sets the default values for all components.

- **(add-db db-name)** A procedure for adding a record to the database. The program prompts the user for values for each element in the data structure.

- **(query-db db-name)** A procedure for retrieving information from the database. The user identifies a specific existing record and the program lists its contents. It also provides the user the opportunity to update the contents of the record, or delete the record entirely.

```
> (create-db)
..db-name? tasks
..record-name? task
..task-element 1? 'name
..task-element 2? 'resources
..task-element 3? 'status
..task-element 4? date-stype
....element name for DATE? 'completion-date
..task-element 5? (quit-db)
Enter default values:
..NAME? nil
..RESOURCES? '(1 day)
..STATUS? 'active
..COMPLETION-DATE-DAY? nil
..COMPLETION-DATE-MONTH? nil
..COMPLETION-DATE-YEAR? 1986

Created database: TASKS
```

```
> (add-db tasks)
TASK0
Enter values:
..NAME? "Wash the car"
..RESOURCES? '(1 hour)
..STATUS? 'active
..COMPLETION-DATE-DAY? 4
..COMPLETION-DATE-MONTH? 7
..COMPLETION-DATE-YEAR? 1986
TASK1
Enter values:
..NAME? "Buy groceries"
..RESOURCES? '((1 hour) (50 dollars))
..STATUS? 'pending
..COMPLETION-DATE-DAY? nil
..COMPLETION-DATE-MONTH? nil
..COMPLETION-DATE-YEAR? 1986
TASK2
Enter values:
..NAME? (quit-db)

> (query-db tasks)
Task id: nil
Component name: 'status
Component value: 'active

TASK0
    NAME            "Wash the car"
    RESOURCES       (1 HOUR)
    STATUS          ACTIVE
    COMPLETION-DATE (4 7 1986)

Action: 'delete

Deleting record TASK0
```

There are a number of problems the programmer will face in building these procedures. Some issues to think about include:

- *Sorting and Searching.* How can the database be implemented to facilitate effective retrieval and update of records?

- *Recursive data structures.* How should the program handle data structures that contain recursive record elements – either directly or indirectly?

• *Data checking.* How can the program be extended to perform error checking to ensure the validity of the input?

12.4.6   Defining define-structure-type [8]

The special form `define-structure-type` is a macro. Here is an example of how it would expand.

```
(define-structure-type score home visitor)
```

would expand into

```
(block (define score-stype    (make-stype 'score '(home visitor)))
       (define make-score     (stype-constructor score-stype))
       (define score?         (stype-predicator score-stype))
       (define score-home     (stype-selector score-stype 'home))
       (define score-visitor  (stype-selector score-stype 'visitor))
       score-stype)
```

Define your own macro which does everything that `define-structure-type` does, but also sets the default values, as specified by component-value pairs. Here is an example.

```
(my-structure-type score (home . 0) (visitor . 0))
```

The default scores would then be set at 0-0.

12.4.7   default Macro [6*]

Another approach to setting default values is to use T's `define-structure-type`, but have a second macro for assigning default values. Here is such a macro.

```
> (default score home 0 visitor 0)
()

> (set x (make-score))
#{Structure SCORE 196}

> (score-home x)
0

> (score-visitor x)
0
```

The `default` macro takes an odd number of arguments: a structure type name followed by any number of pairs of components and values. Write the `default` macro.

12.5   Chapter Summary

- Data abstraction is a useful and powerful programming technique. T allows the programmer to implement new data structures directly.

- The special form `(define-structure-type name . slots)` creates a new data structure with type `name-stype`, and associated operations: a constructor `make-name`, selectors `name-slot`, and predicate `name?`.

- Values of structures can be set indirectly through the selectors.

- T provides a set of general operations for manipulating structures.

```
(stype-id structure-type)
(stype-constructor structure-type)
(stype-master structure-type)
(stype-predicator structure-type)
(stype-selector structure-type component)
(stype-selectors structure-stype)
(selector-id selector)
(structure-type structure)
(structure? object)
(make-stype name components)
```

- The components of a structure may be any object, including other structures.

Chapter 13

Objects and Operations

Wordsworth says somewhere that wherever Virgil
seems to have composed 'with his eye on the object,'
Dryden fails to render him. Homer invariably composes 'with
his eye on the object,' whether the object be a moral or a
material one: Pope composes with his eye on his style, into
which he translates his object, whatever it is.

⋄ MATTHEW ARNOLD, *On Translating Homer (1861)*

To find the length of an object, we have to perform certain
physical operations. The concept of length is therefore fixed when
the operations by which length is measured are fixed: that is,
the concept of length involves as much as and nothing more than
the set of operations by which length is determined.

⋄ PERCY WILLIAMS BRIDGMAN, *The Logic of Modern Physics (1927)*

In the course of this book, we have adopted an implicit view of program execution, namely, that a computer program consists of procedures that manipulate data. This procedural perspective for programming is found in almost all programming languages, and most programmers consider it to be the only way one can write programs.

However, there is an alternative to procedural programming, namely, *object-oriented programming*. To understand the difference, first consider the way in which a person might determine the age of a tree by counting its rings. This is a procedural approach. The object, in this case a tree, is inspected in a specified manner. The procedure entails examination of the object.

Compare this approach with determining the age of a man simply by asking him how old he is. In this second case, you can rely on several facts. First, people know their own age. Second, people understand requests for personal information.

Finally, people can respond to such requests. Trees, for better or worse, fail on all three counts.

In procedural programming, an object is a passive data element which is manipulated by procedures. In object-oriented programming, the object plays an active role of responding to requests from other objects.

13.1   Object-Oriented Programming Languages

The precursor of object-oriented programming was the language Simula [5], developed as an extension to Algol-60. Simula provided a method of describing a collection of processes which could be considered to operate in parallel. Each process contained its own data and could execute actions. The motivation was to simulate complex systems, whose components interacted. Simula was built on top of the Algol programming language, and permitted the programmer to combine Algol procedure calls and Simula processes.

The first language to exploit the object-oriented paradigm fully was the Smalltalk language [9], developed at the Palo Alto Research Center of the Xerox Corporation. The Smalltalk philosophy promoted the extreme view that everything in the system should be viewed as objects that send messages to each other. Even simple arithmetic was eventually implemented to conform to this message-passing metaphor. Thus, a simple expression like "3 + 4" might be interpreted as the number 3 receiving a message of the form "+4", which would mean "answer this message with the sum of your value and the argument 4."

Smalltalk organizes its objects in a class hierarchy, and each class has methods or protocols for answering messages sent to instances of that class. In the example just given, the number 3 would be an instance of the class *SmallInteger*, which itself is a member of the class *Integer*, which is of the class *Number*, which belongs to *Magnitude*, which (finally) is a member of the root class *Object*. The actual method used for addition might differ based on the class of the object. Integer arithmetic may vary quite a bit from floating point arithmetic.

The point is, in Smalltalk, the objects themselves decide how the arithmetic operations would be performed. In procedural languages, the procedures make that decision based on the *type* of the objects. The terminology is significant: the words *class* and *type* both refer to categories of objects, but *type* views objects from the perspective of procedures, while *class* is the object-oriented view.

13.2   Object-Oriented Programming in T

As the reader may have surmised, object-oriented programming in T lives side-by-side with procedural programming. T, like Simula, offers the programmer both alternatives.

We have seen the procedural approach in T in the preceding chapters. Here is an example of object-oriented programming in T. We create a simple object that can tell us its name and age.

```
(define-predicate person?)

(define-settable-operation (age-of self)
    (cond ((tree? self) 'count-the-rings)
          (else 'try-carbon-dating)))
(define-operation (set-age self val))
(define set-age (setter age-of))

(define (make-person name)
  (let ((age nil))
    (object (lambda () name)
      ((person? self) T)
      ((setter self)
       (lambda (val) (set name val)))
      ((age-of self)
       age)
      ((set-age self val)
       (set age val))
      ((print self stream)
       (format stream "#Person ~A ~A Age: ~A"
               (object-hash self) name age)))))

> (set u (make-person 'jim))
#{Person 114 JIM Age: ()}

> (person? u)
#t

> (name-of u)
JIM

> (age-of u)
()

> (set-age u 19)
19

> (age-of u)
19

> u
#{Person 114 JIM Age: 19}
```

```
> (age-of 'hills)
TRY-CARBON-DATING

> (age-of 'oak)
COUNT-THE-RINGS

> (u)
JIM

> (set (u) 'jane)
JANE

> u
#{Person 80 JANE Age: 19}

> (set (age-of u) 30)
30

> u
#{Person 80 JANE Age: 30}
```

The **define-operation**, **define-settable-operation**, and **define-predicate** special forms create operations, that is, ways of sending messages or requests to objects. In this example, we provide default methods for the **age-of** operation for objects that do not themselves know how to respond to this message. Also, the predicate **person?** will respond false for any object that has no method for handling it.

The procedure **make-person** itself returns as a value an object which can respond to the messages. This object has several noteworthy features.

- *Local variables.* The variable **age** and the procedural argument **name** are local to the object. These variables can be accessed and set within the object.

- *Procedural component.* The first argument to the **object** special form is a procedural expression to be evaluated every time the object itself is invoked as a procedure. In this example, the procedure is a simple lambda expression which merely returns the value of the **name** variable. When there is no procedure, we use **nil** as the first argument to **object**.

- *Method clauses.* Following the procedural component are a series of method clauses of the form

```
((operation . variables) . expression-body)
```

Note that the first variable refers to the object itself. In these examples, we adopt the convention of naming that argument **self**. When the object is invoked as an argument to an operation, each of these method clauses are checked to see if any of them apply. If so, the respective **expression-body** is executed.

- **define-settable-operation** is analogous to **define-operation**, except that the operation allows **set** to alter the resulting location indirectly. The operation which is used to set the settable operation must be defined as the **setter** for that operation. In this example, **set-age** is the **setter** for **age-of**.

- *Setter method.* It is also possible to make the object itself settable. Here we use the **setter** operation within the object definition. Note that the expression body for the **setter** clause must be a lambda expression. In this case, setting the object results in changing the **name** variable.

- *Print method.* Notice that **print** is defined as an operation of a method clause. When the programmer prints a **make-person** object, it is the object that specifies how it is to be printed.

The print method in **make-person** calls the procedure **object-hash**, which returns a unique integer identifier for the given object. The companion procedure, **object-unhash**, reverses this process, as shown here.

```
> (object-hash u)
114

> (object-unhash 114)
#{Person 114 JIM Age: 19}

> (object-unhash 113)
#{Procedure 113 MAKE-PERSON}

> (object-hash (object-unhash 113))
113
```

As the programmer may have surmised, **object-hash** is the source of the sequential integers that T includes in the print names of procedures and other objects. Using **object-unhash**, the programmer can retrieve objects by their hash numbers and put them to work.

```
> (lambda (x) (* x 2))
#{Procedure 115}

> ((object-unhash 115) 3.1)
6.2
```

Furthermore, the accessor operation **age-of** and the object itself are *settable*. As we saw in chapter 5, some accessor operations, such as **car** and **cdr**, allow the programmer to **set** the values that they access. T allows the programmer to create new settable operations using **setter** and **define-settable-operation**, as shown above.

We can now try an example that is slightly more realistic. Using the **symbol-generator** procedure, we create objects which behave similarly to T's **generate-symbol**.

```
(define-operation (all-symbols object))
(define-operation (decrement-counter object))
(define-operation (reset-counter object))
(define-operation (last-symbol object))
(define-settable-operation (current-counter object))
(define-operation (set-counter object val))
(define set-counter (setter current-counter))
(define-predicate symgen?)

(define (symbol-generator prefix)
 (let ((counter 0)
       (symbol nil))
   (object (lambda ()
              (set symbol (concatenate-symbol prefix counter))
              (increment counter)
              symbol)
           ((symgen? self) T)
           ((current-counter self) counter)
           ((last-symbol self) symbol)
           ((reset-counter self) (set counter 0))
           ((decrement-counter self) (decrement counter))
           ((set-counter self n) (set counter n))
           ((all-symbols self)
            (do ((count (-1+ counter) (-1+ count))
                 (result '()
                         (cons (concatenate-symbol prefix count)
                               result)))
                ((<0? count) result)))
           ((print self port)
            (format port
                    "#{Symbol-generator: ~A ~D}" prefix counter)))))
```

In this example, we did not make the object itself to be settable.

We can now exercise our new object.

```
> (set nodegen (symbol-generator 'node))
#{Symbol-generator: NODE 0}

> (nodegen)                        ;  invoking the object's procedure
NODE0

> (nodegen)
NODE1

> (symgen? nodegen)                ;  predicate operation
#t

> (current-counter nodegen)        ;  accessor operation
2

> (all-symbols nodegen)
(NODE0 NODE1)

> (last-symbol nodegen)
NODE1

> (reset-counter nodegen)
0

> (current-counter nodegen)        ;  the counter is zero
0

> (decrement-counter nodegen)      ;  the counter is negative
-1

> (nodegen)
NODE-1

> (nodegen)
NODE0

> (set nodegen2 (symbol-generator 'node))
#{Symbol-generator: NODE 0}

> (nodegen2)              ;  a second symbol-generator object
NODE0

> (set (current-counter nodegen) 7)
7
```

```
> (nodegen)
NODE7

> (set (current-counter nodegen2) 999)
999

> (nodegen2)
NODE999

> (print nodegen (standard-output))
#{Symbol-generator: NODE 8}**VALUE-OF-FORMAT**

> (print nodegen2 (standard-output))
#{Symbol-generator: NODE 1000}**VALUE-OF-FORMAT**
```

In this sample session, we see examples of the object being called as a procedure, and being invoked as an argument to operations.

13.3   Object-Oriented Property Lists

We now define an object that is more complex, and more useful: a property list
object.

We have used property lists in several places in this volume; however, we have
tried to warn the programmer of the problems that can arise from the fact that
property lists are global objects. It is difficult for the programmer to maintain
control over any global object. We now define an object-oriented approach to
property lists that allows the programmer to create, manipulate, and control access
to multiple property lists.

We give the definition, with annotation. Then we give examples. Note that
this version of property lists provides more functionality than is normally available.

There is a lot going on. We shall take it one step at a time. We begin by using
define-operation and friends to let T know what new operations we are going to
be using. Note that we do not need to say anything about existing operations like
print and **pretty-print**.

```
(define-predicate plist?)
(define-operation (clear-plist self))
(define-settable-operation (reveal self))
(define-operation (set-plist self new-plist))
(define set-plist (setter reveal))
(define-operation (all-symbols self))
(define-operation (pp-sym self sym port))
(define-settable-operation (pget self sym prop))
(define-operation (pput self sym prop val))
(define pput (setter pget))

(define (make-plist)
  (labels ((plist (copy-tree '((())) ))
           ((sym-plist sym)
            (cond ((assq sym plist)
                   =>
                   cdr)
                  (else
                   (push (cdr plist)
                         (cons sym nil)))))))
```

We define the procedure `make-plist`, which returns a property list object.

There are two `labels` variables. The first is `plist`, which is the name of the list structure – an association list – that will actually contain the property lists themselves. It is set to a *copy* of the initial nested empty list; the copying is to guarantee that subsequent calls to `make-plist` do not result in shared data structures. The second `labels` variable is `sym-plist`, which is a procedure of one argument for looking up symbols in `plist`. If a symbol is not found, it is added to the front of the list.

```
(object ()
    ((plist? self) T)
```

Following the `labels` variables, we introduce the `object` form. This object has no procedure associated with it. Thus, the first argument following `object` is nil.

We now begin defining the operations to which the property list object will respond, starting off with the simple predicate `plist?`.

```
((clear-plist self)
 (set plist '((()))))
```

`clear-plist` sets the `plist` back to its initial value.

```
((set-plist self new-plist)
 (set plist new-plist))
```

set-plist replaces the current value of **plist** with a new one. This is the setter method for **reveal** as well. **reveal** simply returns the current value of **plist**.

```
((reveal self) plist)
```

all-symbols returns a list of all the current symbol keys in **plist**.

```
((all-symbols self)
 (map car (cdr plist)))

((pp-sym self sym port)
 (format port "~%~A" sym)
 (map (lambda (x)
        (format t "~%~5t~A ~15T~A" (car x) (cdr x)))
      (sym-plist sym))
 repl-wont-print)
```

pp-sym "pretty-prints" a given symbol's property list on the given port.

pretty-print is a standard T operation. In this case, it calls **pp-sym** on all symbol keys in **plist**.

```
((pretty-print self port)
 (map (lambda (x) (pp-sym self x port))
      (all-symbols self))
 repl-wont-print)

((print self port)
 (format port "#{Private property list ~A}"
   (object-hash self))
 repl-wont-print)
```

print is a standard T operation. Here, it prints out a T-style tag, using the built-in T procedure **object-hash** to create a unique integer label for the object. **object-unhash** reverses this process.

```
((pget self sym prop)
 (cond ((assq prop (sym-plist sym))
        =>
        cdr)
       (else nil)))
```

pget corresponds to the normal **get** procedure. However, the reader should notice that **pget** takes an additional argument – the property list object. The normal **get** implicitly uses a global property list. The **pget** operation can apply to many different instances of private property lists.

```
((pput self sym prop obj)
 (block0 obj
   (cond ((assq prop (sym-plist sym))
          =>
          (lambda (x) (set (cdr x) obj)))
         (else
          (set (cdr (assq sym plist))
               (cons (cons prop obj)
                     (sym-plist sym)))))))))))
```

pput sets new values in the property list. It is the setter method for **pget**. We can now take our property list objects out for a test drive.

```
> (set p (make-plist))
#{Private property list 62}

> (plist? p)
#t                              ; p  is a property list object

> (plist? 'p)
()                              ; 'p  is not.

> (all-symbols p)
()                              ; plist  is empty

> (pput p 'iago 'age 'ancient)   ;   add data to the property list
ANCIENT

> (pput p 'othello 'age 'old-enough-to-know-better)
OLD-ENOUGH-TO-KNOW-BETTER

> (pp p)                         ; pp  calls pretty-print

OTHELLO
     AGE        OLD-ENOUGH-TO-KNOW-BETTER
IAGO
     AGE        ANCIENT

> (set p1 (reveal p))
((()) (OTHELLO (AGE . OLD-ENOUGH-TO-KNOW-BETTER))
(IAGO (AGE . ANCIENT)))

> (pget p 'iago 'profession)
()
```

```
> (set (pget p 'iago 'profession) '(management consultant))
(MANAGEMENT CONSULTANT)

> (pp p)

OTHELLO
    AGE         OLD-ENOUGH-TO-KNOW-BETTER
IAGO
    PROFESSION
                (MANAGEMENT CONSULTANT)
    AGE         ANCIENT

> (set p1 (copy-tree (reveal p)))
((()) (OTHELLO (AGE . OLD-ENOUGH-TO-KNOW-BETTER)) (IAGO
(PROFESSION MANAGEMENT CONSULTANT) (AGE . ANCIENT)))

> (set (pget p 'othello 'profession) 'ceo)
CEO

> (pp p)

OTHELLO
    PROFESSION
                CEO
    AGE         OLD-ENOUGH-TO-KNOW-BETTER
IAGO
    PROFESSION
                (MANAGEMENT CONSULTANT)
    AGE         ANCIENT

> (set-plist p p1)               ;  restore previous plist value
((()) (OTHELLO (AGE . OLD-ENOUGH-TO-KNOW-BETTER)) (IAGO
(PROFESSION MANAGEMENT CONSULTANT) (AGE . ANCIENT)))

> (pp p)

OTHELLO
    AGE         OLD-ENOUGH-TO-KNOW-BETTER
IAGO
    PROFESSION
                (MANAGEMENT CONSULTANT)
    AGE         ANCIENT
```

```
> (all-symbols p)
(OTHELLO IAGO)

> (pp-sym p 'iago (standard-output))

IAGO
     PROFESSION
                  (MANAGEMENT CONSULTANT)
     AGE          ANCIENT

> (set q (make-plist))                     ;   create a second plist object
#{Private property list 63}

> (pput q 'iago 'age 28)
28

> (pput q 'othello 'age 42)
42

> (pp q)

OTHELLO
     AGE          42
IAGO
     AGE          28

> (pp p)                           ;  p  and q   are separate plists

OTHELLO
     AGE          OLD-ENOUGH-TO-KNOW-BETTER
IAGO
     PROFESSION
                  (MANAGEMENT CONSULTANT)
     AGE          ANCIENT

> p
#{Private property list 62}

> q
#{Private property list 63}
```

```
> (reveal p)
((()) (OTHELLO (AGE . OLD-ENOUGH-TO-KNOW-BETTER)) (IAGO
(PROFESSION MANAGEMENT CONSULTANT) (AGE . ANCIENT)))

> (reveal q)
((()) (OTHELLO (AGE . 42)) (IAGO (AGE . 28)))

> (object-hash p)
62

> (object-unhash 62)
#{Private property list 62}

> (object-unhash (object-hash q))
#{Private property list 63}
```

This extended example demonstrates the utility of the object-oriented approach to data structures.

13.4 Joining Objects

T allows the programmer to create new objects by joining old objects together. The result is an object which handles the union of methods of the constituent objects. The T procedure join creates the combined objects.

Here is an example. We first create a simple programmer object description.

```
(define-settable-operation (knows self))
(define-operation (set-languages self val))
(define set-languages (setter knows))

(define (programmer languages)
    (object nil
      ((knows self)
        languages)
      ((print self stream)
       (format stream "#{Programmer ~A Languages: ~A}"
               (object-hash self) languages))
      ((set-languages self val)
       (set languages val))))
```

We now combine a programmer object with our earlier person object description.

```
> (set joe (join (make-person 'joe) (programmer '(pascal t))))
#{Person 102 JOE Age: ()}
```

```
> (knows joe)
(PASCAL T)

> joe
#{Person 102 JOE Age: ()}

> (joe)
JOE

> (set (age-of joe) 45)
45

> joe
#{Person 102 JOE Age: 45}

> (set (knows joe) (cons 'basic (knows joe)))
(BASIC PASCAL T)

> (set tom (join (programmer '(fortran)) (make-person 'tom)))
#{Programmer 104 Languages: (FORTRAN)}

> (knows tom)
(FORTRAN)

> (tom)

** Error: attempt to call a non-procedure
   (())
>> *** EOF ***

> (set (age-of tom) 33)
33

> (age-of tom)
33

> tom
#{Programmer 104 Languages: (FORTRAN)}
```

We have created two programmer-people: Joe and Tom. Their behavior differs
according to the order of argument to join. Note that Joe is a person first, and a
programmer second, while Tom is the reverse. In responding to messages, T scans
the constituent objects from left to right and uses the first method it encounters.

Both the programmer and person objects have **print** methods; thus Joe prints as
a person, and Tom prints as a programmer.

When T tries to execute an object as a procedure, only the first object is used.
In this case, Joe is executable as a person, but Tom's programmer object cannot
execute. An error results.

The ability to join objects allows the programmer to create hierarchies of
method clauses. For example, if the programmer had methods for handling different
types of animals, he might describe a mouse object as follows.

```
(define (make-mouse)
    (join (object
            (lambda () 'squeak-squeak)
            ((print self stream)
             (format stream "~%#{Mouse ~A}"
                    (object-hash self))))
          (make-rodent)
          (make-small-mammal)
          (make-mammal)
          (make-animal)
          (make-organism)))
```

It is more likely that **make-rodent** would be sufficient for **make-mouse**, since rodent
itself could be defined in terms of small mammal. Then small mammal could be
defined in terms of mammal, and so forth.

With this simple inheritance mechanism, the programmer could quickly populate the world.

13.5   Structures as Objects in T

We can now reveal some more about structures and objects: structures *are* objects.
That is to say, structures in T are implemented as objects. As such, they can
respond to messages or operations. We can add method clauses to the definition of
a structure, in a manner similar to the method clauses in objects.

```
(define-operation (winner self))
(define-structure-type score home visitor
    (((pretty-print self port)
      (format port "Home: ~A   Visitor: ~A"
         (score-home self) (score-visitor self))
      repl-wont-print)
```

```
  ((winner self)
   (cond ((> (score-home self) (score-visitor self))
           'home)
          ((< (score-home self) (score-visitor self))
           'visitor)
          (else 'tie)))

  ((print self port)
   (format port "#{Score ~A"
     (object-hash self))
   repl-wont-print)))

(set (score-home (stype-master score-stype)) 0)
(set (score-visitor (stype-master score-stype)) 0)
```

We define the **score** structure as before, but we have added a final argument which is a list of three method clauses. We then set default values for the components as before.

```
> (set x (make-score))
Home: 0  Visitor: 0

> (pp x)
Home: 0  Visitor: 0

> x
#{Score 74}

> (winner x)
TIE

> (set (score-home x) 7)
7

> (winner x)
HOME

> (set (score-visitor x) 9)
9

> (winner x)
VISITOR
```

Structures, when combined with methods for handling operations, can be an effective and elegant method for object-oriented programming.

13.6 Exercises

13.6.1 Symbol Generator Revisited [3*]

At the end of the symbol generator example on page 244, what would T return as values to (all-symbols nodegen) and (all-symbols nodegen2)?

13.6.2 Removing Property Values [5]

Add an operation **premove**, which eliminates a property-value pair from the property list. Here is an example.

```
> (pp x)

MARY
        AGE        45
JOHN
        SON        JOE
        AGE        199

> (premove x 'john 'age)
199

> (pp x)

MARY
        AGE        45
JOHN
        SON        JOE
```

13.6.3 Object-Oriented Database [8]

Exercise 12.4.5 entailed the interactive construction of a database management system. While it may have been fairly clear how to implement the underlying data structures for the records, there were no specifications for the implementation of storage and retrieval of the records themselves.

In the current chapter, we saw how to use objects to implement a simple property list retrieval mechanism. Implement the database system described in exercise 12.4.5 using this method.

13.6.4   Queue Object [6*]

A queue is a *first-in, first-out* or *FIFO* data structure. By contrast, a stack is a *last-in, first-out* or *LIFO* data structure. A queue is like a pipe: items enter at one end and exit at the other.

   We can use lists and objects to implement a queue object. Write the procedure **make-queue** which creates an object that handles the predicates **queue?** and **queue-empty?**, and the operations **enqueue**, **dequeue**, **q-head**, and **print**, as demonstrated below.

```
> (set y (make-queue))
#{Queue 180 ()}

> (queue? y)
#t

> (queue-empty? y)
#t

> (enqueue y 1)
(1)

> (enqueue y 2)
(2)

> (enqueue y 3)
(3)

> y                        ;  The queue now has three elements.
#{Queue 180 (1 2 3)}

> (q-head y)
1

> (dequeue y)              ;  We remove the first element.
1

> y
#{Queue 180 (2 3)}

> (dequeue y)
2

> (queue-empty? y)         ;  The queue is not empty.
()
```

```
> (dequeue y)
3

> (dequeue y)
()

> (queue-empty? y)           ;  The queue is now empty.
#t

> (dequeue y)
()
```

13.6.5   make-better-plist [5*]

The property list storage and retrieval objects created by `make-plist` require that the key and property objects be restricted to symbols. In particular, the programmer cannot use lists and strings as retrieval keys or properties.

Write `make-better-plist`, which remedies this deficiency. Here are examples of its use.

```
> (set b (make-better-plist))
#{Private property list 70}

> (pput b '(things i like) "at the beach" '(sand sun))
(SAND SUN)

> (pput b '(things i like) "in the city" '(movies restaurants))
(MOVIES RESTAURANTS)

> (pput b "things i hate" '(at the beach) '(flies trash))
(FLIES TRASH)

> (pput b "things i hate" '(in the city) "flies trash")
"flies trash"

> (pp b)

things i hate
     (IN THE CITY)
              flies trash
     (AT THE BEACH)
              (FLIES TRASH)
```

```
(THINGS I LIKE)
    in the city
            (MOVIES RESTAURANTS)
    at the beach
            (SAND SUN)


> (pget b "things i hate" '(at the beach))
(FLIES TRASH)

> (set (pget b '(things i like) "at the beach") 'me)
ME

> (pp b)

things i hate
    (IN THE CITY)
            flies trash
    (AT THE BEACH)
            (FLIES TRASH)

(THINGS I LIKE)
    in the city
            (MOVIES RESTAURANTS)
    at the beach
            ME
```

13.6.6 Object-Oriented Structures [7]

Given the fact that structures can be extended with methods for handling operations, rewrite the `print-standings` procedure on page 229 in an object-oriented fashion.

13.7 Chapter Summary

- Object-oriented programming was originally explored in the Simula and Smalltalk programming languages.

- In procedural programming, data objects are manipulated by procedures. In object-oriented programming, objects actively engage in computation by sending and responding to messages.

- T provides the programmer with a seamless combination of procedural and object-oriented programming.

- New operations on objects are defined using

  ```
  (define-operation (name . args) . body)
  (define-settable-operation (name . args) . body)
  (define-predicate name)
  ```

  The **body** clause is optional, and can be used to specify the default behavior of the operation.

- Objects can be defined as values returned by the form

  ```
  (object procedure . method-clauses)
  ```
  where **method-clauses** are of the form
  ```
  ((operation-name . args) . body)
  ```

  The **procedure** clause is evaluated when the object is invoked as a procedure. The operations specify how the object will respond to their respective messages. The initial argument in the operation refers to the object itself, and, by convention, is referred to as **self**.

- An accessor operation can be "settable" by defining a **setter** operation with the accessor as argument. Then, the value referenced by the accessor can be altered indirectly using **set**.

- **object-hash** returns a unique integer for its object argument, and **object-unhash** reverses the process, returning the object corresponding to the given integer. These object hash numbers are used throughout T in object print names.

- The T procedure **join** creates the combined objects.

- Structures are in fact objects, and the programmer can enable structures to respond to messages by defining methods for handling operations. A list of method clauses may be appended as a final argument to **define-structure-type**.

Chapter 14

Vectors

All are most beautiful, of a thousand shapes,
and all accessible,
and filled with trees of a thousand kinds.

◇ CHRISTOPHER COLUMBUS, *Letter to the Sovereigns on the First Voyage (1493)*

I derived   the method   I use
for writing   music by tossing   coins   from the method used   in   the
Book of Changes   for obtaining   oracles.

◇ JOHN CAGE, *A Year From Monday (1963)*

THEY SAID ONE THING INVOLVING
SYMBOLS — LINEAR   RELATION-
SHIPS — WHICH MADE ME THINK
THEY DIDN'T UNDERSTAND.   BUT
THEN THEY SAID SOMETHING ELSE
— THAT THE SCHOOL'S DAYS OF
BEING OPEN WOULD BE UNPRE-
DICATABLY ARRANGED. THE RESULT
WAS WE HAD A PLEASANT DAY
TOGETHER.

◇ JOHN CAGE, *A Year From Monday (1963)*

By this point, the reader has witnessed a broad range of T objects that can be manipulated to build programs. We have symbols, numbers, lists, characters, strings, ports, procedures, and general objects which can themselves control computations

– a diverse array of objects. We now turn our attention to a data structure which serves as the mainstay of many programming languages – the array itself. T has one primitive array type, the vector, which is a linear array.

In many programming languages, such as FORTRAN, the array is the primary data structure. It is most commonly used for numerical data, often representing matrices. The vector object in T can be applied to such linear algebra problems.

A vector is a linear, random access data structure. The programmer can access any element of a vector directly by specifying that element's location in the vector. It is just as easy to get the last element of a vector as the first.

By contrast, a list is a linear, sequential access data structure. Even if a programmer knows the location of an element in a list, he must still sequentially traverse the list to access the given element. The time required to access an element in a list will be proportional to its distance from the front of the list.

In this chapter, we use vectors in exploring four other programming topics: rectangular arrays, hash tables, random numbers, and lazy evaluation.

14.1   Vectors in T

Vectors are similar to lists, and in T, they are similarly notated. A vector is indicated by a # followed by a list.

```
> '(1 2 3)              ;  The list (1 2 3)
(1 2 3)

> '#(1 2 3)             ;  The vector #(1 2 3)
#(1 2 3)

> (list->vector '(1 2 3))
#(1 2 3)

> (vector->list '#(1 2 3))
(1 2 3)
```

The last two examples give the coercion routines for converting a list to a vector, and vice versa.

The basic accessors for lists are **car** and **cdr**. Vectors are referenced with **vref**. The arguments to **vref** are a vector and an index. Vectors in T, like strings, are *zero-based*. That is, the elements of a vector of length n are numbered from 0 through $n - 1$.

```
> (set x '#(0 1 2 3 4))
#(0 1 2 3 4)

> (vector? x)
#t
```

```
> (vref x 2)
2

> (vref x 0)
0

> (vector-length x)
5

> (set (vref x 0) 10)
10

> x
#(10 1 2 3 4)
```

Above we have created a five-element vector x. The value of each element happens to correspond to its respective index. vector? is the predicate for vectors. The vector-length procedure gives the number of elements, and vref can be used with set to change the value of the given element.

It is also possible to find an element of a vector by its contents, without knowing its location. The procedure vector-posq takes two arguments, an object and a vector, and returns the index of the element of the vector which is eq? to the given object. If no such element is found, vector-posq returns (), as shown here.

```
> (set x '#(11 12 13 14))
#(11 12 13 14)

> (vector-posq 14 x)
3

> (vref x 3)
14

> (vector-posq 10 x)
()

> (vector-pos < 12 x)          ; vector-pos  takes a predicate
2

;  find the element equal to twice 6:
> (vector-pos (lambda (x v) (= v (* x 2))) 6 x)
1
```

```
> (vref x 1)
12
```

The more general form of `vector-posq` is `vector-pos`, which takes a two-place
predicate as an additional argument. `(vector-posq obj vec)` is the same as
`(vector-pos eq? obj vec)`. These procedures allow one conveniently to search
vectors.

14.2   Two-Dimensional Arrays

The elements of a vector can be any T object, including other vectors. Here is a
procedure for creating a two-dimensional, rectangular array object, also called a
matrix.

```
(define-predicate 2d-array?)
(define-settable-operation (2d-ref self x y))
(define-operation (2d-set self x y val))
(define 2d-set (setter 2d-ref))
(define-operation (2d-array-fill self val))

(define (make-2d-array x y)
   (labels ((2d-array (make-vector x))
            ((2d-initialize vector index size)
             (cond ((= index 0) vector)
                   (else
                    (decrement index)
                    (set (vref vector index) (make-vector size))
                    (2d-initialize vector index size)))))
      (set 2d-array (2d-initialize 2d-array x y))
      (object nil
        ((print self port)
         (format port "#{2d-array ~A ~A}"
            (object-hash self) 2d-array))
        ((2d-array? self) T)
        ((2d-ref self x y)
         (vref (vref 2d-array x) y))
        ((2d-set self x y val)
         (set (vref (vref 2d-array x) y) val))
        ((2d-array-fill self val)
         (walk-vector
           (lambda (v) (vector-fill v val)) 2d-array)
         2d-array))))
```

```
> (set x (make-2d-array 3 4))
#{2d-array 72 #(#(0 0 0 0) #(0 0 0 0) #(0 0 0 0))}

> (2d-array-fill x 9)
#(#(9 9 9 9) #(9 9 9 9) #(9 9 9 9))

> (set (2d-ref x 0 0) nil)
()

> x
#{2d-array 72 #(#(() 9 9 9) #(9 9 9 9) #(9 9 9 9))}
```

This example demonstrates several other vector operations.

- (make-vector length) creates a vector of the specified length.

- (vector-fill vector value) sets every element of the vector to the given value.

- (walk-vector procedure vector) applies the given procedure to every element in the vector.

In exercises 14.7.4 and 14.7.5, we examine arrays of higher dimensions.

14.3 Hash Tables

The main advantage of vectors over lists is the relative speed of access. Sequential search is usually slower. For example, if you are looking for someone's office in a large building, it is usually not advisable to search through the building room by room. However, if you know the room number, you can go directly to the right floor, and then find the office directly. The room number provides information about the number of the floor.

Just as a building can be organized with room numbers to correspond to floors, it is possible to use a vector to organize information in a table which can be indexed by keys. Previously, we have used association lists to make tables which are key-indexed. However, association lists are inefficient for large quantities of data because of the sequential search problem.

We can use vectors to implement a key-indexed list using *hash tables*. The name *hash* comes from the method of generating the table index from the key: the key is chopped up and converted into a number, which in turn is used to specify the element (or *bucket*) in the array for storing the information.

There are many hash methods, as discussed in [13]. A common technique involves adding up the numerical values of the characters in the key. We shall use T's **tree-hash** procedure, which converts a T object into an integer, or *hash code*.

Here we create a hash table for storing ages.

```
> (set age-table (make-vector 10))
#(0 0 0 0 0 0 0 0 0 0)

> (tree-hash 'john)
10125466

> (tree-hash 10125466)  ;  numbers hash to themselves
10125466

> (tree-hash 'mary)
10109082

> (set (vref age-table (mod (tree-hash 'john) 10)) '(john 22))
(JOHN 22)

> (set (vref age-table (mod (tree-hash 'mary) 10)) '(mary 21))
(MARY 21)

> age-table
#(0 0 (MARY 21) 0 0 0 (JOHN 22) 0 0 0)

> (vref age-table (mod (tree-hash 'john) 10))
(JOHN 22)
```

The resulting integer from **tree-hash** is usually a good bit larger than the length of the hash table vector, and an error would result if we used that integer directly as the index. Therefore, we take that integer modulo the size of the table to get a number in the proper range. In this case, since the table is of size 10, the index is simply the last digit of the hash code.

Note that the last expression shows that information can be retrieved from the table without giving its explicit location. The location is implicit in the key itself. Furthermore, this method of access is generally much quicker than searching through an association list.

The reader may have already noticed a potential problem in this method. What would happen if John and Mary had the same index? That is, their hash codes could have been distinct, but the last digits could have matched. In that case, the second entry would have clobbered the first. They would have hit the same bucket.

There are several methods for handling these collisions. One method is to check for a collision at the time of entry or retrieval. If a collision is found, check the current bucket to see if it matches the specified key. If it does not, try the next bucket in sequence.

Here is a T procedure for creating hash table objects which implements this strategy.

```
(define-predicate hash-table?)
(define-operation (table-get self key))
(define-operation (table-put self key value))
(define-operation (reveal self))

(define (make-hash-table size)
    (labels ((table (vector-fill (make-vector size) nil))
             ((next-number number)
              (increment number)
              (cond ((= number size) 0)
                    (else number)))
             ((get-bucket number)
              (vref table number))
             ((get-number key number)
              (cond ((null? number)
                     (set number (mod (tree-hash key) size))))
              (let ((bucket (get-bucket number)))
                 (cond ((null? bucket) number)
                       ((eq? key (car bucket)) number)
                       (else
                        (get-number key (next-number number)))))))
        (object nil
          ((reveal self) (vector->list table))
          ((hash-table? self) T)
          ((table-get self key)
             (cdr (get-bucket (get-number key nil))))
          ((table-put self key value)
           (set (vref table (get-number key nil)) (cons key value)))
          ((print self port)
           (format port "#{Hash table ~A}"
               (object-hash self))
            repl-wont-print) )))

> (set y (make-hash-table 10))
#{Hash table 41}

> (hash-table? y)
#t

> (table-get y 'john)
()

> (table-put y 'mary 21)
(MARY . 21)
```

```
> (table-put y 'john 39)
(JOHN . 39)

> (table-get y 'john)
39

> (reveal y)
(() () (MARY . 21) () () () (JOHN . 39) () () ())
```

We have created a 10-element hash table, and made two entries. We now add another record, which collides with John at index position 6.

```
> (tree-hash 'hank)
13287626                              ;  last digit is 4

> (table-put y 'hank 11)
(HANK . 11)

> (reveal y)
(() () (MARY . 21) () () () (JOHN . 39) (HANK . 11) () ())
```

We see that Hank's record was inserted sequentially after John's.

There are many issues involved in designing effective hash tables. The method just given suffers on several counts. First, as the table fills up, the insertion and retrieval rapidly converges to slow sequential search.

Second, there is no good way to delete items from the table. Removing an item may result in making some other item inaccessible. For example, if you deleted John's entry in the table above, the program would no longer find Jane.

Finally, the table can fill up. The only way to enlarge the table would be to build a new, bigger table and reenter the existing data in the new table – an expensive proposition. In exercise 14.7.9, we present a method for building extensible hash tables.

T actually provides a convenient table mechanism. Here is an example.

```
> (set joe (make-table))
#{Table 19 ()}

> (table? joe)                 ; JOE  is a table.
#t

> (set (table-entry joe 'age) 23)
23

> (set (table-entry joe 'weight) 150)
150
```

```
> (set (table-entry joe 'father) 'joe-sr)
JOE-SR

> (table-entry joe 'age)
23

> (table-entry joe 'height)
()
```

There are three basic procedures.

- (make-table . id) produces a table. The id argument is an optional identifier.

- (table? object) is a predicate for tables.

- (table-entry table key) is a settable accessor function for tables. It is
  analogous to get.

Tables provide an efficient mechanism for storing and retrieving data. They
are implemented as hash tables. We can use tables to implement property lists.

```
(define *property-list* (make-table))

(define (prop-check node)
    (cond ((null? (table-entry *property-list* node))
           (set (table-entry *property-list* node)
                (make-table)))))

(define (get node property)
    (prop-check node)
    (table-entry (table-entry *property-list* node)
                 property))

(define (put node property value)
    (prop-check node)
    (set (table-entry (table-entry *property-list* node)
                      property)
         value))
```

We first make *property-list* a global table. The procedure prop-check is
called by both get and put to ensure that the given node has been entered as a
table in the global property list.

14.4   Testing Random Numbers

Can a computer flip a coin? Can it make a random choice?

Random numbers are used in a variety of applications in computer programs. Many computer simulations require random data. Other programs require random sampling of input. In exercise 8.7.3, we showed a method of making a deck of cards. How could the computer shuffle the cards? Presumably if you wrote a bridge program, you would not care to be dealt the same hand every time.

In point of fact, computers cannot flips coins. However, they can produce *pseudo*-random numbers. That is, it is possible to specify an algorithm to generate a sequence of numbers that appear to be random, but that algorithm, given the same initial data, will always produce the same sequence of random numbers.

Hash functions share many properties with pseudo-random number generators. The difference is that the hash function always retains its initial state. The pseudo-random number generator uses each new number it produces to determine the next number.

How random is random? There are numerous methods for designing and testing random number generators. These techniques are discussed in [14]. Here we present a random number generator given in [14] and a simple procedure for checking its randomness.

The procedure make-random uses two procedures which are not defined here: lastchar and time. See exercise 6.6.2 for the procedure lastchar. time is a system routine which is implementation dependent and not strictly a part of T. In this example, time returns the current time as a string. The programmer can give the seed value as a second parameter to make-random, and thus dispense with the call to time. The latter method provides the programmer a means of reproducing an exact pseudo-random sequence.

```
(define-predicate random?)
(define-operation (range-of self))
(define-settable-operation (seed-of self))
(define-operation (set-seed self new-seed))
(define set-seed (setter seed-of))
```

```
;; generates a pseudo-random number such that 0 <= random < range
(define (make-random range)
   (let ((modulus 65536)
         (multiplier 25173)
         (incr 13849)
         (seed (char->digit (lastchar (time)) 10))
         (coerce
           (cond ((float? range) ->float)
                 ((integer? range) ->integer)
                 (else identity)))))
```

```
      (object
        (lambda ()
          (set seed
              (mod (+ incr
                      (* multiplier seed))
                   modulus))
          (coerce (/ (* seed range) modulus)) )
        ((print self port)
         (format port "#{Random ~A}"
                 (object-hash self)))
        ((random? self) T)
        ((range-of self) range)
        ((setter self)
         (lambda (new-range) (set range new-range)))
        ((seed-of self) seed)
        ((set-seed self new-seed)
         (set seed new-seed)) )))

> (set x (make-random 10))
#{Random 54}

> (x)                          ; x  is an object which returns a random number
2                              ;    between 0 and 9, inclusive.

> (x)
7

> (set (x) 100)                ; We extend the range of results.
100

> (x)
47

> (x)
26
```

Based on these few pseudo-random samples, we can feel fairly confident that the numbers are coming out at random. However, we can put the generator to a test based on a very simple notion: If the numbers generated are random, then every number in the range is equally likely to appear. With a large enough sample of numbers, we should expect an equal distribution of all numbers in the range. Here is a program to implement this test.

```
(define (test-rand randgen trials)
  (labels ((testv (vector-fill
                     (make-vector (range-of randgen)) 0))
           ((trial-run randgen trials)
             (cond ((zero? trials) testv)
                   (else
                     (increment (vref testv (randgen)))
                     (trial-run randgen (- trials 1)))))))
    (trial-run randgen trials)))

> (test-rand (make-random 10) 1000)
#(87 89 95 121 104 91 88 110 116 99)

> (test-rand (make-random 10) 2000)
#(185 181 189 217 215 179 199 208 220 207)

> (test-rand (make-random 10) 3000)
#(281 290 285 312 329 275 306 300 308 314)
```

The **test-rand** procedure simply counts the number of times each possible outcome occurs. These results are stored conveniently in a vector, which is returned as the value of the procedure. In each test case, we generate random numbers between 0 and 9. In the first case, we have 1000 trials, which means that we expect each number to occur about 100 times. With 2000 trials, we expect about 200 occurrences, and with 3000 trials, we should see around 300 occurrences.

How can we evaluate the results? Taking the *average* doesn't tell us anything. The average number of occurrences will be exactly the total number of trials divided by the number of outcomes, that is, 100, 200, and 300, respectively. Even if the random number generator always produced the number 8 each and every trial, this average would be unaffected.

We need a method to judge how much the actual results vary from the predicted results. A standard way of measuring this difference is the *chi-squared* test, which is discussed in [14] and in most texts on statistics and probability. To compute a chi-squared statistic, we perform the following calculation. For each possible outcome, we subtract the predicted number of occurrences from the observed number of occurrences. This difference is then squared and divided by the predicted number of occurrences. The sum of the resulting values gives the chi-squared statistic.

Here is a program for performing this calculation, where **vec** is a vector of observed occurrences (such as produced by **test-rand**), and **n** is the predicted number of occurrences for each outcome.

```
(define (chi-sq vec n)
   (labels ((total 0)
              ((square-dif x y)
               (let ((dif (- x y)))
                 (* dif dif))))
       (walk-vector
         (lambda (v)
           (set total (+ total (/ (square-dif v n) n)))))
         vec)
       (->float total)))
```

```
> (chi-sq '#(87 89 95 121 104 91 88 110 116 99) 100)
13.54
```

```
> (chi-sq '#(185 181 189 217 215 179 199 208 220 207) 200)
10.88
```

```
> (chi-sq '#(281 290 285 312 329 275 306 300 308 314) 300)
8.64
```

A detailed interpretation of a chi-squared test requires referring to a table which indicates how likely a given value is as a function of the number of possible outcomes. In the case of random numbers, the lower the value, the better — it indicates a more even distribution. Here we observe that the chi-squared value drops as we increase the number of trials. This too is to be expected. Local differences tend to average out in the long run. This is an example of the "Law of Large Numbers," a fundamental precept of statistics.

Also, the value of the chi-squared statistic is proportional to the number of possible outcomes. In this case, we have 10 possible outcomes. If we reduce the number of possible outcomes and use the same random number generator, we should get a lower chi-squared value.

```
> (test-rand (make-random 5) 1000)
#(176 216 195 198 215)
```

```
> (chi-sq '#(176 216 195 198 215) 200)
5.43
```

```
> (test-rand (make-random 2) 1000)
#(496 504)
```

```
> (chi-sq '#(496 504) 500)
0.064
```

14.5   Using Random Numbers: Math Quiz

In this section we present a simple application for our random number generator which also allows us to use vectors in two new ways. We create a vector of random number generators, and another set of vectors containing strings to be used as interactive responses.

The sample program, called **prob**, is a simple math drill for subtraction, addition, and multiplication. It uses the random number generator to chose both the test numbers, and the positive or negative response after the student has replied. Here are three sample runs — one for each for subtraction, addition, and multiplication.

In the first session, the student chooses subtraction problems with numbers less than 20. Note that the answer is always positive.

```
> (prob - 20)
How much is 4 minus 1? 3              ;  The student enters 3.
OK.  That's good.                     ;  The program responds.

How much is 14 minus 3? 10
Wrong.  Try again.

How much is 14 minus 3? 11
Of course!  (Why didn't I think of that?)

How much is 9 minus 2? quit           ;  The student terminates the session.

First tries: 1 correct out of 2.     ;  The program prints the score.

Have a nice day!
```

In the second session, the student selects addition problems with numbers less than 100.

```
> (prob + 100)
How much is 21 plus 4? 25
Close enough. (In fact, exactly right.)

How much is 74 plus 15? 89
OK.  That's good.

How much is 47 plus 10? q

First tries: 2 correct out of 2.

Have a nice day!
```

In the final run, we have multiplication of numbers less than 10.

```
> (prob * 10)
How much is 2 times 0? 0
OK.  That's good.

How much is 7 times 1? 7
Yep.  Nice work.

How much is 4 times 1? 4
Of course!  (Why didn't I think of that?)

How much is 2 times 2? stop

First tries: 3 correct out of 3.

Have a nice day!
```

This program is not profound, but it does illustrate some ways in which vectors and random numbers can be employed. The main underlying structure in this program is a vector of random number generators, produced by the procedure `make-random-vector`, given here.

```
(define (make-rand-vector size)
   (labels ((rand-vector (make-vector size))
            ((rand-vector-fill slot)
             (cond ((= slot size) rand-vector)
                   (else
                    (set (vref rand-vector slot)
                         (make-random (+ 1 slot)))
                    (rand-vector-fill (+ 1 slot)))))))
      (rand-vector-fill 0)))
```

This procedure creates a vector of the given size, each element of which is a random number generator whose range is one more than its own index. Thus, executing the generator in element 5 will produce a random number between 0 and 5. We can select our first number from the entire range, and then use that number to specify the generator used for the second number. We use this (cumbersome) approach to guarantee that the second number chosen will never be greater than the first. (For another, more efficient means, see exercise 14.7.16.)

Most of the program is taken up with processing the replies. Here is the code for **prob**.

```
(define (prob func size)
  (labels ((randv (make-rand-vector size))
           ((randbig)
            ((vref randv (- size 1))))
           ((randsmall num)
            ((vref randv num)))
           (func-name (select func
                        ((*) "times")
                        ((-) "minus")
                        ((+) "plus")))
           (right-answers 0)
           (wrong-answers 0)
           ((make-prob lastbig lastsmall)
            (let* ((big (randbig))
                   (small (randsmall big))
                   (ans (func big small)))
              (cond ((and (= big lastbig)
                          (= small lastsmall))
                     (make-prob lastbig lastsmall))
                    (else
                     (ask-question big small ans t)))))
           ((print-score)
            (format t "~%First tries: ~A correct out of ~A.~%"
              right-answers (+ right-answers wrong-answers)))
           ((ask-question big small ans flag)
            (format t "How much is ~A ~A ~A? " big func-name small)
            (let ((resp (read (standard-input))))
              (cond ((and (number? resp)
                          (= resp ans))
                     (cond (flag (increment right-answers)))
                     (right-reply)
                     (make-prob big small))
                    ((memq? resp '(q qu qui quit stop exit nil ()))
                     nil)
                    (else
                     (cond (flag (increment wrong-answers)))
                     (wrong-reply)
                     (ask-question big small ans nil)))))))
    (make-prob 0 0)
    (print-score)
    (format t "~%Have a nice day!~%")
    repl-wont-print))
```

The procedures **right-reply** and **wrong-reply** are both generated as executable objects using `make-reply`.

```
(define (make-reply reply-vector)
    (let ((rand (make-random (vector-length reply-vector))))
        (object
            (lambda ()
                (write-string (standard-output)
                        (vref reply-vector (rand)))
                (format t "~%~%")))))

(define right-reply
    (make-reply
    '#("Right!"
        "OK.  That's good."
        "Just what I would have said!"
        "Close enough. (In fact, exactly right.)"
        "Great!  Super!  Let's keep going..."
        "Of course!  (Why didn't I think of that?)"
        "Yep.  Nice work.")))

(define wrong-reply
    (make-reply
    '#("Wrong.  Try again."
        "In a word: no."
        "Not quite right.  One more time."
        "Try again.  You can get it right.")))
```

These procedures print out randomly selected responses taken from the initial vector of strings.

14.6 Infinite Objects and Lazy Evaluation

How many random numbers can a random number generator produce? Presumably, it can keep cranking out random numbers forever, as long as someone pays the electric bill.

Random number generators are examples of infinite data objects. That is, they *implicitly* represent an infinite amount of data. Even with the dropping costs of disk storage, few programmers opt for an *explicit* representation of infinite data.

Using objects, we can create an infinite list of integers.

```
(define (make-integers n)
    (let ((next (->integer n)))
      (object
        (lambda () (block0 next (increment next)))
        ((print self port)
         (format port "#{Next-integer: ~A}" next)))))
```

```
> (set x (make-integers 0))
#{Next-integer: 0}
```

```
> (x)
0
```

```
> (x)
1
```

```
> x
#{Next-integer: 2}
```

The argument to make-integers is the initial number in the series. The result is an object which, when evaluated, gives the successive integers. Notice that this object does not contain a list of all the integers; instead, it contains a *method* for generating all the integers. This method for generating integers is an implicit representation of those integers.

The code that generates integers is executed only as needed. The program does not produce the *nth* integer in the series until the $n-1$ has already been used. At each cycle of evaluation, the procedure produces two things: a result and a method for producing the next result. This type of delayed execution is termed *lazy evaluation*. T provides a specific method for implementing lazy evaluation. It uses the constructs delay and force, demonstrated here with the procedure integers.

```
(define (integers n)
  (cons n (delay (integers (+ 1 n)))))
```

```
> (set x (integers 0))
(0 . #{Delayed 143})
```

```
> (car x)
0
```

```
> (delay? (cdr x))
T
```

```
> (set x (force (cdr x)))
(1 . #{Delayed 144})

> (car x)
1
```

We define `integers` to be a recursive procedure. However, when `integers` itself is called, the recursive call is not immediately executed due to `delay`. Instead, the result is postponed until `force` is applied. We then get another delayed object, which likewise can be forced to evaluate. The predicate `delay?` identifies delayed objects.

We can define a simple macro which facilitates this lazy evaluation strategy. We call it `lazy-pop`, and test it out with an odd-number generator.

```
(define-syntax (lazy-pop n)
   `(block0
       (car ,n)
       (set ,n (force (cdr ,n)))))

(define (odd-numbers n)
    (cons n (delay (odd-numbers (+ n 2)))))
```

```
> (set x (odd-numbers 1))
(1 . #{Delayed 177})

> (lazy-pop x)
1

> (lazy-pop x)
3

> (lazy-pop x)
5

> x
(7 . #{Delayed 178})
```

Another useful application of implicit objects is data structures. Sometimes a programmer may have a very large data structure that is only sparsely populated. For example, a scientific problem may call for a very large two-dimensional array, with only a few dozen non-zero elements. The programmer should not have to allocate the space for the entire array just to represent a few dozen values.

The answer to this problem is lazy data structures — data representations that allocate space only when needed. Here is a simple example using the two-dimensional arrays described at the beginning of the chapter.

```
(define-predicate 2d-larray?)
(define-settable-operation (2d-ref self x y))
(define-operation (2d-set self x y val))
(define 2d-set (setter 2d-ref))
(define-operation (2d-larray-fill self val))

(define (make-2d-larray x y)
    (labels ((2d-larray (make-vector x))
             (2d-fill-value 0)
             (2d-fill-flag nil)
             ((lref x)
              (cond ((delay? (vref 2d-larray x))
                     (set (vref 2d-larray x)
                          (force (vref 2d-larray x)))
                     (cond (2d-fill-flag
                            (vector-fill (vref 2d-larray x)
                                         2d-fill-value)))))
              (vref 2d-larray x))
             ((2d-initialize vector index size)
              (cond ((= index 0) vector)
                    (else
                     (decrement index)
                     (set (vref vector index)
                          (delay (make-vector size)))
                     (2d-initialize vector index size)))))
      (set 2d-larray (2d-initialize 2d-larray x y))
      (object nil
        ((print self port)
         (format port "#{Lazy-array ~A}"
            (object-hash self)))
        ((2d-larray? self) T)
        ((2d-ref self x y)
         (cond ((delay? (vref 2d-larray x))
                2d-fill-value)
               (else
                (vref (vref 2d-larray x) y))))
        ((2d-set self x y val)
         (set (vref (lref x) y) val))
```

```
    ((2d-larray-fill self val)
     (walk-vector
       (lambda (v)
         (cond ((delay? v)
                (set 2d-fill-flag T)
                (set 2d-fill-value val))
               (else
                (vector-fill v val))))
         2d-larray)
       2d-larray))))
```

```
> (set x (make-2d-larray 3 10))
#{Lazy-array 198}

> (2d-larray-fill x 10)
#(#{Delayed 201} #{Delayed 202} #{Delayed 203})

> (2d-ref x 2 2)
10

> (set (2d-ref x 2 2) 5)
5

> (2d-ref x 2 2)
5

> (2d-ref x 2 3)
10
```

Lazy evaluation provides a means to create virtual data structures. The program can use these structures in much the same way as fully allocated data structures, but with economies of space and time.

14.7 Exercises

14.7.1 Expression Drill [4]

Evaluate the following expressions, first by hand, then with the help of the T interpreter.

```
(set x (make-vector 10))
(vector-fill x 1)
(vector-posq (+ 1 1) '#(0 1 2 3 4))
(vector-pos < (+ 1 1) '#(0 1 2 3 4))
(walk-vector (lambda (n) (+ n 1)) x)
```

```
(set (vref x 0) (walk-vector (lambda (n) (+ n 1)) x))
(tree-hash (tree-hash 123456789))
(define (eager-integers n) (cons n (eager-integers (+ 1 n))))
(eager-integers 0)
```

14.7.2   Tic-Tac-Toe [7]

Using a 3 by 3 two-dimensional array, write a program which plays tic-tac-toe. The program should have the following basic cycle:

1. Determine if game is over. If so, stop.

2. Determine whose move it is.

3. If it is the machine's move, select legal move. Otherwise, solicit legal move from opponent.

The program should know both the rules (what constitutes a legal move), and strategy (what constitutes a good move). The program should never lose.

14.7.3   More Tic-Tac-Toe [9]

Modify the previous program for tic-tac-toe. Remove the strategy knowledge and replace it with a procedure for evaluating and learning new strategies. The program should begin with a random strategy (using the random number generator presented above). The program should notice what succeeds and what fails — both from its own moves and those of its opponent.

The program should learn from its experience. It may be useful to have the program play games with itself to speed up the acquisition of experience.

14.7.4   Three-Dimensional Arrays [5*]

Extend the two-dimensional array object to three dimensions. That is, create a procedure **make-3d-array** which takes three arguments, the x, y, and z dimensions of a rectangular array, and creates an object analogous to the **2d-array**.

14.7.5   n-Dimensional Arrays [6*]

Rather than methodically create special array objects for specific dimensions, we shall simply solve the problem once and for all. Create a procedure **make-nd-array** which takes a variable number of arguments for the dimensions of the array. Thus, (make-nd-array 2 2 2) would create a three-dimensional array object, and (make-nd-array 2 2 2 2 2), would create a six-dimensional array object. The array object should respond to the appropriate operations, namely, **print, nd-ref, nd-set, nd-array-fill,** and also **dimensions-of**, which returns the respective dimensions of the array-object.

```
> (set x (make-nd-array 2 2 2 2))
#{nd-array 174 #(#(#(#(0 0) #(0 0)) #(#(0 0) #(0 0)))
#(#(#(0 0) #(0 0)) #(#(0 0) #(0 0))))}

> (nd-array? x)
#t

> (dimensions-of x)
(2 2 2 2)

> (set (nd-ref x 1 1 0 1) 9)
9

> (nd-ref x 1 1)                    ; nd-ref  can return subarrays
#(#(0 9) #(0 0))

> (nd-ref x 1 1 0)
#(0 9)

> (nd-ref x 1 1 0 1)
9

> (nd-array-fill x 8)
#(#(#(#(8 8) #(8 8)) #(#(8 8) #(8 8))) #(#(#(8 8) #(8 8))
#(#(8 8) #(8 8))))
```

14.7.6   Hash Tables [3*]

Modify the hash table given previously in this chapter to handle keys other than identifiers. Specifically, it should allow numbers, strings, and lists as keys. Here is an example.

```
> (set y (make-hash-table 10))
#{Hash table 40}

> (table-put y '(mary smith) 21)
((MARY SMITH) . 21)

> (table-get y '(mary smith))
21

> (table-put y "Jane Doe" 39)
("Jane Doe" . 39)
```

```
> (reveal y)
(() () () () ("Jane Doe" . 39) () () () ((MARY SMITH) . 21) ())

> (table-put y 39 "age of john")
(39 . "age of john")

> (reveal y)
(() () () () ("Jane Doe" . 39) () () ()
((MARY SMITH) . 21) (39 . "age of john"))
```

14.7.7 Searching Hash Tables [4*]

Modify the hash table object presented in this chapter to handle the operation **table-find**. Given a hash table object and a value, **table-find** returns the first key in the table that has the specified value, as shown below.

```
> (set y (make-hash-table 10))
#{Hash table 53}

> (table-put y 'mary 21)
(MARY . 21)

> (table-put y 'john 39)
(JOHN . 39)

> (table-find y 21)
MARY

> (table-find y 39)
JOHN

> (table-find y 100)
()
```

14.7.8 Random Hash Tables [2*]

What are advantages and disadvantages of using a random number generator as part of a hashing function?

14.7.9 More Hash Tables [5*]

Above we created a hash table which handled collisions through sequential search of the hash table itself. Another method is to allow each bucket to contain multiple items and to search each bucket sequentially. Implement a bucket-search hash table using an association list for the bucket.

14.7.10   new-hash [5*]

Write your own version of `tree-hash`. This should be a recursive procedure which traverses the input, converting it to a number. Here is a hash algorithm similar to T's own `tree-hash`.

- If the input is an integer, then no change is made.

- If the input is a character, then it returns the ASCII value of that character.

- The empty string hashes to 1.

- The empty list hashes to the magic number 31415926.

- If the input is a symbol, it is converted to a string which is then hashed.

- If the input is a string, then it returns the sum of the hash value of the first character and twice the hash value of the rest of the string.

- Lists and vectors should be hashed in a manner similar to strings.

Note that embedding changes the hash value.

```
> (new-hash '(a b c))
251327887

> (new-hash '((a b c)))
314159739

> (new-hash '(((a b c))))
376991591
```

14.7.11   Hashed Databases [8]

In exercise 12.4.5, we presented the programmer with the task of developing an interactive database management system. One of the problems highlighted in that discussion was the efficient update and retrieval of records.

Hash tables provide a convenient strategy for database retrieval. If the database is updated rarely, but frequently queried, then it may be advisable to have a hash table for each of the fields in the record. Each table would index the master record.

Implement this strategy. Incorporate hash tables as the primary indexing and search mechanism for the database system described in exercise 12.4.5.

14.7.12   Generalized Chi-Squared [5*]

We can simulate flipping a coin using a random number generator with a range of 2. Heads would be 0 and tails would be 1. To simulate the flipping of two coins, we can use two calls to the same generator and then sum the results. Thus, 0 would be two heads, 1 would be one heads and one tails, and 2 would be two tails.

```
> (set coin (make-random 2))
#{Random 54}

> (coin)
0

> (define (make-two-coins)
    (object
        (lambda () (+ (coin) (coin)))
        ((range-of self) 3)))
#{Procedure 68 MAKE-TWO-COINS}

> (define two-coins (make-two-coins))
#{Procedure 69}

> (two-coins)
0

> (range-of two-coins)
3
```

If we toss two coins, A and B, there are four possible outcomes, with three possible values, as shown here.

	B Heads	B Tails
A Heads	0	1
A Tails	1	2

If we now want to evaluate the effectiveness of our **two-coins** simulator, we must modify our previous chi-squared program. Previously, we had assumed that all possible values were equally likely. In this case, however, there should be twice as many 1's (one head and one tail) as either 0's or 2's.

Modify the **chi-sq** procedure to use a vector of expected values as the second argument to allow for varying values of predicted outcomes. The procedure should still handle the optional case of a single integer to represent all expected values.

```
> (test-rand two-coins 100)
#(27 52 21)
```

```
> (chi-sq '#(27 52 21) '#(25 50 25))
0.88
> (chi-sq '#(176 216 195 198 215) 200)
5.43
```

The second example shows that the new version of **chi-sq** produces the same results as the old one.

14.7.13 Shuffling Cards [5*]

Write a procedure which takes a list, and permutes the order of a list through a specified number of two-element swaps, using T's **exchange** form.

```
> (set x 1)
1

> (set y 2)
2

> (exchange x y)      ;  switches values of x and y
2

> x
2

> y
1

> (set z '(a . b))
(A . B)

> (exchange (car z) (cdr z))
B

> z
(B . A)

> (shuffle '(1 2 3 4 5 6 7 8 9) 9)
(1 2 3 4 5 9 7 8 6)

> (shuffle '(1 2 3 4 5 6 7 8 9) 200)
(2 7 4 8 5 1 9 3 6)
```

```
;; make-deck  is from exercise 8.7.3
> (set deck (make-deck *ranks* *suits*))
((TEN . CLUBS) (JACK . CLUBS) (QUEEN . CLUBS) (KING . CLUBS)
(ACE . CLUBS) (TEN . DIAMONDS) (JACK . DIAMONDS) (QUEEN . DIAMONDS)
(KING . DIAMONDS) (ACE . DIAMONDS) (TEN . HEARTS) (JACK . HEARTS)
(QUEEN . HEARTS) (KING . HEARTS) (ACE . HEARTS) (TEN . SPADES)
(JACK . SPADES) (QUEEN . SPADES) (KING . SPADES) (ACE . SPADES))

> (shuffle deck 200)
((QUEEN . DIAMONDS) (JACK . SPADES) (TEN . DIAMONDS) (QUEEN . CLUBS)
(QUEEN . HEARTS) (JACK . CLUBS) (JACK . DIAMONDS) (KING . HEARTS)
(KING . CLUBS) (ACE . CLUBS) (KING . DIAMONDS) (QUEEN . SPADES)
(KING . SPADES) (TEN . HEARTS) (TEN . CLUBS) (ACE . SPADES)
(TEN . SPADES) (JACK . HEARTS) (ACE . DIAMONDS) (ACE . HEARTS))
```

14.7.14   Card Games [8]

Now that we have a deck of cards and a way to shuffle them, we can deal a couple of hands. Write a program which plays your favorite card game. Gin rummy, blackjack, poker, and solitaire games are reasonable choices. Card games can have many subtleties. Even "Go Fishing" proves to be challenging to program well.

14.7.15   Chance Music [6*]

As practiced by composers such as John Cage, music composed at random is termed *aleatoric* music. Write a procedure music which takes three arguments: a list of pitches, a list of durations, and a positive integer indicating the desired number of notes. It returns a list of the given size containing a random sequence of notes. Here is an example.

```
(define *pitches* '(a-flat a b-flat b c d-flat d
                    e-flat e f g-flat g rest))

(define *durations* '(whole half quarter eighth sixteenth))
```

```
> (music *pitches* *durations* 10)
((B-FLAT . HALF) (F . EIGHTH) (D . QUARTER) (B . HALF)
(B-FLAT . HALF) (REST . SIXTEENTH) (G-FLAT . EIGHTH)
(D . QUARTER) (D . QUARTER) (B . HALF))
```

The musically inclined programmer might wish to explore ways of constraining the random composition process to produce music that satisfies rules of tonality, counterpoint, meter, or harmony.

14.7.16   New Math [4*]

The vector of random number generators used in the math quiz program was both illustrative and inefficient. There really is not any need to have a multitude of random number generators to guarantee that subtraction problems never have negative answers. Devise a solution which requires only one random number generator.

14.7.17   Lazy n-Dimensional Arrays [7*]

In exercise 14.7.5 above, we defined n-dimensional array objects. The space for each array was completely allocated at the time the array was created. This could result in a waste of both space and effort if only a small percentage of the array is actually used.

In this chapter, we saw how to use lazy evaluation to delay the allocation of space in a two-dimensional array. Extend this method to an arbitrary, positive number of dimensions. Here is an example.

```
> (set x (make-nd-larray 2 2 2 2 2))
#{nd-larray 241 #(#{Delayed 242} #{Delayed 243})}

> (nd-larray? x)
T

> (dimensions-of x)
(2 2 2 2 2)

> (nd-ref x 1 1 1 1 1)
0

> (nd-larray-fill x 8)
#(#{Delayed 242} #{Delayed 243})

> (nd-ref x 1 1 1 1 1)
8

> (set (nd-ref x 1 1 1 1 1) 9)
9

> x
#{nd-larray 241 #(#{Delayed 242} #(#{Delayed 244} #(#{Delayed 245}
#(#{Delayed 246} #(#{Delayed 247} #(8 9))))))}
```

14.7.18 Executable Data Structures [5*]

Through a simple change in our definitions of array and hash table objects, we can make these data structures executable for reference and storage.[1] Here are some examples.

```
> (set john (make-xhash-table 20))
#{Hash table 138}

> (set (john 'age) 30)
30

> (john 'age)
30

> (set (john 'sister) 'mary)
MARY

> (john 'sister)
MARY
```

We have created an executable hash table. The table itself is a settable accessor procedure. We can have the same effect with arrays.

```
> (set xx (make-xnd-array 2 2 2))
#{nd-array 141 #(#(#(0 0) #(0 0)) #(#(0 0) #(0 0)))}

> (xx 1 1 1)
0

> (set (xx 1 1 1) 'something)
SOMETHING

> (xx 1 1 1)
SOMETHING

> (xx 1 1 0)
0
```

Modify the hash table and array definitions in this chapter to give them this functionality.

---

[1] James Philbin informed the author of this technique.

14.8   Chapter Summary

- Vectors provide an efficient, random access data structure.

- Vectors in T are notated by # followed by a list. For example, #(1 2 3) is a simple three-element vector.

- T provides an array of operations for vectors.

```
(list->vector list)
(vector->list vector)
(vref vector index)          ; [vector-elt]
(vector? object)
(vector-length vector)
(make-vector size)
(vector-fill vector value)
(walk-vector procedure vector)
(copy-vector vector)
(vector-pos predicate object vector)
(vector-posq object vector)
```

- Vectors may be used to implement multidimensional arrays.

- Hash tables provide an efficient means for implementing key-indexed tables. T's **tree-hash** is a convenient hashing method.

- Random numbers are useful in a variety of computer applications, such as simulations and games. Over a large number of trials, a random number generator should produce an even distribution of possible outcomes. The *chi-squared* statistic is an appropriate measure of this distribution.

- Lazy evaluation provides a method for building infinite objects and virtual data structures. A T programmer can implement lazy evaluation with three basic constructs.

```
(delay? object)
(delay expression)
(force delay)
```

- Values of two T objects can be swapped using **exchange**.

Chapter 15

Environments and EVAL

All the vital mechanisms, varied as they are,
have only one object, that of preserving constant
the conditions of life in the internal environment.

◇ CLAUDE BERNARD, *Lessons on Reactions Common to Animals and Plants*
(1878)

The first is, that through a vitalizing spirit,
a painting should possess the movement of life.
The second is, that by means of the brush,
the structural basis should be established.
The third is, that the representation should so conform with the objects
as to give their likenesses.
The fourth is, that the coloring should be applied according to their characteristics.
The fifth is, that through organization, place and position should be determined.
The sixth is, that by copying the ancient models should be perpetuated.

◇ HSIETH HO, Concerning the Six Principles of Painting. *Notes Concerning the*
Classification of Old Paintings (c. 500)

Computers do not tolerate ambiguity. When a programmer uses an identifier to refer to a value, there must be exactly one such identifier, and it must have exactly one value. Right? Well, yes and no.

Most programmers write code in which the same identifier is used repeatedly in separate procedures. For example, a programmer may use "**lst**" to identify list arguments, "**vec**" to identify vectors, and so forth. These identifiers may occur dozens of times in separate procedures, but they should never be confused with one another — either by the programmer or by the computer.

The problem of ambiguous reference occurs regularly outside computer programs. How many people do you know named John or Mary or Joe or Jane? A colleague of the author has five different friends named "Stephen." His secretary has learned that the terse message "Steve called." will be met with bewilderment and frustration.

15.1 Lexical Scoping

The computer should never have to ask "Which Steve?" or rather "Which **vec**?" At any given point in a program, there is always a one-to-one relationship between identifiers and values. The programmer's desire to reuse names must be reconciled with this requirement to maintain uniqueness of reference. The answer is for the programmer to control the context of an identifier through its *scope* of reference.

In chapter 5, we discussed the dichotomy of global and local reference. Global variables have indefinite scope – they may be referenced throughout a program. Local variables in T normally are *lexically* scoped. That means that the scope of a local variable can be determined by its textual setting at the time it is defined. We have seen that T provides a number of ways of creating local variables, such as with **let**, **lambda**, and **labels**. Here are some examples.

```
> (define x 0)          ; x  is defined as a global value
0

> (let ((x 3))          ; x  here is local to this let
     (let ((x 4))        ; x  here is local to the second let
        (* x x)))        ; x  is within the scope of the second let
16

> (let ((x 3))
     (let ((x 4)))       ; this let expression ends on this line
     (* x x))            ; x  here is within the scope of the first let
9

> (let ((y x))          ; x  gets its value here from the global
     (let ((x 3))
     (let ((x 4)))
     (* y y)))           ; y  got its value from the global value of x
0
```

A more general way to view the scope of variables is as hierarchical *contours*. Global variables are bound within the outer contour, or environment. When local variables are created, such as with **let** or **lambda**, the bindings of those variables are in effect within the inner contour. These contours can be nested. Here is a schematic example.

```
(block
   ...                                ; Outer contour.
   (let ((x 1) (y 2))
      ...                             ; Contour 1.
      (lambda (u v w)
         ...                          ; Contour 2.
         (labels ((x 2) (y 1))
            ...                       ; Contour 3.
            )
         ...                          ; Contour 2.
         (lambda (w)
            ...                       ; Contour 4.
            ))))
```

This code fragment begins with a **block**, which is part of the outer (global) contour. We then introduce a **let** which creates two local variables, **x** and **y**, which have bindings within contour 1. Next, **lambda** introduces an embedded inner contour with three additional local variables. The values of **x** and **y** are still accessible from contour 1. Then, we have a **labels** which creates two new bindings for **x** and **y** which *shadow* the previous bindings. That is, within contour 3, the new values of **x** and **y** supersede the earlier values. The bindings of the contour 2 variables, **u**, **v**, and **w**, are also available within contour 3. When contour 3 ends, contour 2 is still in effect, as are the previous bindings of x and y. Finally, in contour 4, begun by **lambda**, we get a new binding for w which shadows the earlier contour 2 value.

We may now offer a more precise definition of lexical scoping. At the time of definition, a local identifier's binding is in effect only in the textual body of the defining form, e.g., **let** or **lambda**.

We earlier stated that local variables in T are *normally* lexically scoped. There is an alternative. A contrasting method is *dynamic scoping,* in which non-local reference is resolved at execution time, instead of at the time of definition. T allows the programmer the option of dynamic scoping with the **bind** form. The syntax of **bind** is the same as **let**. Here are examples comparing the two approaches.

```
> (let ((x 100))
      (define (x-times n)
         (* n x)) )
#{Procedure 36 X-TIMES}

> (x-times 5)
500

> (let ((x 200)) (x-times 5))      ; x-times  ignores the new value of x
500
```

```
> (set y 8)
8

> (define (y-times n) (* n y))
#{Procedure 37 Y-TIMES}

> (y-times 5)
40

> (let ((y 10)) (y-times 5))    ; y-times  ignores the new value of y
40

> (bind ((y 10)) (y-times 5))   ; bind  replaces the outer binding of y
50
```

The **bind** form for dynamic binding can be viewed as analogous to the following.

```
    (bind ((location value)) . body)
;  is the same as
    (let ((saved-value location))
       (set location value)
       (unwind-protect (block . body)
                    (set location saved-value)))
```

The programmer should note that **bind** assumes that **location** has previously been bound.

   Lexical scope is of great benefit for optimizing compilers, as we shall see in the next chapters. However, for years most LISP dialects used dynamic binding, which allowed the programmer to get away with obscure programming habits, such as implicit parameter passing. The T programmer can dabble in such debauched practices using the **bind** form. Here is an example.

   In good T style, we had previously defined the procedure **son-of-zeller** (see exercise 2.11.11), which calls the procedure **zeller**.

```
(define (son-of-zeller day month year)
    (zeller day month (quotient year 100) (remainder year 100)
                    (cond ((leap-year? year) 1)
                          (else 0))))
```

```
; zeller  was defined with explicit parameters, like this:
(define (zeller d m c y l)
    . . .
```

However, using **bind** we can dispense with the explicit passing of parameters. Instead, we can redefine **zeller** to take no arguments, and simply bind exact identifiers before calling **zeller**.

```
(define (son-of-zeller day month year)
    (bind ((d day)
           (m month)
           (c (quotient year 100))
           (y (remainder year 100))
           (l (cond ((leap-year? year) 1)
                    (else 0))))
          (zeller)))
```

```
; zeller is now defined without any arguments:
(define (zeller)
    ...
```

The programmer should avoid such usage. It becomes pardonable under rare circumstances, such as in porting large amounts of LISP code from some other dialect that exploits such properties of dynamic scoping.

15.2 Environments

We have been referring to global variables and outer contours in a way that might lead the reader to infer a universal, or boundless extent. Actually, global variables are local to an *environment*. An environment is simply a collection of bindings between identifiers and values. T also uses the term *locale* to specify environments. T provides a set of mechanisms for creating and manipulating environments. Here are some examples.

```
> (define x 21)
21

> x
21

> (define *l* (make-empty-locale '*l*))
#{Locale 42 *L*}

> (locale? *l*)
#t

> (*define *l* 'x 100)
100

> (*value *l* 'x)
100
```

```
> (locale? user-env)
#t

> (*value user-env 'x)
21

> (import *L* x)
100

> (*value user-env 'x)
100
```

These examples start off innocently enough. We first define x to have the value 21, and then we verify that simple transaction. After that, we enter the world of locales.

- (make-empty-locale id) As its name implies, this procedure creates an unpopulated locale. The id argument is used in debugging.

- locale? This is the predicate for locales.

- (*define locale id value) This procedure is similar to the **define** form, except that it requires an explicit locale name, and it evaluates all of its arguments. Here we give x the value 100 in the *L* locale.

- (*value locale id) The *value procedure simply retrieves the value of the given identifier in the given locale.

- user-env This global identifier is the name of the default environment. Note that it answers true to locale? and that the value of x in user-env is still 21, at least for a while.

- (import env . vars) As should be apparent, import sets the values of the identifiers in the current environment to the respective values found in the given environment. Here is a definition of the import special form.

```
(define-syntax (import env . vars)
  (let ((g (generate-symbol 'import)))
    `(let ((,g ,env))
       ,@(map (lambda (var)
                (let ((var (check-arg symbol? var 'import)))
                  `(define ,var (*value ,g ',var))))
              vars))))
```

The companion to import is export, which is discussed in exercise 15.7.1.

The programmer can also create copies of environments using the `make-locale` procedure. The settable procedure `repl-env` determines the environment in which the read-eval-print loop operates. Here are examples.

```
> (define *my-env* (make-locale standard-env '*my-env*))
#{Locale 127 *MY-ENV*}

> (define george-washington 'president)
PRESIDENT

> (*define *my-env* 'george-washington 'druggist)
DRUGGIST

> george-washington
PRESIDENT

> (set (repl-env) *my-env*)
#{Locale 127 *MY-ENV*}

> george-washington
DRUGGIST

> (set (repl-env) user-env)
#{Locale 123 USER-ENV}

> george-washington
PRESIDENT
```

We first create a new locale called *my-env*, which is a copy of the standard environment, standard-env. (The user-env is likewise a copy of the standard environment.) In the standard environment, george-washington is President, but in *my-env*, george-washington is a druggist. We can change the default value simply by changing default environments. When the read-eval-print loop is set to look up bindings in *my-env*, it finds the druggist; in the standard environment, Reagan is President.

When loading a file, the programmer can specify the binding environment with an optional second argument to load. The default value is (repl-env). Here is an example.

Assume the file test.t contains the following expression.

```
(define george-washington 'commander-and-chief)
```

We execute the following code.

```
> (*value *my-env* 'george-washington)
DRUGGIST

> (load "test.t" *my-env*)

;Loading "test.t" into *MY-ENV*
[Redefining GEORGE-WASHINGTON]
COMMANDER-AND-CHIEF COMMANDER-AND-CHIEF

> (*value *my-env* 'george-washington)
COMMANDER-AND-CHIEF

> george-washington
PRESIDENT
```

The **load** has affected the bindings in **my-env**, and left (**repl-env**) untouched.

Another way to create a local environment is with T's **locale** form. Here is an example. We use **lset** to assign values to local variables that may shadow bindings in the outer environment. Note the difference among **set**, **lset**, and **define**.

```
> (define x 100)
100

> (locale () (+ x x))
200

> (locale name (define x 2) (+ x x))
[Assigning NAME] [Shadowing X] 4

> x
100

> (locale () (set x 2) (+ x x))
[Assigning X] 4

> x
2

> (locale () (lset x 22) (+ x x))
[Shadowing X] 44

> x
2
```

We first give a global value to x. In the first **locale**, this global value is used. In the second **locale** form, we shadow the global value with a local **define**. We also

give a local name to the locale. This name can be referenced within the locale's
lexical scope. In the third locale, we use set, which changes the global value of
x. In the last locale, we use lset, which affects only the local environment.

For a detailed look at the distinction among lset, set, and define, the reader
is directed to the definition of t-eval later in this chapter.

15.3   eval

In the preceding section, we saw how the same identifier can simultaneously have
different values in different environments. This multiplicity of values does not create
a conflict because expressions are always evaluated within a specific environment.

As the reader may recall, the basic cycle of the T interpreter is the read-
eval-print loop. That is, expressions are read from the input port, evaluated, and
the results are printed to the output port. In chapter 7, we encountered read and
print. The remaining member of the central triumvirate is eval. Here is how they
can be plugged together.

```
(print
  (eval
    (read (standard-input))
    (repl-env))
  (standard-output))
```

eval takes two arguments: an expression and an environment, which need
not be the (repl-env). The eval form may be called directly with an expression
and environment. Here are examples.

```
> (define *crazy-env* (make-empty-locale '*crazy-env*))
#{Locale 6 *CRAZY-ENV*}

> (*define *crazy-env* '- +)
#{Procedure 7 ADD}

> (*define *crazy-env* '+ -)
#{Procedure 8 -}

> (eval '(+ (- 22 20) 2) user-env)
4

> (eval '(+ (- 22 20) 2) *crazy-env*)
40
```

In a truly perverse example, we have created a new environment *crazy-env*,
in which the definitions of addition and subtraction are switched. Then, the exact same expression produces different results depending on which environment is
specified to eval.

15.4   eval Example: T Workspace

Generally, the programmer does not need to make explicit calls to **eval**. The regular read-eval-print loop usually provides sufficient functionality. However, there are occasions when the programmer can properly exploit **eval**. We here present a basic example, that of making a simple workspace.

Some interpreted languages, like APL, provide a convenient mechanism for keeping track of global variables and procedure definitions. During the course of a programming session, the programmer may have defined or modified several definitions, and created or updated some global variables. In a *workspace*, the computer can keep track of variables and procedures so that the programmer can save his work when he is done, and later restart his previous session from where he left off. Normal workspace functions include saving a workspace, restoring a workspace, defining new procedures, editing procedure definitions, and creating and modifying global variables.

T already allows the programmer to create and modify procedures and variables through the interpreter. Editing definitions of procedures and variables is discussed in exercise 15.7.4. Here we present a trivial mechanism for saving and restoring the state of a programming session.

First, we shall look at a sample session. We use the **make-workspace** procedure, which takes a single filename argument. The workspace expressions will be logged to that file. We will terminate the workspace session with **(save-ws)**.

```
> (make-workspace "testfile")
Starting workspace.  End with (save-ws)

WS> (define pi 3.14159)
3.14159

WS> pi
3.14159

WS> (define (area r) (* pi r r))
#{Procedure 28 AREA}

WS> (area 2)
12.56636

WS> (area 3)
28.274309999999996

WS> (put 'joe 'age 23)
23

WS> (save-ws)
```

```
Workspace saved in file: testfile
END-WORKSPACE
```

Here are the contents of the workspace file, `testfile`.

```
(herald workspace)
(DEFINE PI 3.14159)
(DEFINE (AREA R) (* PI R R))
(AREA 2)
(AREA 3)
(PUT (QUOTE JOE) (QUOTE AGE) 23)
```

This file can be read back into T using **load** to reproduce the final state of the variables and procedures. Furthermore, the programmer could edit this file directly to remove those expressions which do not result in side effects, such as the calls to the AREA procedure.

We now present the definition of **make-workspace**.

```
(define (make-workspace filename)
  (catch stop
    (format t "Starting workspace.  End with (save-ws) ~%")
    (labels ((port (open filename '(out)))
             (ws-prompt "WS> ")
             ((ws-fn? input)
              (cond ((eq? (car input) 'save-ws)
                     (close port)
                     (stop nil)))))
      (format port "(herald workspace)")
      (iterate loop ()
        (format t "~%~A" ws-prompt)
        (let ((input (read (standard-input))))
          (cond ((list? input)
                 (ws-fn? input)
                 (format port "~%~A" input)))
          (print (eval input (repl-env)) (standard-output))
          (loop)))))
    (format t "~%Workspace saved in file: ~A~%" filename)
    'end-workspace)
```

The procedure performs the following.

1. Prints out initial message.

2. Opens an output port to the given file.

3. Defines a local predicate `ws-fn?` which checks to see if the command **save-ws** was input. If it was, then it closes the output port, and throws control to the **catch** expression.

4. The `iterate` clause contains a modified read-eval-print loop. It prints out the special prompt, and then reads the input. If the input is a list, then the `ws-fn?` checks the input and the input is copied to the output file. (Non-list expressions, such as symbols, are not copied to the file since their evaluation does not alter the state of session.) Finally, the input is evaluated and the results are printed to the standard output.

This example demonstrates how the programmer can insinuate his own code into the read-eval-print loop. Exercise 15.7.3 provides another example.

15.5 Locatives

As previously stated, bindings are associations between identifiers and values. To specify how that correspondence is implemented, we need to introduce *locatives*. Locatives are T's version of pointers, as found in other programming languages such as Pascal and C.

A locative specifies a location where a value may be stored. Here are some examples.

```
> (define a '(1 2 3))
(1 2 3)

> (locative a)
#{Vcell 34 A}

> (contents (locative a))
(1 2 3)

> (locative (car a))
#{Locative 42}

> (set (contents (locative (car a))) 5)
5

> a
(5 2 3)

> (locative? a)
()
```

```
> (locative? (locative a))
#t
```

We first create an identifier "**a**" with a given value. We then explore and modify "**a**" using various mechanisms.

- (locative location) This is a special form which returns a locative giving the address of the location. The notation #{Vcell} refers to a "value cell" address, whereas #{Locative} refers here to a list structure address.

- (contents locative) This is a settable operation which returns the stored value.

- (locative? object) This is the predicate for locatives.

The behavior of **locative** with value cells is analogous to the following.

```
    (locative identifier)
;   is equivalent to
(define-settable-operation (contents self))
(define-operation (set-contents self value))
(define set-contents (setter contents))
    . . .
    (object nil
        ((contents self) identifier)
        ((set-contents)
         (lambda (value) (set identifier value)))
        ((locative? self) t))
```

Locatives also provide a way to circumvent the normal protection afforded by lexical scoping. With locatives, the programmer may pass locative arguments to procedures which in turn change the original value. Here is an example.

```
> (define (test1 x)
      (set x (+ x 2)))
#{Procedure 30 TEST1}

> (set y 6)
[Binding Y] 6

> (test1 y)
8

> y                        ;  The value of y is not changed.
6
```

```
> (define (test2 x)
    (set (contents x) (+ (contents x) 2)))
#{Procedure 31 TEST2}

> (test2 (locative y))
8

> y                      ;  The value of y is changed.
8
```

Thus, locatives provide a method for the programmer to write procedures that can destructively alter values outside of their lexical scope.

In the next section, we see how locatives can be applied in implementing variable binding.

15.6   eval Exposed

As evidence of the underlying elegance and simplicity of the design of LISP, it is possible to define **eval** in a page or so of LISP code. This basic definition contains the essential components, such as **car**, **cdr**, **cond**, and **eq?**, from which more complex procedures can be defined.

Our definition of **eval** is both recursive and circular. It is like a dictionary that defines "cat" to be a feline, and "feline" to be a cat. For example, we use **cond** in the process of defining **cond**, and even **define** to define **define**! The point of the definition is to demonstrate the way in which **eval** works, and to show the role of the environment in the process of evaluation.

In this section, we actually present two definitions of **eval**. The first is a simple version, based on the original definition of LISP. It uses an association list to maintain the bindings between identifiers and values. The second **eval** is closer to T, and uses an object-based environment. Here is **simple-eval**.

```
(define (simple-eval exp env)
   (cond ((number? exp) exp)
         ((string? exp) exp)
         ((char? exp) exp)
         ((atom? exp)
          (simple-env-lookup exp env))
         ((eq? (car exp) 'quote)
          (cadr exp))
         ((eq? (car exp) 'cond)
          (simple-eval-cond (cdr exp) env))
         (else
          (simple-apply (car exp)
                        (simple-eval-list (cdr exp) env) env)))))
```

```
(define (simple-env-lookup id env)
    (cdr (assq id env)))

(define (simple-eval-cond exp env)
    (cond ((simple-eval (caar exp) env)
             (simple-eval (cadar exp) env))
            (else (simple-eval-cond (cdr exp) env))))

(define (simple-eval-list exp env)
    (cond ((null? exp) nil)
            (else
             (cons (simple-eval (car exp) env)
                      (simple-eval-list (cdr exp) env)))))
```

The algorithm for **simple-eval** is straightforward. Numbers, strings, and characters evaluate to themselves. Atoms (symbols) return their respective values from the environment. In this case, the environment is just an association list of identifier-value pairs. (Note that the value could be a lambda-expression.) A quoted expression falls through. A **cond** clause is evaluated in the expected fashion – the first test clause is evaluated, and then either the result clause or the remaining conditional clauses are evaluated. If the expression being evaluated does not match any of those categories, then it is assumed to be a procedure call. In that case, the procedure is applied to its arguments, which are first evaluated with **simple-eval-list**.

```
(define (simple-apply proc args env)
    (cond ((atom? proc)
            (case proc
                ((car)   (caar args))
                ((cdr)   (cdar args))
                ((cons)  (cons (car args) (cadr args)))
                ((atom?) (atom? (car args)))
                ((eq?)   (eq? (car args) (cadr args)))
                (else
                 (simple-apply (simple-eval proc env) args env))))
          ((eq? (car proc) 'lambda)
           (simple-eval (caddr proc)
                        (pairlis (cadr proc) args env)))
          ((eq? (car proc) 'define)
           (simple-apply (caddr proc)
                 args
                 (cons (cons (cadr proc) (caddr proc)) env)))))
```

```
(define (pairlis x y env)
   (cond ((null? x) env)
         (else
          (cons (cons (car x) (car y))
                (pairlis (cdr x) (cdr y) env)))))
```

The procedure **simple-apply** is quite similar to **simple-eval** itself. We have directly defined the primitive procedures like **car** and **cdr** inside **simple-apply**. Other procedures can be specified in the environment, as shown below. The evaluation of lambda-expressions requires the binding of identifiers and arguments with the simple procedure **pairlis**, which simply adds pairs to the front of the environment association list.

The evaluation of **define** adds the given definition to the environment before applying the procedure to its arguments. A defined procedure has an identifier in the environment bound to its definition. Thus, **define** provides a mechanism for recursion. The reader should note that in this version of **eval**, the procedure definitions are local – they do not persist.

Here are some examples. We first see that numbers, strings, and characters evaluate to themselves.

```
> (simple-eval 9 nil)
9

> (simple-eval "a string" nil)
"a string"

> (simple-eval #\a nil)
#\a

; Symbols get their values from the environment.
> (simple-eval 'x '((x . 5)))
5

; The default value for symbols is ().
> (simple-eval 'x nil)
()

> (simple-eval '(quote lisp) nil)
LISP

; Note that we must specify values for else and t.
> (simple-eval '(cond ((eq? x 0) t) (else nil))
               '((x . 0) (else . t) (t . t)))
T
```

```
;   The primitive list operations are built into simple-eval.
> (simple-eval '(car (cdr x)) '((x . (1 2 3))))
2


> (simple-eval '(car (cons x x)) '((x . "hello")))
"hello"


;   The heart of procedure application is lambda expressions.
> (simple-eval '((lambda (n) (car n)) '(a b c)) nil)
A


;   We can introduce new procedure names into the environment.
> (simple-eval '(zero? x)
               '((x . 0) (zero? . (lambda (n) (eq? n 0)))))
#t


> (simple-eval '(head '(1 2 3))
               '((head . (lambda (n) (car n)))))
1


;   or more succinctly:
> (simple-eval '(head '(1 2 3))
               '((head . car)))
1


;   Finally, we can define recursive procedures.
;   For clarity, we first make the environment a global variable.
> (set env '((else . t) (null? . (lambda (n) (eq? n nil)))))
((ELSE . T) (NULL? LAMBDA (N) (EQ? N NIL)))


;   We next define the last procedure, and invoke it on a short list.
> (simple-eval
   '((define last
       (lambda (l)
         (cond ((null? (cdr l)) (car l))
               (else (last (cdr l))))))
     '(1 2 3))
   env)
3
```

To get a full appreciation of the workings of **simple-eval**, the reader should enter the code and trace it during execution. The simple evaluation of **last** resulted in *38* calls to **simple-eval**!

We now turn our attention to a more complex **eval** definition, based on the definition provided in *The T Manual*. The primary difference between **t-eval** and **simple-eval** is the representation of the environment. In **t-eval**, the environment is represented as linked objects which can respond to the **env-lookup** operation.

```
(define (t-eval exp env)
    (cond ((or (number? exp)
               (char? exp)
               (string? exp))
           exp)
          ((symbol? exp)
           (value env exp))
          ((pair? exp)
           (case (car exp)
             ((quote)   (cadr exp))
             ((if)      (t-eval-if      exp env))
             ((block)   (t-eval-block   exp env))
             ((locale)  (t-eval-locale  exp env))
             ((lambda)  (t-eval-lambda  exp env))
             ((define)  (t-eval-define  exp env))
             ((lset)    (t-eval-lset    exp env))
             ((set)     (t-eval-set     exp env))
             ((object)  (t-eval-object  exp env))
             ((case)    (t-eval-case    exp env))
             ((cond)    (t-eval-cond    exp env))
             ((and)     (t-eval-and     exp env))
             ((or)      (t-eval-or      exp env))
             ((let)     (t-eval-let     exp env))
             (else      (t-eval-call    exp env)))))))
```

At this point, there is not much difference between **t-eval** and **simple-eval**. Numbers, characters, and strings are self-evaluating. Symbols return their value from the environment. There are more special cases, but as we shall see, they are generally straightforward.

```
(define (t-eval-call exp env)
    (apply (t-eval (car exp) env)
           (map (lambda (arg) (t-eval arg env))
                (cdr exp))))
```

In the procedure **t-eval-call**, we go ahead and use T's own **apply** and **map**.

```
(define (t-eval-if exp env)
    (if (t-eval (cadr exp) env)
        (t-eval (caddr exp) env)
        (t-eval (cadddr exp) env)))
```

```
(define (t-eval-block exp env)
   (t-eval-sequence (cdr exp) env))

(define (t-eval-sequence exps env)
   (cond ((null? (cdr exps))
          (t-eval (car exps) env))
         (else
          (t-eval (car exps) env)
          (t-eval-sequence (cdr exps) env)))))
```

These definitions are trivial. The reader should note that the termination test in
t-eval-sequence is deliberately not **(null? exps)**, so as to allow the definition
to be properly *tail-recursive* – an optimization discussed in the next chapter.

In order to understand most of the remaining definitions, we now turn our
attention to the representation of environments and the mechanism for binding
variables.

Here are the primary procedures that manipulate the environment:

- **t-eval-locale**, which creates environment objects which can handle the
  t-env-lookup operation. For the purposes of this implementation on top
  of T, the **t-env-lookup** operation defaults to T's **env-lookup** operation.

  The **t-env-lookup** operation uses two flags, **local?** and **create?**, to specify
  the initialization. If the initial call to a locale is for a local binding that does
  not require creation, then there obviously is no such value – it returns **nil**.
  If the initial call is for a non-local binding, then the call is passed on to the
  outer environment. Finally, if the call requires the creation of a binding, the
  locale's environment is replaced by the object returned by **bind-variable**,
  which includes the new binding and a link to the initial locale environment.

- **t-bind-variables**, which recursively adds variable bindings to the environment.

- **t-bind-variable**, which creates environment objects linked to other environment objects. The object responds to the **t-env-lookup** operation by
  checking to see if it has the binding for the specified identifier. If it does,
  it returns the appropriate locative. If not, it passes the operation on to its
  superior environment.

- **value**, which returns the contents of the locative returned by **t-env-lookup**.

- **set-value**, which stores a value in a variable binding.

Here is the code.

```
(define-operation (t-env-lookup self id local? create?)
                  (env-lookup self id local? create?))

(define (t-eval-locale exp env)
    (let ((the-env nil))
      (set the-env
          (object nil
            ((t-env-lookup self id local? create?)
             (cond ((and local? (not create?))
                      nil)
                   ((and (not local?)
                         (t-env-lookup env id nil nil)))
                   (create?
                    (set the-env
                        (bind-variable id (undefined-value)
                                       the-env))
                    (t-env-lookup the-env id local? create?))
                   (else nil)))))
      (let ((the-locale
              (object nil
                ((t-env-lookup self id local? create?)
                 (t-env-lookup the-env id local? create?)))))
          (if (cadr exp)
              (set-value (cadr exp) the-locale the-locale t))
          (t-eval-sequence (cddr exp) the-locale))))

(define (bind-variables ids values env)
    (cond ((pair? ids)
            (bind-variable (car ids)
                           (car values)
                           (bind-variables (cdr ids)
                                           (cdr values)
                                           env)))
          ((null? ids) env)
          (else
           (bind-variable ids values env))))
```

```
(define (bind-variable identifier value env)
    (object nil
        ((t-env-lookup self id local? create?)
         (cond ((eq? id identifier)
                (locative value))
               (else
                (t-env-lookup env id local? create?)))))))
```

```
(define (value id env)
    (contents (t-env-lookup env id nil nil)))
```

```
(define (set-value id env val local?)
    (set (contents (t-env-lookup env id local? t)) val))
```

We now finish with the code for handling **lambda**, **set**, **lset**, **define**, and
object.

```
(define (t-eval-lambda exp env)
    (lambda args
        (t-eval-sequence (cddr exp)
            (bind-variables (cadr exp) args env))))
```

```
(define (t-eval-set exp env)
  (let ((place (cadr exp)))
    (cond
      ((atom? place)
       (set-value place env (t-eval (caddr exp) env) nil))
      (else
       (t-eval `((setter ,(car place)) ,@(cdr place) ,(caddr exp))
               env)))))
```

```
(define (t-eval-lset exp env)
    (set-value (cadr exp) env (t-eval (caddr exp) env) t))
```

```
(define (t-eval-define exp env)
    (let ((pattern (cadr exp)))
        (cond ((atom? pattern)
               (t-eval-lset exp env))
              (else
               (t-eval-lset
                 `(lset ,(car pattern)
                        (lambda ,(cdr pattern) ,@(cddr exp)))
                 env)))))
```

```
(define (t-eval-object exp env)
   (t-eval-object-aux (t-eval (cadr exp) env) (cddr exp) env))

(define (t-eval-object-aux proc clauses env)
  (cond
    ((null? clauses)
     (object proc))
    (else
     (let ((clause (car clauses)))
       (join (object proc
              (((t-eval (caar clause) env) self . args)
                    (t-eval-sequence (cdr clause)
                                     (bind-variables (cdar clause)
                                        (cons self args)
                                        env))))
             (t-eval-object-aux nil (cdr clauses) env))))))
```

In exercise 15.7.6, we invite the reader to provide the remaining definitions for **t-eval-cond**, **t-eval-or**, **t-eval-and**, **t-eval-case**, and **t-eval-let**.

Here is **t-eval** in action.

```
> (t-eval 8 user-env)
8

> (t-eval '(define x 7) user-env)
7

> (t-eval 'x user-env)
7

> (t-eval (quote x) user-env)
7

> (t-eval '(quote x) user-env)
X

> (t-eval '(if nil 1 2) user-env)
2

> (t-eval '(if t 1 2) user-env)
1

> (t-eval '(block x x 3 4 "fhf" (if t 1 2)) user-env)
1
```

```
> (t-eval '(map add1 (quote (1 2 3))) user-env)
(2 3 4)

> (t-eval '(apply + (quote (1 2 3))) user-env)
6
> (t-eval
    '(define (fact n)
       (if (zero? n) 1 (* n (fact (- n 1)))))
    user-env)
#{Procedure 41}

> (t-eval '(fact 6) user-env)
720

> (t-eval '((lambda (x) (* x 5)) 10) user-env)
50
```

15.7   Exercises

15.7.1   Export [5*]

Write a macro export, which is the opposite of import. Here is an example.

```
> (define *my-env* (make-empty-locale '*my-env*))
#{Locale 82 *MY-ENV*}

> (define x 7)
7

> (define (double n) (+ n n))
#{Procedure 78 DOUBLE}

> (export *my-env* x double)
#{Procedure 78 DOUBLE}

> (eval '(double x) *my-env*)
14
```

15.7.2   Cleaning the Slate [3*]

Write a procedure clean-slate, which will effectively restore the environment to its original state, and dirty-slate, which can take you back to your earlier environment, as shown below.

```
> (define x 5)
5

> (clean-slate)
#{Locale 52 *CLEAN-ENV*}

> x

** Error: variable X is unbound

>> (dirty-slate)
#{Locale 53 USER-ENV}

>> x
5
```

15.7.3 Making Transcripts [4*]

Modify the `make-workspace` example given in this chapter to simulate T's `transcript-on` and `transcript-off` procedures. What can the built-in procedures do that this method does not handle?

15.7.4 Workspace Editor [7*]

The workspace procedure described in this chapter provides the minimum function of capturing the state of a session by logging expressions to a file. However, the `make-workspace` method is indiscriminate in the expressions that it saves. The programmer is usually interested only in definitions of procedures and variables.

Another approach to the workspace management problem is to have a method for keeping track of those definitions that are important, and furthermore, making it easier to create and modify those definitions in the first place. One way to provide this functionality is with an interactive editor. Here is an example of one such editor, **ed**.

```
> (ed 'fact)
Creating definition of: FACT
```

```
ED> ?

?        print help information
car | <  move context down by car
cdr | >  move context down by cdr
del      delete car of current context
exit     save current definition and exit
(exp)    evaluate given expression
find     move context to matching expression
i        insert at current context
p        print current context
pd       print definition
quit     exit editor without saving
rep      replace car of current context
save     save current definition
set      set current definition
subst    global substitution in definition
top      move context to top definition
u | ^    move context up
```

The programmer invokes the editor with the call (ed 'fact), and the program responds with the prompt "ED>". The programmer types "?" to get a list of commands. Synonyms are separated by vertical bars, e.g., car | >. The session continues.

```
ED> set

Definition: (define (fact n) (cond ((zero n) 0)
  (else (+ n (fact (- nn 1)))))))

ED> exit

Exiting editor.
> (fact 4)

** Error: variable ZERO is unbound
>> (ret zero?)

** Error: variable NN is unbound
>> (ret 1)

** Error: variable ZERO is unbound
>> (ret zero?)
3
```

The programmer gives an initial definition of **fact**, and exits the editor – saving the definition. When he tests **fact**, he encounters a couple of errors. He then returns to the editor to correct the errors.

```
> (ed 'fact)
Modifying definition of: FACT

ED> pd                          ; print current definition
(DEFINE (FACT N) (COND ((ZERO N) 0) (ELSE (+ N (FACT (- NN 1)))))))
ED> subst                       ; global substitution
Old Expression: nn
New Expression: n

ED> pd
(DEFINE (FACT N) (COND ((ZERO N) 0) (ELSE (+ N (FACT (- N 1)))))))
ED> cdr                         ; move context down to the cdr

ED> cdr

ED> cdr

ED> p                           ; print current context
()
ED> u                           ; too far.  back up one.

ED> p
((COND ((ZERO N) 0) (ELSE (+ N (FACT (- N 1))))))
ED> car                         ; move context down to the car

ED> p
(COND ((ZERO N) 0) (ELSE (+ N (FACT (- N 1)))))
ED> >                           ; synonym for cdr

ED> p
(((ZERO N) 0) (ELSE (+ N (FACT (- N 1)))))
ED> <                           ; synonym for car

ED> p
((ZERO N) 0)
ED> rep                         ; replace car of current context

Expression: (zero? n)
```

```
ED> p
((ZERO? N) 0)
ED> t                       ;  move context to top definition

ED> p
(DEFINE (FACT N) (COND ((ZERO? N) 0) (ELSE (+ N (FACT (- N 1))))))
ED> save                    ;  save current definition
[Redefining FACT] #{Procedure 29 FACT}
ED> (fact 3)                ;  evaluate given expression
6                           ;  looks OK
ED> (fact 6)
21                          ;  hmmm.  Something's wrong here.
ED> p
(DEFINE (FACT N) (COND ((ZERO? N) 0) (ELSE (+ N (FACT (- N 1))))))
```

; We have been adding instead of multiplying.
```
ED> find                    ;  move directly to the scene of the crime.

Expression: +

ED> p
(+ N (FACT (- N 1)))
ED> del                     ;  delete the old +

Deleting: +
ED> ins                     ;  insert the new *

Expression: *

ED> p
(* N (FACT (- N 1)))
ED> pd
(DEFINE (FACT N) (COND ((ZERO? N) 0) (ELSE (* N (FACT (- N 1))))))
ED> save
[Redefining FACT]
ED> (fact 6)                ;  test it again
0                           ;  Another problem arises.
ED> find

Expression: 0
```

```
ED> p
(0)
ED> rep                    ;  replace 0 with 1

Expression: 1

ED> p
(1)
ED> pd
(DEFINE (FACT N) (COND ((ZERO? N) 1) (ELSE (* N (FACT (- N 1))))))
ED> save
[Redefining FACT]
ED> (fact 6)               ;  Finally.
720
ED> quit
Exiting editor.
```

At long last, we have arrived at the correct definition. We now define a simple constant, and then save all our work in a file using the procedure **save-ws**.

```
> (ed 'pi)
Creating definition of: PI

ED> set

Definition: (set pi 3.14159)

ED> save
[Binding PI]
Exiting editor.
> *ws-definitions*         ;  a global list of workspace definitions
(PI FACT)
> (save-ws "outfile")

Workspace saved in file: outfile
```

Here are the contents of "outfile".

```
(herald workspace)

;; Ed definition: PI
(SET PI 3.14159)
;; Ed definition: FACT
(DEFINE (FACT N)
        (COND ((ZERO? N) 1)
              (ELSE (* N (FACT (- N 1)))))))
```

The exercise is to write the procedures **ed** and **save-ws**.

15.7.5   standard-simple-env [6]

It is possible to define many T procedures in terms of the primitive procedures given in **simple-eval**. The reader should create an association list environment containing as many basic T list procedures as possible. Here are some trivial ones to begin with.

```
(define *standard-simple-env*
    '((caar . (lambda (n) (car (car n))))
      (cadr . (lambda (n) (car (cdr n)))))))
```

Other procedures would be **append**, **subst**, **memq**, **assq**, and **reverse**.

15.7.6   The Rest of t-eval [7*]

Write the remaining procedures to complete the meta-circular definition of **t-eval** presented in this chapter. You need to define the following procedures.

```
t-eval-cond
t-eval-case
t-eval-or
t-eval-and
t-eval-let
```

Here are examples of their use.

```
> (define e (repl-env))
#{Locale 6 USER-ENV}

> (t-eval '(cond (nil 1 2) (else 3 4)) e)
4

> (t-eval '(case 2 ((1) 'one) ((2) 'two) (else 'many)) e)
TWO
```

```
> (t-eval '(case 3 ((1) 'one) ((2) 'two) (else 'many)) e)
MANY

> (t-eval '(or (lset x 1) (lset x 2)) e)
1

> (t-eval 'x e)
1

> (t-eval '(and (set x 1) (set x 2)) e)
2

> (t-eval 'x e)
2

> (t-eval '(let ((a 1) (b 2)) (+ a b)) e)
3
```

15.8 Chapter Summary

- Local variables in T are normally lexically scoped.

- T's **bind** form provides a means for dynamic scoping of variables.

- Environments are a collection of variable bindings, organized in a hierarchy of contours. T also refers to environments as locales.

- Global variables are local to an environment.

- T provides a set of mechanisms for creating and manipulating environments.

```
(make-empty-locale id)
(make-locale locale id)
(locale? object)
(*define locale id value)
(*value locale id)        ;  settable
(import env id)
(repl-env)                ;  settable
(locale id . body)
```

- **define** and **lset** shadow variable bindings, whereas **set** does not.

- Standard T environments include

```
user-env
standard-env
```

- The programmer may load a file into a specific environment by giving a second argument to **load**. The default environment is **(repl-env)**.

- Expressions are evaluated within a given environment. The **eval** form may be called directly with an expression and environment.

- The **locative** and **contents** operations in T are equivalent to pointer operations in languages such as Pascal and C. Locatives allow the programmer to manipulate the actual locations of identifiers. The predicate for locatives is **locative?**.

- We can specify a meta-circular definition of **eval**, implementing the binding environment as an association list or as linked objects.

Chapter 16

Efficiency and Compilation

Efficiency of a practically flawless kind
may be reached naturally in the struggle for bread.
But there is a something beyond — a higher point,
a subtle and unmistakable touch of love and pride beyond mere skill;
almost an inspiration which gives to all work that finish which is almost art
— which is art.

⋄ JOSEPH CONRAD, *The Mirror of the Sea (1906)*

Love's herald should be thoughts,
Which ten times faster glide than the sun's beams.

⋄ WILLIAM SHAKESPEARE, *Romeo and Juliet (1594-1595)*

Like Aesop's fox, when he had lost his tail,
would have all his fellow foxes cut off theirs.

⋄ ROBERT BURTON, *Anatomy of Melancholy (1621-1651)*

The late Duchess of Windsor had her motto embroidered on a pillow: "You can never be too rich or too thin." For the programmer, the eternal aphorism is "A program can never be too small or too fast."

In many cases, the programmer is satisfied once his program runs. Period. The question of speed is secondary. After all, computers are fast; therefore, the program must be fast.

This conclusion is illusory. What constitutes a fast program? How long should it take to run? A second? A minute? An hour? For a given problem and set of input, the speed of execution depends on many things: the algorithm, the program itself, the language implementation, and the particular machine.

A discussion of the efficient design of algorithms is beyond the scope of this book. Likewise, we shall not explore machine architecture. In this chapter, we shall first examine some ways to write more efficient T code. Then, we shall introduce the major strategy for producing faster programs: compilation. In the next chapter, we look at implementation details of T's optimizing compiler.

16.1   Coding Optimizations: Arithmetic

There are two qualitative principles involved in estimating the speed of a program. First, some steps take longer than others. Second, the fewer steps to be executed, the faster the execution.

In arithmetic expressions, multiplication usually takes longer than addition. Thus, the statement

```
(* x 2)
```

would probably take longer to execute than

```
(+ x x)
```

Admittedly, we are talking about a difference of a small fraction of a second. However, that piece of code might be executed thousands or millions of times, and those fractions will add up.

Similarly, floating point arithmetic usually takes longer than fixed point arithmetic. Thus, assuming that x is an integer, the code

```
(+ x 2)
```

would probably execute faster than

```
(+ x 2.0)
```

Also, in the first case, the result is an integer, and in the second, it is a floating point number. The procedure + performs generic arithmetic. It checks the types of its arguments, and coerces them as needed. This process of checking and coercion takes time. If you know in advance that your arithmetic expressions will include only integers, you can specify integer arithmetic. This saves the steps involved in coercion and produces faster code. Consider the following segments of code.

```
(do ((i 0 (+ i 1)))          ;  Example 1
    ((> i 10000) i)
    (+ i i))

(do ((i 0 (+ i 1.0)))        ;  Example 2
    ((> i 10000.0) i)
    (+ i i))
```

The second example runs 50% slower than the second. (See table 16.1 on page 330 for details.) The difference is due to the floating point arithmetic required in the second case.

We can achieve even greater speedups by avoiding generic arithmetic altogether in compiled code. There are two ways to do this. The first is to give the compiler a hint — tell it that a given variable will always be of a certain type. The T procedure **proclaim** provides this declaration. The expression

```
(proclaim fixnum? i)
```

tells the compiler that the object i must answer true to the predicate **fixnum?**. The compiler can use this information to produce better code.

The second way to avoid generic arithmetic is to use type-specific arithmetic – either for integers (fixnums) or floating point numbers (flonums). T provides a set of arithmetic operations for both, which are simply the normal arithmetic operations prefixed either with **fx** for fixnums, or with **fl** for flonums. The arithmetic operations for fixnums are:

```
fx+    fx*    fx-    fx/
fx<    fx<=   fx=    fx>    fx>=   fxn=
```

and the flonum operations are:

```
fl+    fl*    fl-    fl/
fl<    fl<=   fl=    fl>    fl>=   fln=
```

In addition to being type specific, these operations also take a fixed number of arguments, namely, 2. Thus, using generic arithmetic, you could write

```
(+ w x y z)
```

but with type-specific arithmetic, you must write something like

```
(fx+ (fx+ w x) (fx+ y z))
```

There is a limit on the size of fixnums in T. This limit is implementation dependent and given by two global variables.

```
> most-positive-fixnum
268435455

> most-negative-fixnum
-268435456

> (fixnum? 268435455)
T
```

```
> (fixnum? -268435456)
T

> (fixnum? -268435457)
()

> (fixnum? 268435456)
()
```

In this case, `most-positive-fixnum` is $2^{28}-1$ and `most-negative-fixnum` is -2^{28}. The predicate `fixnum?` can settle disputes in the mind of the programmer. The moral is that extremely large integers cannot benefit from fixnum arithmetic.

There are several additional fixnum operations which have no corresponding flonum procedures. Their meaning should be apparent.

```
fixnum-remainder          fixnum-abs
fixnum-min                fixnum-max
fixnum-odd?               fixnum-even?
```

The type-specific operations could be defined explicitly using `proclaim`. For example,

```
(fx+ x y)
```

is equivalent to

```
(proclaim fixnum? (+ (proclaim fixnum? x) (proclaim fixnum? y)))
```

Finally, there are explicit coercion outines for converting between fixnums and flonums.

```
fixnum->flonum
flonum->fixnum
```

The main benefit of type-specific arithmetic is derived through compilation.

16.2   Coding Optimizations: Destructive Operations

In the preceding section, we saw that the generic arithmetic operations often perform redundant steps, or rather, steps that could be avoided if we could specify our requirements more exactly.

Similarly, there are common list operations which perform extra steps that can often be avoided. In chapter 14, we discussed applications in which vectors provided faster access than lists. List access commonly requires traversing the list, which is usually slower than accessing elements of a vector. Another list inefficiency comes from the copying of list structure. Most list operations that result in a modification to a list make the changes on a copy of the list, not the original list itself. There are good reasons for this extra effort – primarily safety. If the operation does not result in the intended effect, the programmer still has the old value of the list.

However, copying list structure is expensive, in terms of both time and memory space. We shall see below that the profligate use of space can result in a considerable loss in time spent during memory reclamation.

Therefore, the programmer will occasionally chose to avail himself of *destructive* list operations, which make changes directly to the given list structure, not a copy. In T, these operations are indicated by the suggestive suffix "!". The primary destructive list operations are

```
append!
del!
delq!
map!
reverse!
```

Destructive operations on strings include:

```
map-string!
string-downcase!
string-upcase!
string-tail!
```

Here are some examples.

```
> (set x '(1 2 3 4 5))
(1 2 3 4 5)

> (set y '(6 7 8))
(6 7 8)

> (append x y)              ;  this is the normal append.
(1 2 3 4 5 6 7 8)

> x                         ;  x  is unchanged.
(1 2 3 4 5)

> y                         ;  y  is unchanged.
(6 7 8)

> (append! x y)             ;  this is the destructive append.
(1 2 3 4 5 6 7 8)
```

```
> x                              ; x  has been reused.
(1 2 3 4 5 6 7 8)

> y
(6 7 8)

> (reverse x)                    ;  this is the normal reverse.
(8 7 6 5 4 3 2 1)

> x                              ; x  is unchanged.
(1 2 3 4 5 6 7 8)

> (reverse! x)
(8 7 6 5 4 3 2 1)

> x                              ; x  is clobbered!
(1)

> y                              ;  So is y.
(6 5 4 3 2 1)

> (map! add1 y)                  ; map!  takes only a single list.
(7 6 5 4 3 2)

> y
(7 6 5 4 3 2)
```

The reader should appreciate that the destructive operations on lists and strings are a two-edged sword. They can result in savings of time and space, but they can also result in screwy results. The copying operations are usually safer, but the efficiency-minded programmer may choose to incorporate destructive operations when feasible.

16.3   GC

GC stands for "garbage collection." This unsavory term denotes the process of dynamic memory reclamation.

In many programming languages, the programmer must explicitly allocate and deallocate memory. In T, memory management is implicit and automatic. Whenever the programmer executes some procedure that requires memory, T simply provides it. When T's supply of unused memory runs out, T must then reclaim memory that it had previously allocated, but is no longer in use. This process is known as garbage collection.

Consider a simple analogy, based on normative college student grooming habits. When a student needs a shirt to wear, he simply opens a drawer and pulls out a clean t-shirt. The dirty shirts are deposited in various locales, such as the floor, closet, hallway, bathroom, or fire escape. This t-shirt supply system works quite well until the drawer becomes empty. At that point, the student must engage in t-shirt reclamation, also known as doing laundry. The student canvasses his room and environs, locating all t-shirts. Each t-shirt is categorized as either in-use (currently occupied) or free. The unoccupied shirts are collected, washed, and placed back in the drawer, ready for future service.

Memory allocation and reclamation is a similar process, but instead of t-shirts, we have words of computer memory. T maintains memory in a *heap*. Whenever a procedure, such as **cons** requires new memory, T allocates some from its heap. This process continues until no free space remains. At that time, garbage collection begins. All previously allocated memory is examined to see if it is currently in use. The memory that is no longer active becomes the new available storage.

The process of garbage collection, like doing laundry, is a slow task with no intrinsic reward. There are two basic ways to avoid garbage collection. First, be very efficient in your use of memory. Techniques such as destructive list operations can cut down on memory requirements – just as turning t-shirts inside-out can double their use. Also, the techniques of lazy evaluation, discussed in chapter 14, can be applied to structure allocation to reduce memory requirements.

The second method to cut down on garbage collection is to have lots of memory. T uses a method of garbage collection that involves copying one heap to another. This means that you actually need *twice* the amount of space as a single heap at the time of garbage collection. The larger the heap, the longer between GC's, but when you do GC, it will take longer. The student with 365 t-shirts might wash them only once each year, but what a gruesome task.

Just as some college students have been known to do their laundry before they run out of clean clothes, some programmers may choose to perform garbage collection before necessity calls. The T procedure **gc** invokes garbage collection, as shown here.

```
> (gc)

;Beginning garbage collection.
;(10000) Copying from 5350F5 to 84477D.
;(20000) Copying from 54829D to 866C65.
;Garbage collection finished.
T
```

The "from" and "to" values refer to memory locations.

We shall not go into the details of T's GC. Garbage collection algorithms can be very complex, and must be extremely robust. During garbage collection, it is usually impossible to process errors or interrupt the program. Several methods for garbage collection are presented in [12].

The main lesson of garbage collection is that resources are limited. Even with millions of words of memory, a program will eventually run out of storage. The programmer should learn to practice conservation of space and time in his programs. One of the easiest ways to save space and time in T is with the compiler.

16.4 Compilation

The T compiler is itself a T program, albeit a very large one. To invoke the compiler, the programmer calls **comfile** with an argument of the filename (given without extension) which contains the source code.

We have created a file call **tctest.t**, which has the following definitions.

```
(herald tctest)

;; generic arithmetic with integer constants
(define (test1 n)
 (do ((i 0 (+ i 1)))
     ((> i n) i)
     (+ i i)))

;; fixnum arithmetic with integer constants
(define (test2 n)
 (do ((i 0 (fx+ i 1)))
     ((fx> i n) i)
     (fx+ i i)))

;; generic arithmetic with flonum constants
(define (test3 n)
 (do ((i 0 (+ i 1.0)))
     ((> i n) i)
     (+ i i)))

;; flonum arithmetic with flonum constants
(define (test4 n)
 (do ((i 0.0 (fl+ i 1.0)))
     ((fl> i n) i)
     (fl+ i i)))
```

We now compile this file, and load in the resulting object file.

```
> (comfile 'tctest)

;----- Beginning t compilation on "tctest"

(VARIABLES
  FREE (FL> FL+ > +)
  EARLY-BOUND ()
  DEFINED (TEST4 TEST3 TEST2 TEST1)
  LSET ()
  SET ()
  UNREFERENCED (TEST4 TEST3 TEST2 TEST1))
(AS (IB 46) (SDF 25) (ALIGN 17) (MARK 37) (CLEAN 1)
(DIRTY 7) (BYTES 592))
#t


> (load 'tctest)

;Loading  tctest.mobj into USER-ENV
#t


> (test1 10000)
10001
```

The **comfile** procedure prints out statistics as it goes along, and produces several output files. The most important one is the executable object code — here the file with the extension .**mobj** or "Motorola OBJect" — an object file for the Motorola instruction set. In older versions of the compiler, the programmer must explicitly assemble the output from **comfile**. The current compiler does this automatically. Thus, we may immediately load the object file.

Once we load the compiled code, we can execute the procedures directly. The answers don't change between interpreted and compiled code, but the speed does. Compiling a program results in two time savings: load time and run time. The object file (.**mobj**) loads considerably faster than the corresponding source file (.**t**). However, the major difference comes at run time. In table 16.1, we present comparative timings for interpreted and compiled versions of the four procedures in **tctest**. These results show that compilation always helps, but that it helps fixnum arithmetic most dramatically — a factor of 200!

16.5 More Compilation: Files and herald

The compiler generates extra files besides the executable object file. These other files share the same filename, but differ in their extensions. The original source file has an extension of .**t**, and the rest of the files have extensions that are machine dependent, as shown in table 16.2.

Procedure Call	Interpreted	Compiled
`(test1 1000)`	5079	1506
`(test2 1000)`	5206	24
`(test3 1000.0)`	7144	3583
`(test4 1000.0)`	5973	2488

Table 16.1: Comparative Execution Times (milliseconds)

CPU	Noise	Support	Object
M68000	`.mnoi`	`.minf`	`.mobj`
VAX11	`.vnoi`	`.vinf`	`.vobj`

Table 16.2: Compiler File Extensions

The files themselves are the following.

- *Noise File:* A transcript of the terminal messages written by the compiler, plus some statistics and cross-referencing information. Here are the contents of the noise file produced from compiling `tctest.t`.

```
;----- Beginning t compilation on "tctest"

;;; TEST1
;;; TEST2
;;; TEST3
;;; TEST4
(VARIABLES
  FREE (FL> FL+ > +)
  EARLY-BOUND ()
  DEFINED (TEST4 TEST3 TEST2 TEST1)
  LSET ()
  SET ()
  UNREFERENCED (TEST4 TEST3 TEST2 TEST1))
;;; 0 IBs queued, 3 IBs unqueued
(AS (IB 46) (SDF 25) (ALIGN 17) (MARK 37) (CLEAN 1)
(DIRTY 7) (BYTES 592))
;;; Writing support file
;;; Needed support tables: ()
```

- *Support File:* Compiled, executable code describing early binding information, which the compiler can use in compiling other files that refer to definitions in the present file. The **env** clause in the **herald** form cites this information, as discussed below. This file contains binary data and is not in human-readable form.

- *Object File:* The executable code. This file can be loaded into T, and the procedures will run like the wind. We cannot reproduce its binary contents here.

As we shall see in the next chapter, the T compiler knows a lot about the basic T procedures, and uses this information to produce optimized code. Given the fact that T programmers often have programs that entail more than one source file, it is sometimes necessary to tell the compiler about those other files. For example, we might now create a file **tctest2.t**, which contains procedures that call the procedures defined in **tctest.t**.

```
(herald tctest2
    (env t (mss/t tctest)))

(define (test-driver)
    (format t "~%Beginning test1...")
    (test1 10000)
    (format t "done.~%"))
```

The **env** keyword specifies the support environment for compiling the file. The first argument is the environment name, which should normally be **T**. This is followed by an optional list of file specifications which have appropriate support environments. The file specification given here is a directory path (**mss/t**) followed by the filename without extension.

Here is a TC session in which we compile this file. Note that the referenced support file is loaded at the start.

```
> (comfile 'tctest2)

;----- Beginning t compilation on "tctest2"

(VARIABLES
  FREE (FORMAT)
  EARLY-BOUND (TEST1)
  DEFINED (TEST-DRIVER)
  LSET ()
  SET ()
  UNREFERENCED (TEST-DRIVER))
(AS (IB 8) (SDF 4) (ALIGN 4) (MARK 6) (CLEAN 0)
(DIRTY 0) (BYTES 136))
#t
```

```
> (load 'tctest2)

;loading "tctest2.mobj" into USER-ENV
#t

> (test-driver)

Beginning test1...

** Error: attempt to call an undefined procedure
   (TEST1 10000)
>> *** EOF ***              ; The programmer types ^Z

> (load "tctest.bin")     ; The programmer forgot to load this before.

;Loading "tctest.mobj" into USER-ENV
#{Procedure 29 TEST4}

> (test-driver)

Beginning test1...done.
**VALUE-OF-FORMAT**
```

This method of specifying support files in the **herald** works for referring to external compiled procedures. It does not work for external macro definitions – compiled or otherwise. If you wish to compile a file that includes calls to user-defined macros, you must first load those macro definitions into the compiler.

16.6   Definition Declarations

In addition to making type declarations for arithmetic, the programmer can also help the compiler by explicitly declaring constants with the **define-constant** form. This is analogous to **define** for variables, but tells the compiler that the programmer does not intend ever to change the value. Thus, the compiler can substitute the constant's value directly in the code. This optimization technique is called *constant-folding*.

There is analogous form for procedure definitions: **define-integrable**. This declaration tells the compiler that the definition is not likely to change. More to the point, when this procedure is called by other procedures, the code may be directly integrated in-line during compilation. For reasons that should be clear, recursive procedures are not integrable.

Here is an example which calculates the area of a circle and the volume of a cylinder.

```
(define-constant pi 3.14159)

(define-integrable (area radius)
   (* pi radius radius))

(define-integrable (volume rad height)
   (* height (area rad)))
```

In this case, the compiler can produce better code since it can assume that the value of **pi** will never change, and the definitions of **area** and **volume** may be directly inserted in the code that calls them. Here is the support file created when these procedures are compiled. (This output was produced by an earlier version of the compiler which generated text in support files. The **CPUT** expressions store values in a special database used by the compiler.)

```
(CPUT 'PI 'CONSTANT (QUOTE 3.14159))
(CPUT 'PI 'DEFINED T)
(CPUT 'AREA 'INTEGRABLE-FUNCTION (QUOTE (LAMBDA (RADIUS)
(* 3.14159 RADIUS RADIUS))))
(CPUT 'AREA 'DEFINED (QUOTE (1 . 1)))
(CPUT 'VOLUME 'INTEGRABLE-FUNCTION (QUOTE (LAMBDA (RAD HEIGHT)
(* HEIGHT (* 3.14159 RAD RAD)))))
(CPUT 'VOLUME 'DEFINED (QUOTE (2 . 2)))
```

Note that the value of **pi** has been put into the definitions of **area** and **volume**, and that the definition of **area** has been incorporated in the definition of **volume**, with appropriate changes to the argument names.

16.7   Tail Recursion

In the preceding section, we saw how the compiler can optimize integrable procedures by replacing the procedure call with the literal code from the procedure definition. Thus, the definition of **volume** that resulted from this substitution was

```
(define-integrable (volume rad height)
   (* height (* 3.14159 rad rad)))
```

Why should this definition be faster than the one that called **area**? Because there is a cost to procedure calls. A procedure call requires bookkeeping, which uses up time and memory space. Recursive procedure calls can be especially expensive.

However, it is possible to limit significantly the recursive procedure call overhead under certain circumstances, namely when the procedure call is the *last* expression executed in a given procedure. Consider the following two definitions of factorial.

Procedure Call	(length z) = 100	(length z) = 500
(r-map abs z)	129	613
(tr-map abs z)	60	276
(tr-map! abs z)	54	213
(map abs z)	45	196

Table 16.3: Comparative Compiled Execution Times (milliseconds)

```
(define (fact n)
   (cond ((zero? n) 1)
         (else (* n (fact (- n 1)))))))

(define (tr-fact n)
  (labels (((tr-fact-aux count result)
           (cond ((zero? count) result)
                 (else (tr-fact-aux (- count 1)
                                    (* result count)))))))
    (tr-fact-aux n 1)))
```

Both definitions are recursive, but the second one is *tail recursive*. Specifically, the definition of **tr-fact-aux** calls itself as the last branch of the **cond** clause. That means that *the value returned by the first recursive call will be the same as the value returned by the last recursive call.* This identity does not hold for the recursive calls in **fact** since results returned by recursive calls to **fact** are then multiplied by the current value of **n**.

Tail recursion is effectively the same as iteration. The compiler can optimize the tail recursion calls into direct jumps. The procedure call overhead disappears, and the code runs like the wind.

Why should tail recursion make such a difference? Consider an analogy. In chapter 4, we discussed a census taker who had to ask 10 questions at each household. Clearly, it would be best to ask all 10 questions at one time rather than visit each house 10 times – once per question. By not returning to any house a second time, the census taker is saving not only the time required to come back to each house, but also the record-keeping required to keep track of which houses have answered what questions. When the census taker leaves a house, he should not have to return.

So it is with tail recursion. Less overhead results in faster code. Here is another example. We first write a simple recursive definition of **map** that takes a procedure and just one list as arguments. We then write two tail recursive versions; the first one uses **reverse** and the second uses **reverse!**, a destructive operation.

```
(define (r-map proc lst)
   (cond ((null? lst) nil)
         (else
           (cons
             (proc (car lst))
             (r-map proc (cdr lst))))))

(define (tr-map proc lst)
   (labels (((tr-map-aux proc lst result)
            (cond ((null? lst)
                    (reverse result))
                  (else
                    (tr-map-aux proc (cdr lst)
                        (cons (proc (car lst)) result)))))))
     (tr-map-aux proc lst nil)))

(define (tr-map! proc lst)
   (labels (((tr-map-aux proc lst result)
            (cond ((null? lst)
                    (reverse! result))
                  (else
                    (tr-map-aux proc (cdr lst)
                        (cons (proc (car lst)) result)))))))
     (tr-map-aux proc lst nil)))
```

In table 16.3 we present comparative execution speeds of our compiled procedures. Note that the regular tail recursive version is twice as fast as the simple recursive code. The use of the destructive operation **reverse!** is a significant help as well. Also, there are minor economies of scale: a 500-element list takes less than five times as long to execute as a 100-element list.

16.8   Exercises

16.8.1   Compilation Experiments [5]

In this chapter we have discussed a number of ways to write more efficient code. In this exercise, we ask the obstreperous question: *How much more efficient?*

This exercise is open ended. The reader is asked to design procedures that can be implemented in several contrasting ways to produce a range of execution speeds. Appropriate methods to compare would include the following.

- Multiplication vs. addition. For example, (* x 2) compared with (+ x x).

- Vectors vs. lists. Rewrite some of the vector code from chapter 14 using lists instead of vectors, and compare the execution speeds of the two versions.

- `proclaim` and `define-constant`. Compile programs with and without `proclaim` and `define-constant` declarations. When does it help? How much?

- Type-specific vs. generic arithmetic. Compile programs with and without type-specific arithmetic operations.

- Recursive vs. iterative. In section 9.4, we discussed differences between recursive and iterative control mechanisms. Compile procedures to test the relative efficiency of these contrasting methods. Finally, write the code in a tail recursive fashion for comparison with the normal iterative and recursive versions.

- `labels` vs. secondary procedures. The `labels` form allows the programmer to create local named procedures — as does `let` with lambda expressions. Compare the efficiency of these approaches with `define`'d subprocedures.

The programmer should provide a method for calling the test procedures repeatedly, to get an accurate aggregate execution time greater than a few seconds. An obvious way to do this is with the `repeat` macro described in chapter 11. If the programs are executed on time-shared machines, the programmer should take the machine load into account when comparing execution times.

16.8.2   Tail Recursive reverse [4*]

Write a tail recursive version of `reverse`.

16.8.3   Tail Recursive append [4]

Write a tail recursive version of `append`.

16.8.4   Tail Recursive last [4*]

Write a tail recursive version of `last`.

16.8.5   Tail Recursive nth [4]

Write a tail recursive version of `nth`.

16.8.6   Tail Recursive remove-duplicates [4*]

Write a tail recursive version of `remove-duplicates`, described in exercise 4.7.9, page 74.

16.9   Chapter Summary

- The compiler can benefit from knowing the type of the objects in a procedure. The programmer can use **proclaim** to provide this information.

      (proclaim predicate object)

- Type-specific arithmetic operations can be more efficient than generic arithmetic. These procedures take only two arguments. The fixnum operations are:

      fx+   fx*   fx-   fx/
      fx<   fx<= fx=   fx>   fx>= fxn=

- The flonum operations are:

      fl+   fl*   fl-   fl/
      fl<   fl<= fl=   fl>   fl>= fln=

- Additional fixnum operations include:

      fixnum-remainder   fixnum-abs
      fixnum-min   fixnum-max
      fixnum-odd?   fixnum-even?

- There are explicit coercion routines for converting between fixnums and flonums.

      (fixnum->flonum fixnum)
      (flonum->fixnum flonum)

- The range of fixnums in T is implementation dependent, and given by the global variables **most-positive-fixnum** and **most-negative-fixnum**. Fixnums are tested with the predicate **fixnum?**.

- Most list operations do not make changes directly on a given list structure, but instead on a copy. Destructive operations save space and time by changing the original structure. Destructive list operations include:

      (append! . lists)
      (del! predicate object list)
      (delq! object list)
      (map! procedure list)   ; Note: Takes only a single list.
      (reverse! list)

- Destructive operations on strings include:

  ```
  (map-string! procedure string)
  (string-downcase! string)
  (string-upcase! string)
  (string-tail! string)
  ```

- T performs dynamic memory management, also known as garbage collection. The **(gc)** procedure can be invoked explicitly by the programmer.

- Compilation produces code that executes faster. The compilation command is **comfile**.

- The compiler produces output files termed noise, support, and object.

- The **herald** form at the beginning of a source file has an **env** option, which allows the compiler to reference information about external compiled files.

  ```
  (env support-env-name . filespecs)
  ```

- The **define-constant** and **define-integrable** forms are another method for providing helpful declarations for the compiler.

  ```
  (define-constant variable value)
  (define-integrable (variable . args) . body)
  ```

- The overhead expense of recursive procedure calls can be obviated in T through the use of tail recursion.

Chapter 17

Implementation of T

> *Take, for instance, a twig and a pillar,*
> *or the ugly person and the great beauty, and all*
> *the strange and monstrous transformations.*
> *These are all leveled together by Tao. Division*
> *is the same as creation; creation is the same as destruction.*
>
> ◇ CHUANG TZU, *On Leveling All Things (c. 300 B.C.)*

> *One may quote till one compiles.*
>
> ◇ ISAAC D'ISRAELI, *Curiosities of Literature*

> *A little inaccuracy sometimes saves tons of explanation.*
>
> ◇ SAKI, *The Square Egg (1924)*

In the last chapter, we discussed how compiled code can be made more efficient. In the present chapter, we discuss the technology behind T's compiler, which results in highly optimized code.

By way of introduction, table 17.1 presents a set of benchmarks comparing the performance of T's current compiler, Orbit, with other LISP systems. The benchmark programs are from Richard Gabriel's study of LISP performance [8]. These performance figures come from [8] and [15].

It is difficult to draw detailed conclusions from these numbers, since there are other factors involved in overall performance such as variations in memory size, processor speed, and efficiency of garbage collection. The Sun-3 uses a MC68020 processor, which is much less expensive than the other processors listed. The qualitative assessment is that the Orbit compiler produces much more efficient code to achieve performance comparable to higher-priced LISP engines. How does T do it?

Language:	T	ZetaLISP	InterLISP	CommonLISP	CommonLISP
Compiler:	Orbit	ZetaLISP	InterLISP	VAX LISP	VAX LISP
Manufacturer:	SUN	Symbolics	Xerox	DEC	DEC
Machine:	SUN-3	3600 +IFU	Dorado	VAX 8600	VAX 780
Program					
Tak	0.25	0.43	0.52	0.45	1.83
Takl	1.63	4.95	3.62	2.03	7.34
Boyer	15.84	9.40	17.08	12.18	46.79
Browse	40.28	21.43	52.50	38.69	118.51
Destructive	1.24	2.18	3.77	2.10	6.38
Deriv	3.62	3.79	15.70	4.27	13.76
Dderiv	4.92	3.89	17.70	6.58	19.00
IDiv2	0.24	1.51	3.43	1.65	5.00
RDiv2	0.36	2.50	4.08	2.52	9.84
Triangle	84.36	116.99	252.20	99.73	360.85
Fprint	2.18	2.60	2.93	1.08	3.94
Fread	2.62	4.60	1.57	2.34	7.24
Tprint	1.66	4.89	5.55	0.70	2.85

Table 17.1: Benchmarks: T's Compiler vs. Other LISP's

17.1   T for Two

T was initially implemented for two distinct machines simultaneously: the VAX and the MC68000 (the processor found in workstations such as Apollo, HP-9000, and Sun). This feat of versatility was made feasible by several factors.

First, most of the T system is written in a machine-independent, high-level programming language (namely, T itself), and requires minimal machine language code. This T-in-T principle facilitates language portability — a dynamite idea.

Second, the compiler produces extremely efficient code. The only machine-dependent parts of the compiler are the code generator, certain parameter values (such as the number of registers available), and foreign procedure call mechanisms to interface with the operating system.

Before we go into the details of T's compiler and its predecessors, we shall first present a simple overview of a typical compiler. There are three basic stages.

1. *Lexical Analysis or Lexer.* The lexer reads in the source program and converts the characters to a series of tokens, classified according to the syntax of the language. Typical token categories would be identifiers, numbers, and operators.

2. *Parsing.* The parser takes the results of the lexer, and produces a parse tree, reflecting the order of execution.

3. *Code Generation.* The parse tree is traversed, and machine instructions are generated according to the correspondence between tokens and the instruction set of the given machine. For example, the simple expression "`a:=b+c`" — which is equivalent to (`set a (+ b c)`) in T — might result in the following machine instructions:

```
load  b
add   c
store a
```

which means "place the value of b in the accumulator; add the value of c to the contents of the accumulator; store the contents of the accumulator in location a."

A smart compiler – one that generates efficient code – is always on the lookout for shortcuts. In the previous example of "`a:=b+c`", a smart compiler might ask questions such as "Is b or c a constant? Are b and c equal? Is the value of a ever referenced again? If so, how soon?" The answers to these questions may enable the compiler to produce faster, more efficient code.

In the preceding chapter we saw that certain operations were faster than others. For example, integer arithmetic is faster than floating point arithmetic, and addition is faster than multiplication. Another significant efficiency difference is found in the speed of accessing values stored in registers versus values in memory. Registers are faster. Therefore, the smart compiler wants to use its registers as much as possible, and minimize memory references.

With these thoughts in mind, we shall now look at the history of the T compiler.

17.2 BLISS/11 and RABBIT

The T compiler owes a lot to previous compiler technology. The primary influences have been the BLISS/11 compiler, by Wulf et al. [25], and Steele's RABBIT compiler for Scheme [21].

The BLISS/11 compiler combined a number of optimizing methods connected in a pipeline process. Each step would pass its results on to the next step, involving a total of eight representations of the program – the initial source code, six intermediate representations, and the final object code. Many of the processes introduced temporary names, or TN's, which were used to identify common subexpressions, user variables, or intermediate results. The problem of register allocation then became one of binding TN's to registers. Register allocation was based on factors such as evaluation order of commutative operators, number of registers available, and indexing capabilities of target machine. The last stage of compilation involved peephole optimizations, such as rerouting jumps to jumps, and removing unreachable code, also known as dead-code limination.

The lesson of the BLISS/11 effort was that there is no one simple way to produce efficient code. There are lots of factors that the compiler must take into account. This lesson was applied by Steele in his RABBIT compiler for Scheme.[1]

With a LISP-based compiler for a LISP-based language, the first two steps of compilation — lexical analysis and parsing — come for free. The LISP reader provides a parse tree in the form of a list of expressions. Therefore, the compiler can concentrate on generating efficient code.

Given the fact that many of the procedures in Scheme could be defined in terms of other Scheme procedures, it was possible to transform Scheme source code into equivalent source code expressions. This process of source-to-source transformation would converge to a minimal set of expressions. Thus, the compiler would need to know two things: how to generate optimal code for a handful of expressions, and how to convert all other expressions to this kernal set.

Here are some of RABBIT's transformations. We first look at **block**, **or**, and **and**. Read "==>" as "is transformed to."

```
1.  (block x)           ==> x

2.  (block x . rest)    ==> ((lambda (a b) b)
                            x
                            (lambda () (block . rest)))

3.  (or)                ==> 'nil

4.  (or x . rest)       ==> ((lambda (v r) (if v v (r)))
                            x
                            (lambda () (or . rest)))

5.  (and x . rest)      ==> ((lambda (v r) (if v (r) 'nil))
                            x
                            (lambda () (and . rest)))
```

There are simpler ways of defining some of these transformations, but these definitions have the drawback of being wrong. See exercises 17.5.1 and 17.5.2.

The definition of **cond** takes advantage of **or** and **block**, as well as the primitive **if**.

```
6.  (cond)              ==> 'nil

7.  (cond (x) . rest)   ==> (or x (cond . rest))

8.  (cond
        (x . r) . rest) ==> (if x (block . r) (cond . rest))
```

---

[1]RABBIT etymology note: Compiled LISP code was called LISP Assembly Program or LAP code, and was loaded into LISP with the command LAPIN.

In RABBIT, these expressions were defined as macros that were expanded during the first stage of compilation. At this time, the compiler generates temporary names (TN's) for all bound variables. The TN's are symbols, and their property lists are used to store information about the variables. This first phase of compilation is known as *alpha conversion*.

The next phase of compilation involves analysis of variable references, trivial expressions, and side-effects. The user program is of course a list expression, and can be traversed as a tree. There are three passes through the tree at this stage. The first is to label variable references. At each node in the tree, the compiler identifies all variable references that are local to that node, that is, those variables that are referenced at or beneath that node. This information is stored on the TN property lists.

The second pass during analysis locates *trivial* parts of the program. These include constants and variables, and **if**-expressions whose three arguments are trivial.

The third pass identifies possible side-effects for each node in the tree. Side-effects can result from a variety of operations, including input/output, **set**, and **cons**. Normal accessing operations such as **car** and **cdr** do not cause side-effects. Identifying nodes that do not have side-effects provides the compiler with greater latitude in ordering code and allocating registers.

After this three-pass analysis, the compiler performs certain optimizations. The initial source-to-source transformations may have introduced lambda-expressions. At this point, the compiler tries to get rid of those same lambda-expressions, albeit in a principled manner. Consider the following transformations.

9. `((lambda () body)   ==> body`

10. `((lambda (x y z) body) a b c)`
    `==>`
    `((lambda (x z) body) a c)`

if **y** is not referenced in **body**, and **b** produces no side-effects.

11. `((lambda (x y z) (. . . y . . .)) a b c)`
    `==>`
    `((lambda (x z) (. . . b . . .)) a c)`

if **y** is referenced only once inside the lambda-body, or if **b** has no side-effects.

The latter transformations depend on the side-effect analysis of the previous phase.

During the following phase, the compiler converts the program into continuation-passing style, or CPS. In the CPS version of the program, each function is changed so that it does not return a value, but rather executes a *continuation* in a tail-recursive fashion. This continuation becomes an additional (procedural) argument to each procedure. The CPS conversion algorithm is given in [21]. As a result of CPS conversion, control flow is made explicit in the tree.

The next phase, which precedes actual code generation, is a final analysis. This phase performs a variety of functions, including analysis of variable references introduced during CPS-conversion, register allocation, and environment allocation.

Finally, the compiler generates actual code. At this time, it performs peephole optimization to improve inefficient constructs. For example,

```
(set x x)
```

would be eliminated, and

```
12.     (car (cdr (cdr x)))
        ==>
        (caddr x)
```

In RABBIT, Steele showed that the BLISS/11 compiler techniques could be exploited and extended in an elegant fashion in Scheme, given Scheme's simple syntax and coherent, well-defined semantics.

17.3   S-1, TC, Tau, and Orbit

RABBIT was not a full compiler. Rather, it was built on top of MIT's MacLISP, and depended on the MacLISP compiler to produce final code. Together with Rodney Brooks and Richard Gabriel, Steele applied the ideas in RABBIT to a LISP compiler for the S-1 computer at the Lawrence Livermore National Laboratory.

T's initial compiler, TC, was an extension of the S-1 compiler. TC was part of a larger implementation of T. This initial T implementation by Jonathan Rees and Norman Adams was called *Tau*. Tau had to implement the T constructs that were not found in the Scheme language, such as macros, objects, and structures. Objects, in particular, pervade the implementation of T. T's implementation is object-oriented. Objects are used for a wide variety of tasks, including arithmetic, car/cdr chains, debugging operations, environments, evaluation, files, list accessors, reading, ports, and structures. James Philbin, Richard Kelsey, and David Kranz extended the work of Rees and Adams to produce the current version of the T compiler, known as Orbit.

The TC and Orbit compilers provided a number of extensions to the RABBIT/S-1 compiler, including

- Assignment conversion – an extension to CPS conversion which introduces cells to hold the values of assigned variables, making it easier to analyze side-effects.

- A register allocation strategy that optimizes register usage across forks and joins. This scheme is based on *trace scheduling* [7,6].

- Early binding – saving information gathered during compilation of one file to be used when compiling subsequent files. (See discussion of support files and the **env** clause in **herald** form in preceding chapter.)

- Simplification methods, including constant folding, algebraic simplification, lambda hoisting, and boolean short-circuiting. We give an example of the last method below.

Boolean short-circuiting transformations reduce the complexity of conditional expressions. Here are some examples of boolean short-circuiting.

13. `(if nil a b)`   `==> b`

14. `(if t a b)`   `==> a`

15. `(if a (if a b c) d) ==> (if a b d)`

16. `(if a b (if a c d)) ==> (if a b d)`

17. `(if (if a b c) d e) ==> (if a (if b d e) (if c d e))`
    or even better, avoiding duplication of **d** and **e**
    which might be complex expressions
    `==>`
    ```
    (let ((x (lambda () d))
          (y (lambda () e)))
       (if a (if b (x) (y)) (if c (x) (y))))
    ```

18. `(if (let ((. . .)) a) b c)`
    `==>`
    `(let ((. . .)) (if a b c))`

We now present an example of this technique in practice. First, we give a definition for **not**, then we transform the expression `(if (not x) 0 1)`.

19. `(not x)`   `==> (if x nil t)`

```
(if (not x) 0 1)
  ==>     (if (if x nil t) 0 1)        ; Definition 19.
  ==>     (if x (if nil 0 1) (if t 0 1)) ; Definition 17.
  ==>     (if x 1 (if t 0 1))          ; Definition 13.
  ==>     (if x 1 0)                   ; Definition 14.
```

For more details of the implementation of T and its compiler, the reader is referred to [15] and the sources to the T system itself. The fact that almost all of T is written in T provides the inquisitive T programmer with a wealth of expository examples.

17.4   Summary

In the beginning of this book, we discussed several dimensions on which to judge computer languages, including speed of program development and speed of program execution. We believe these two related criteria to be at the heart of a programmer's primary concern: writing programs.

Throughout this book, we have presented T as a collection of tools to help the programmer with his task. These tools are not a disparate collection, but an integrated body of materials and methods. Our belief is that the programmer who has mastered these tools will discover two things. First, it is now easier to write programs. Second, those programs will run faster.

What more could a programmer ask for?

17.5   Exercises

17.5.1   Either or [4*]

Here is how the T compiler defines the source-to-source transformation for (and x . rest).

```
(and x . rest)      ==> (if x (and . rest) 'nil)
```

What's wrong with the similar source-to-source transformation for **or**?

```
(or x . rest)       ==> (if x x (or . rest))
```

17.5.2   Another block [4*]

What's wrong with the following source-to-source transformation for **block**?

```
(block x . rest)    ==> ((lambda (v) (block . rest)) x)
```

17.5.3   Transformational Programming [6]

Write a procedure which takes a T expression as an argument and applies the transformation rules given in this chapter, returning the result. It should call itself recursively until no further transformations can be applied.

17.6   Chapter Summary

- The T compiler, Orbit, produces extremely efficient code, and, as a result, provides high-quality performance on less expensive hardware.

- The primary predecessors of the T compiler are the BLISS/11 compiler and the RABBIT compiler for Scheme. These two compilers demonstrated the effectiveness of multiple, pipelined optimization strategies.

- RABBIT utilized source-to-source transformations both to convert most expressions in the language into a minimal kernal set of expressions, and to optimize the resulting kernal expressions. Other optimizations included register allocation and peephole optimization.

- RABBIT utilized continuation passing style to provide more efficient control flow — especially for tail recursion.

- The Tau system was the initial T language implementation, including a compiler descended from the RABBIT prototype. The implementation of T exploits the object-oriented capabilities of T.

- The Orbit compiler for T provides additional optimization techniques that result in efficient code.

Appendix A

List of LISPs

Throughout this book we have focused on the T programming language. Many of the features of T can be found in other dialects of LISP as well. In this appendix, we compare and contrast T with two other modern versions of LISP: Scheme and Common LISP.

A.1   T

The main purpose of this appendix is to help the reader execute the code given in this text. The best way to use this book is with T itself. Currently, T has been implemented on the following processors.

- DEC VAX, under both the UNIX and VMS operating systems.

- Motorola 68000, for the Apollo, Sun, and Hewlett-Packard workstations.

For information about obtaining T, the reader should contact:

T Project
Yale Department of Computer Science
Box 2158
New Haven, CT 06520
(203) 432-1278

Also, readers who have access to appropriate networks can send electronic mail to any of the following network addresses:

ARPANET:	`t-book-questions@yale.ARPA`
BITNET:	`t-book-questions@yalecs.BITNET`
USENET/uucp:	`...!decvax!yale!t-book-questions`
or	
USENET/uucp:	`...!ihnp4!hsi!yale!t-book-questions`

where "..." indicates programmer-specified routing information.

The content of that electronic mail might include

- errata.

- requests for information about obtaining T.

- requests for on-line distribution of source code from this book, such as the compatibility packages given in this appendix, and the procedure definitions given in the book.

- requests for inclusion in an electronic mailing list for information about this book and T, including errata and release notes.

All such requests will be serviced to the limit of available resources.

The examples and exercises given in this book were developed under T version 2.8, and then tested and modified under a beta-release of T version 3. The primary difference between these versions is the improved performance of the compiler. However, there were also a number of changes made to the language itself. For the benefit of those programmers who may be using earlier versions of T with this book, we present a brief list of those changes.

- Streams are now called ports (in keeping with the Scheme terminology). The names of stream procedures have changed accordingly.

- Global system constants no longer have surrounding asterisks. For example, `*repl-wont-print*` is now `repl-wont-print`.

- The value of the symbol T is now `#t` instead of the symbol T itself.

- The compiler is no longer a separate system, but rather is part of the regular T system.

- The compiler produces loadable files, rather than relying on an external assembler.

- Property lists are no longer included in the main T system. A general table facility is available instead. A simple definition of property lists using tables is given in section 14.3 on page 267.

- Methods can be defined for structures directly, thus eliminating the need for `define-methods`.

- Objects can be combined using `join`.

- A few names have changed. For example, `div` is now `quotient`.

- Undefined values, such as the value of `define`, may print differently in T3.

Here is a brief compatibility package providing T3 synonyms for T2.8 entities.

```
(define repl-wont-print        *repl-wont-print*)
(define eof                    *eof*)
(define standard-read-table    *standard-read-table*)
(define standard-syntax-table  *standard-syntax-table*)
(define standard-env           *standard-env*)
(define user-env               *scratch-env*)
(define quotient               div)
(define most-positive-fixnum   *max-fixnum*)
(define most-negative-fixnum   *min-fixnum*)
(define port?                  stream?)
(define string->input-port     string->input-stream)
(define input-port?            input-stream?)
(define output-port?           output-stream?)
(define port-read-table        stream-read-table)
(define-syntax (with-open-ports . 1)
   `(with-open-streams ,@1))
```

A.2 Scheme

The Scheme dialect is the parent of T. Scheme was developed as an experimental vehicle to test ideas of language design [24,18,19,2] and compiler optimization [17,20,21]. Scheme programming style is eloquently explained and explored in Abelson and Sussman's textbook on programming [1].

Scheme contains an essential core required for computation. It is the refined and elaborated intersection of LISP dialects.

Scheme, as described in *The Revised Revised Report on SCHEME: An Uncommon Lisp* [2], does not provide a standard for such features as macros, structures, object-oriented programming, and debugging tools. There was no consensus on these issues, and different implementations of Scheme might vary on the design of these features. Scheme provides the underlying tools and an elegant formalism. Viewed in this way, T is one possible Scheme implementation, or alternatively, Scheme is a subset of T.

It is possible to make Scheme more closely resemble T. Below we present a "T-in-Scheme Compatibility Package." The programmer can create a file containing this code, load it into Scheme, and execute most of the programs given in this text.

It is important that the code be executed in the order given, since the later code often depends on earlier definitions. The order of presentation here mirrors the chapter order in this book. For efficiency, we recommend that the programmer compile the code given here.

```
;;   ----------------------------------
;;   T-in-Scheme Compatibility Package
;;   ----------------------------------

;;   Load this code into Scheme to make it resemble T.

;;   Chapter 2    --   Tutorial Introduction
;;   ---------------------------------------
;;        true prints as #!true
;;        false prints as #!false
(define ->integer        truncate)
(define (not-equal? x y) (not (= x y)))
(define not-less?        >=)
(define not-greater?     <=)
(define (float? x) (and (real? x) (not (integer? x))))))))
(define ratio?          rational?)
(define add1            1+)
(define subtract1       -1+)

;;   Chapter 3    --   Lists
;;   ----------------------
;;   no primitive definitions for
;;        any?, every?, mem?, delq, del, subst, substq
;;   no push or pop
;;   no property lists
(define list?           pair?)
(define (proper-list? l) (null? (cdr (last-pair l))))
(define alikev?         equal?)           ;;   sort of ...
(define nth             list-ref)
(define nthcdr          list-tail)
(define last            last-pair)
(define (lastcdr list) (cdr (last list)))
```

```scheme
(define (sublist l start count)
    (cond ((positive? start)
           (sublist (nthcdr l start) 0 count))
          ((zero? count) nil)
          (else
           (cons (car l)
                 (sublist (cdr l) 0 (- count 1))))))
(define memq?           memq)
(define walk            for-each)


;;  Chapters 4 - 6  --  Recursion, Let/Set, Characters and Strings
;;  ------------------------------------------------------------
;;  Note:
;;      no indirect set
;;      set === set!
;;      no string-posq primitive
(define (concatenate-symbol . args)            ;; sort of ...
    (string->symbol (apply string-append args)))
(define alphabetic?     char-alphabetic?)
(define digit?          char-numeric?)
(define uppercase?      char-upper-case?)
(define lowercase?      char-lower-case?)
(define char=          char=?)
(define char<          char<?)
(define char>          char>?)
(define (charn= ch1 ch2) (not (char= ch1 ch2)))
(define char>=          char>=?)
(define char<=          char<=?)
(define string-empty?   string-null?)
(define string-equal?   string=?)
(define (string-head string) (string-ref string 0))
(define (string-tail string)
    (substring string 1 (- (string-length string) 1))))
(define string-elt      string-ref)
(define (string-nthtail string n)
    (substring string n (- (string-length string) 1))))
(define t-substring     sublist)            ;; defined above
(define (string-upcase str)
    (map-string char-upcase str))
(define (string-downcase str)
    (map-string char-downcase str))
(define (map-string proc str)
    (list->string (map proc (string->list str))))
```

```
(define char->ascii        char->integer)
(define ascii->char        integer->char)
(define (char->string char)
    (list->string (cons char nil)))

;;  Chapter 7   --  Ports, Input and Output
;;  ------------------------------------
;;  Note:
;;     Absent or implementation dependent:
;;        write-spaces, format, string->input-port
;;        pretty-print, file-exists?, repl-wont-print
;;        hpos, line-length
;;        unread-char, peek-char, read-line
(define (standard-input)    (current-input-port))
(define (standard-output)    (current-output-port))
(define (port? obj)
    (or (input-port? obj) (output-port? obj)))
(define print               write)
(define (write-string port string)
    (display string port))
;;  no append option on open
(define (open filename mode-list)
    (cond ((memq? 'in mode-list)
           (open-input-file filename))
          (else (open-output-file filename))))
(define (close port)
    (cond ((input-port? port)
           (close-input-port port))
          (else (close-output-port port))))
(define eof?               eof-object?)

;;  Chapter 8   -- Lambda and Labels
;;  ------------------------------
;;  Note:
;;      may support special cond syntax
;;      labels === letrec, but with lambda-binding syntax, e.g.,
;;  T:       (labels (((foo x) . body) ...) . body)
;;  Scheme: (letrec ((foo (lambda (x) . body)) ...) . body)
```

```
;;   Chapter 9   -- Control
;;   ----------------------
;;   Note:
;;       block === begin or sequence
;;       no block0, unwind-protect, iterate
;;       no select form
;;       catch === call-with-current-continuation
;;           but with lambda-binding syntax, e.g.,
;;   T:      (catch exit . body)
;;   Scheme: (call-with-current-continuation
;;               (lambda (exit) . body))

;;   Chapter 10  -- Debugging
;;   ------------------------
;;   Note:
;;       implementation dependent, except for transcripts.

;;   Chapter 11  -- Macros
;;   ---------------------
;;   Note:
;;       implementation dependent.

;;   Chapter 12  -- Structures
;;   -------------------------
;;   Note:
;;       implementation dependent.

;;   Chapter 13  -- Objects
;;   ----------------------
;;   Note:
;;       implementation dependent.

;;   Chapter 14  -- Vectors
;;   ----------------------
;;   Note:
;;       no vector-pos, vector-posq
;;       no exchange
;;       no tree-hash
(define vref          vector-ref)
(define vset          vector-set!)
(define vector-fill   vector-fill!)
```

```
(define (walk-vector proc vector)
    (list->vector (walk proc (vector->list vector))))
(define (copy->vector vector)
    (list->vector (vector->list vector)))

;; Chapter 15  -- Environments and EVAL
;; ------------------------------------
;; Note:
;;     Scheme is lexically scoped.
;;     Other features are implementation dependent.

;; Chapter 16  -- Efficiency and Compilation
;; -----------------------------------------
;; Note:
;;     implementation dependent.
```

A.3   Common LISP

Just as Scheme may be viewed as an extended intersection of LISP dialects, Common LISP is the refined union of LISP dialects. Common LISP is the result of a great collaboration on the part of representatives from the disparate LISP dialects, including MacLISP, Scheme, SpiceLISP, ZetaLISP, Standard LISP, and others. The product of their congress is described in detail in [22].

Though Common LISP is a fairly new dialect, there are many machines – including microcomputers – that support it. The reader is advised to consult his hardware vendor to determine if his own machine runs Common LISP.

The reader of this book who has access to Common LISP will encounter the following differences between T and Common LISP.

- *Procedural arguments.* Common LISP does not support procedures in a manner uniform with other argument types. Common LISP has a special syntax for referring to procedures as arguments, namely #'. To call a passed procedure, the programmer must invoke funcall. Here is a simple example, using T's define form and atom? predicate, the Common LISP versions of which we shall present shortly.

  ```
  (define (test-me predicate argument)
      (funcall predicate argument))

  > (test-me #'atom? 'x)
  T
  ```

  It is possible to get around the #' syntax by defining the value of a procedure

name to be the syntactic name of the procedure.[1] For example, the predicate
atom? is defined to be the same as the Common LISP predicate **atom**, and
the symbol **atom?** is given the value of **#'atom?**. Then the following two
expressions would be equivalent.

```
(test-me atom? 'x)
(test-me #'atom 'x)
```

We incorporate this indirect naming approach in our **define** form given below.

- *Object-oriented programming.* Common LISP does not support object-oriented programming. However, Stefik and Bobrow [23] have proposed an object-oriented extension to Common LISP called *CommonLoops* which is similar to T's object-oriented approach. Also, structures can be used as objects in many applications.

- *Locales and Environments.* The Common LISP correlate is called *packages*, which provide a method for organizing name spaces, but from a slightly different perspective.

- *Default filename extensions.* Common LISP files normally end with .lsp instead of .t.

- *Naming conventions.* The most obvious difference is with predicate morphology: T predicates always end in ?, while Common LISP predicates usually end in p or -p. We present the synonyms below.

- *Order of arguments.* There are several Common LISP procedures which have the same name as the corresponding T procedure, but switch the order of arguments. For example, the **nth** procedure takes two arguments in T: a list and an index. In Common LISP, **nth** takes the index first, then the list. In these cases, we refrain from clobbering the Common LISP definition, and instead create a new procedure with the prefix **t-**, e.g., **t-nth**. Similarly, there are a few cases in which the Common LISP procedure having the same name as a T procedure does something entirely different, as with **map**. Here too, we choose not to kill off the existing Common LISP procedure. In the case of **map**, though, we have renamed the Common LISP version to **cl-map**, and use it in defining other T procedures.

Those differences aside, Common LISP and T share a great deal. The following pages of code comprise a "T-in-Common LISP Compatibility Package." The programmer can create a file containing this code, load it into Common LISP, and execute most of the programs given in this text.

It is important that the code be executed in the order given, since the later code often depends on earlier definitions. The order of presentation here mirrors

---

[1]James Meehan pointed this out to the author.

the chapter order in this book. The comments serve to point out differences as discussed above. For example, **"fn problem"** indicates a procedure which takes functional arguments, and thus requires use of the **#'** syntax.

```
;; --------------------------------------
;; T-in-Common LISP Compatibility Package
;; --------------------------------------

;; Load this code into Common LISP to make it resemble T.

;; Preliminaries
;; -------------

;; the symbol else is given the value T
(defconstant else T)

;; T's define special form.
;; This definition of define makes it simple and efficient
;;     to give T names to Common LISP procedures.
;; It also allows the procedures to be passed as arguments
;;     without #'ing them.
(defmacro define (name &rest body)
    (cond ((and (atom name)
                (functionp (car body)))
          `(progn
            (setf (symbol-function ',name)
                  (symbol-function ',(car body)))
            (defvar ,name #',name)))
          ((atom name)
          `(defvar ,name ,@body))
          ((null (cdr (last name)))      ;; proper-list?
          `(progn
            (defun ,(car name) ,(cdr name) ,@body)
            (defvar ,(car name) #',(car name))))
          (else
          `(progn
            (defun ,(car name)
             ,(append (subseq name 1 (length name))
                      (list '&rest (cdr (last name))))
             ,@body)
            (defvar ,(car name) #',(car name)))))))
```

```
;;  Chapter 2  --  Tutorial Introduction
;;  ------------------------------------
;;  Note:
;;     reset and stop are implementation dependent in Common LISP
;;     no herald form in Common LISP
(define  remainder        rem)
(define  quotient         truncate)
(define  ->integer        truncate)
(define  ->float          float)
(define  add1             1+)
(define  subtract1        1-)
(define  equal?           eql)
(define  less?            <)
(define  greater?         >)
(define  not-equal?       /=)
(define  not-less?        >=)
(define  not-greater?     <=)
(define  zero?            zerop)
(define  positive?        plusp)
(define  negative?        minusp)
(define  number?          numberp)
(define  integer?         integerp)
(define (ratio? obj) (and (rationalp obj) (not (integerp obj)))))
(define  float?           floatp)
(define  even?            evenp)
(define  odd?             oddp)


;;  Chapter 3  --  Lists
;;  --------------------
(define  symbol?          symbolp)
(define  pair?            consp)
(define  atom?            atom)
(define  list?            listp)
(define (proper-list? l) (and (pair? l) (null? (cdr (last l)))))
(define  null?            null)
(define  eq?              eq)
(define  alikev?          equalp)        ;;  sort of ...
(define (t-nth list n) (nth n list))     ;;  switch arguments
(define (t-nthcdr list n) (nthcdr n list))  ;;  switch arguments
(define (lastcdr list) (cdr (last list)))
```

```
(define (sublist l start count)
    (subseq l start (+ start count)))
(define  any?               some)       ;; fn problem
(define  every?             every)      ;; fn problem
(define  memq?              member)
(define (mem? pred obj list)            ;; fn problem
    (member  obj list :test pred))
(define  delq               delete)
(define (del pred obj list)             ;; fn problem
    (delete obj list :test pred))
(define  cl-map             map)        ;; ** switch **
(define  map                mapcar)     ;; fn problem
(define  substq             subst)
(define (t-subst pred new old tree)     ;; switch arguments
    (subst new old tree :test pred))
(defmacro t-push (l obj)                ;; switch arguments
    `(push ,obj ,l))
(define  assq               assoc)
(define (ass pred item a-list)          ;; fn problem
    (assoc item a-list :test pred))
(define (put x y z) (setf (get x y) z))

;; Chapters 4 - 6  --  Recursion, Let/Set, Characters and Strings
;; --------------------------------------------------------------
;; Note:
;;    set is an existing CL function with a different meaning
(defmacro t-set (loc val) `(setf ,loc ,val))
(define (string-append . args)
    (apply #'concatenate 'string args))
(define (concatenate-symbol . args)
    (intern (apply #'string-append
                    (mapcar #'princ-to-string args))))
(define  char?              characterp)
(define  string?            stringp)
(define  alphabetic?        alpha-char-p)
(define  digit?             digit-char-p)
(define  uppercase?         upper-case-p)
(define  lowercase?         lower-case-p)
(define  charn=             char)
(define (string-empty? string) (string= string ""))
(define  string-equal?      string=)
(define  string-length      length)
```

```lisp
(define (string-head string) (char string 0))
(define (string-tail string) (subseq string 1))
(define  string-elt          elt)
(define (string-nthtail string n) (subseq string n))
(define  substring           sublist)              ;; defined above
(define  string-posq         position)
(define (map-string proc str)
    (cl-map 'string proc str))                      ;; cl-map defined above
(define  char->ascii         char-code)
(define  ascii->char         code-char)
(define (list->string l) (coerce l 'string))
(define (string->list s) (coerce s 'list))
(define  symbol->string      string)
(define  string->symbol      intern)
(define  char->string        string)


;;   Chapter 7    --   Ports, Input and Output
;;   ----------------------------------------
;;   Note:
;;       eof check built into read functions
;;       unread-char takes character argument
;;       peek-char takes type argument
;;       open slightly different
;;       implementation dependent: hpos, line-length
;;       reverse arguments:  write-string, write-char
(define (standard-input)     *standard-input*)
(defsetf standard-input () (val)
    `(setq *standard-input* ,val))
(define (standard-output)    *standard-output*)
(defsetf standard-output () (val)
    `(setq *standard-output* ,val))
(define (write-spaces port count)
    (dotimes (c count repl-wont-print)
          (write-char #  port)))
(define  port?               streamp)
(define  output-port?        output-stream-p)
(define  input-port?         input-stream-p)
(define  newline             terpri)
(define  pretty-print        pprint)
(define  display             princ)
(define  string->input-port  make-string-input-stream)
(define  file-exists?        probe-file)
```

```
(define repl-wont-print (values))    ;; slightly different
(defconstant eof (gensym "EOF"))
(define (eof? x) (eq? x eof))
(define (t-read port) (read port nil eof))
(define (t-read-line port) (read-line port nil eof))
(define (t-read-char port) (read-char port nil eof))
(define (t-peek-char port) (peek-char nil port nil eof))


;; Chapter 8   -- Lambda and Labels
;; --------------------------------
;; Note:
;;     no special cond syntax
;;     labels in CL cannot be used to define variables.
;;         also, syntax is slightly different:
;;     T:  (labels (((fn-name vars) body) ...) . body)
;;     CL: (labels ((fn-name (vars) body) ...) . body)
(define  procedure?          functionp)


;; Chapter 9   -- Control
;; ----------------------
;; Note:
;;     no select form
;;     T-block  : progn
;;     T-catch  : block
;;     T-block0 : prog1


;; Chapter 10  -- Debugging
;; ------------------------
;; Note:
;;     check-arg === check-type + assert
;;     recklessness, akin to (declare (optimize ...))
;;     (load-noisily?) is like *load-verbose*
;;     debug is implementation dependent
(define  argspectrum         describe)
(define  transcript-on       dribble)   ;; !!
(define  transcript-off      dribble)   ;; !!
(define  pp                  pprint)    ;; fn problem
(define  where-defined       describe)  ;; sort of,...
(define  breakpoint          break)
```

```
;;  Chapter 11  -- Macros
;;  ---------------------
;;  Note:
;;      no port-read-table
;;      repl-prompt is implementation dependent
(defmacro define-syntax (name &rest body)
    (cond
      ((null (cdr (last name)))      ;; proper-list?
       `(defmacro ,(car name) ,(cdr name) ,@body))
      (else
       `(defmacro ,(car name)
                  ,(append (subseq name 1 (length name))
                           (list '&rest (cdr (last name))))
                  ,@body))))
(t-set standard-read-table *readtable*)
(define  make-read-table  copy-readtable)
(define (read-table-entry read-table char)
    (get-macro-character char read-table))
(defsetf read-table-entry (read-table char) (function)
    `(set-macro-character ,char ,function ,read-table))


;;  Chapter 12  -- Structures
;;  -------------------------
;;  Note:  Anonymous structures not supported.
(define-syntax (define-structure-type name . slots)
    `(progn
       (defstruct ,name ,@slots)
       (define (concatenate-symbol ',name '?)
               (concatenate-symbol ',name '-p))))
(defmacro increment (x) `(incf ,x))
(defmacro decrement (x) `(decf ,x))


;;  Chapter 13  -- Objects
;;  ----------------------
;;  See Common LOOPS, cited above.
;;  Also, structures can be used as objects for many applications.
(define (generate-symbol x)
    (gensym (princ-to-string x)))
```

```
;;   Chapter 14   -- Vectors
;;   ----------------------
;;   Note:
;;        Common LISP directly supports multidimensional arrays
;;        Common LISP directly supports hash tables
;;        Common LISP directly supports random numbers.
(define (list->vector l) (coerce l 'vector))
(define (vector->list v) (coerce v 'list))
(define  vref               svref)
(define  vector?            vectorp)
(define  vector-length      length)
(define (vset vector index object)
    (setf (svref vector index) object))
(define  make-vector        make-array)
(define  vector-fill        fill)
(define (walk-vector procedure vector)
    (cl-map nil procedure vector))         ;;  defined above
(define  copy-vector        copy-seq)
(define (vector-pos pred obj vec)
    (position obj vec :test pred))
(define  vector-posq        position)
(define  tree-hash          sxhash)
(define  hash-table?        hash-table-p)
(defmacro exchange (x y) `(rotatef ,x ,y))
(defstruct delayed-obj (forced? nil) val proc)
(define  delay?             delayed-obj-p)
(defmacro delay (form)
    `(make-delayed-obj :proc #'(lambda () ,form)))
(define (force x)
  (cond ((not (delay? x)) x)
        ((delayed-obj-forced? x) (delayed-obj-val x))
        (else (setf (delayed-obj-forced? x) t)
              (setf (delayed-obj-val x)
                    (funcall (delayed-obj-proc x))))))

;;   Chapter 15   -- Environments and EVAL
;;   ------------------------------------
;;   Note:
;;        Common LISP is lexically scoped
;;        bind is similar to special, but not the same
;;        packages are like environments
;;        can import and export between packages.
```

```
;;  Chapter 16  -- Efficiency and Compilation
;;  ----------------------------------------
(define  comfile              compile-file)
```

Appendix B

ASCII Character Codes

You have suffered worse things;
God will put an end to these also.

◇ VIRGIL, *Aeneid (Book I)*

Perhaps some day it will be pleasant
to remember even this.

◇ VIRGIL, *Ibid.*

We present here a T program which prints out the ASCII character codes in decimal (base 10), octal (base 8), and hexadecimal (base 16), as well as the read table entries for each character. Refer to section 11.5 for a discussion of read tables. See page 104 for a definition of the procedure `incr-char`.

Finally, we present the output itself for purposes of reference.

```
(define (print-ascii-table)
    (format t "~%Character ~12TDEC ~17TOCT ~22THEX")
    (format t "~27TRead table entry")
    (do ((ch #\null (incr-char ch)))
        ((char> ch #\rubout) repl-wont-print)
        (print-ascii ch)))

(define (print-ascii ch)
    (let ((ch-val (char->ascii ch)))
        (format t "~%~S ~12T~D ~17T~O ~22T~X ~27T~S"
            ch  ch-val ch-val ch-val
            (read-table-entry standard-read-table ch))))

> (print-ascii-table)
```

365

Character	DEC	OCT	HEX	Read table entry
#\NULL	0	0	0	4
#^A	1	1	1	4
#^B	2	2	2	4
#^C	3	3	3	4
#^D	4	4	4	4
#^E	5	5	5	4
#^F	6	6	6	4
#\BELL	7	7	7	4
#\BACKSPACE	8	10	8	4
#\TAB	9	11	9	0
#\NEWLINE	10	12	A	0
#^K	11	13	B	4
#\FORM	12	14	C	0
#\RETURN	13	15	D	0
#^N	14	16	E	4
#^O	15	17	F	4
#^P	16	20	10	4
#^Q	17	21	11	4
#^R	18	22	12	4
#^S	19	23	13	4
#^T	20	24	14	4
#^U	21	25	15	4
#^V	22	26	16	4
#^W	23	27	17	4
#^X	24	30	18	4
#^Y	25	31	19	4
#^Z	26	32	1A	4
#\ESCAPE	27	33	1B	2
#^\	28	34	1C	4
#^]	29	35	1D	4
#^^	30	36	1E	4
#^_	31	37	1F	4
#\SPACE	32	40	20	0
#\!	33	41	21	2
#\"	34	42	22	#{Procedure 20 READ-DELIMITED-STRING}
#\#	35	43	23	#{Procedure 21}
#\$	36	44	24	2
#\%	37	45	25	2
#\&	38	46	26	2
#\'	39	47	27	#{Procedure 22 READ-QUOTATION}
#\(	40	50	28	#{List-reader 23}
#\)	41	51	29	#{List-terminator 24}

#*	42	52	2A	2
#\+	43	53	2B	2
#\,	44	54	2C	#{Procedure 25 READ-COMMA}
#\-	45	55	2D	2
#\.	46	56	2E	2
#\/	47	57	2F	2
#\0	48	60	30	2
#\1	49	61	31	2
#\2	50	62	32	2
#\3	51	63	33	2
#\4	52	64	34	2
#\5	53	65	35	2
#\6	54	66	36	2
#\7	55	67	37	2
#\8	56	70	38	2
#\9	57	71	39	2
#\:	58	72	3A	2
#\;	59	73	3B	#{Procedure 26 READ-COMMENT}
#\<	60	74	3C	2
#\=	61	75	3D	2
#\>	62	76	3E	2
#\?	63	77	3F	2
#\@	64	100	40	2
#\A	65	101	41	2
#\B	66	102	42	2
#\C	67	103	43	2
#\D	68	104	44	2
#\E	69	105	45	2
#\F	70	106	46	2
#\G	71	107	47	2
#\H	72	110	48	2
#\I	73	111	49	2
#\J	74	112	4A	2
#\K	75	113	4B	2
#\L	76	114	4C	2
#\M	77	115	4D	2
#\N	78	116	4E	2
#\O	79	117	4F	2
#\P	80	120	50	2
#\Q	81	121	51	2
#\R	82	122	52	2
#\S	83	123	53	2
#\T	84	124	54	2
#\U	85	125	55	2

#\V	86	126	56	2
#\W	87	127	57	2
#\X	88	130	58	2
#\Y	89	131	59	2
#\Z	90	132	5A	2
#\[	91	133	5B	4
#\\	92	134	5C	3
#\]	93	135	5D	#{List-terminator 27}
#\^	94	136	5E	2
#_	95	137	5F	2
#\`	96	140	60	#{Procedure 28 READ-BACKQUOTE}
#\a	97	141	61	2
#\b	98	142	62	2
#\c	99	143	63	2
#\d	100	144	64	2
#\e	101	145	65	2
#\f	102	146	66	2
#\g	103	147	67	2
#\h	104	150	68	2
#\i	105	151	69	2
#\j	106	152	6A	2
#\k	107	153	6B	2
#\l	108	154	6C	2
#\m	109	155	6D	2
#\n	110	156	6E	2
#\o	111	157	6F	2
#\p	112	160	70	2
#\q	113	161	71	2
#\r	114	162	72	2
#\s	115	163	73	2
#\t	116	164	74	2
#\u	117	165	75	2
#\v	118	166	76	2
#\w	119	167	77	2
#\x	120	170	78	2
#\y	121	171	79	2
#\z	122	172	7A	2
#\{	123	173	7B	4
#|	124	174	7C	2
#\}	125	175	7D	4
#\~	126	176	7E	2
#\RUBOUT	127	177	7F	1

Appendix C

Answers to Selected Exercises

*Keep the faculty of effort alive in you
by a little gratuitous exercise every day.*

◇ WILLIAM JAMES, *The Principles of Psychology (1890)*

*It is better to know some of the questions
than all of the answers.*

◇ JAMES THURBER, *Saying*

Most of the answers given in this appendix are definitions of T procedures. They appear here without comment or annotation. The reader should not assume that this terse manner of presentation be construed as a model to emulate. Rather, the reader should realize that the original exercise cited at each answer elucidates the purpose of the code.

Comments are valuable. Comments are necessary. Comments are a positive force in the universe. Also, if the reader has to rely on this appendix for the answers to the exercises, the least he could do is to write his own comments.

Exercise 2.11.2 Defining New Procedures (p. 28)

```
(define (add2 x) (+ x 2))

(define (add5 x) (+ x 5))

(define (double x) (+ x x))

(define (min-abs4 a b c d)
    (min (min (abs a) (abs b))
         (min (abs c) (abs d))))

(define (max-abs4 a b c d)
    (max (max (abs a) (abs b))
         (max (abs c) (abs d))))
```

Exercise 2.11.3 Foreign Procedure Names (p. 28)

```
(define ajoutez +)
(define retranchez -)
(define hochstmas max)
(define multiplizieren *)
(define njia-ya-kutokea exit)
```

Exercise 2.11.7 cond vs. and/or (p. 30)

Here are three cases in which the **and/or** version of **cond** will return different results:

- When there is no expression clause — it should return the value of the predicate.

```
(cond ((predicate x)))
```

- When there are multiple expression clauses — it should return the value of the last expression clause.

```
(cond ((predicate x) (expression-1 x) ... (expression-n x)))
```

- When the predicate is non-NIL, but value of the expression clause itself is nil.

```
(cond ((predicate x) nil))
```

Exercise 2.11.9 floor and ceiling (p. 30)

```
(define (floor x)
    (cond ((positive? x) (->integer x))
          ((zero? x) 0)
          ((equal? x (->integer x))
           x)
          (else (- (->integer x) 1))))

(define (ceiling x)
    (cond ((negative? x) (->integer x))
          ((zero? x) 0)
          ((equal? x (->integer x))
           x)
          (else (+ 1 (->integer x)))))
```

Exercise 2.11.10 Leap Year (p. 31)

```
(define (leap-year? year)
    (cond ((zero? (remainder year 4))
           (cond ((zero? (remainder year 100))
                  (cond ((zero? (remainder year 400))
                         T)
                        (else nil)))
                 (else T)))
          (else nil)))
```

Exercise 2.11.11 Zeller Revisited (p. 31)

```
(define (son-of-zeller day month year)
    (zeller day month (quotient year 100) (remainder year 100)
                  (cond ((leap-year? year) 1)
                        (else 0))))
```

Exercise 3.10.3 New List Procedures (p. 55)

```
(define (no-zeros lst) (del equiv? 0 lst))

(define (collect-numbers n lst)
    (cond ((number? n) (cons n lst))
          (else lst)))

(define verb-list '(is am are have has go went gone))
```

```
(define (verb-find sent)
    (delq nil
      (map verb-in sent)))

(define (verb-in word)
    (cond ((memq? word verb-list) word)
          (else nil)))
```

Exercise 3.10.4 Association List Personnel File (p. 56)

```
(define (make-person name age weight sex sign children)
    (list
        (cons 'name name)
        (cons 'age age)
        (cons 'weight weight)
        (cons 'sex sex)
        (cons 'sign sign)
        (cons 'children children)))

(define (get-sign pers)
    (list
      (cdr (assq 'sign pers))
      '(I knew it)))

(define (get-age pers)
    (cdr (assq 'age pers)))

(define (get-children pers)
    (cdr (assq 'children pers)))
```

Exercise 3.10.5 Property List Personnel File (p. 56)

```
(define (make-person2 name age weight sex sign children)
        (put name 'age age)
        (put name 'weight weight)
        (put name 'sex sex)
        (put name 'sign sign)
        (put name 'children children)
        name)

(define (get-sign2 pers)
    (list (get pers 'sign)
          '(I knew it)))
```

```
(define (get-age2 pers)
   (get pers  'age ))

(define (get-children2 pers)
   (get pers  'children ))
```

Exercise 3.10.6 More List People (p. 57)

```
(define (get-name+age x)
   (list  x  (get x 'age)))

(define (age-of-children person)
   (map get-age+name  (get-children2 person)))
```

Exercise 3.10.7 Daughter of Zeller (p. 57)

```
(define (daughter-of-zeller month day year)
   (nth '(sunday monday tuesday wednesday thursday
          friday saturday)
     (son-of-zeller
             day
             (cadr (assq month
                 '((january 11)
                   (february 12)
                   (march 1)
                   (april 2)
                   (may 3)
                   (june 4)
                   (july 5)
                   (august 6)
                   (september 7)
                   (october 8)
                   (november 9)
                   (december 10))))
             year)))
```

Exercise 4.7.3 Making Changes (p. 73)

```
(define (make-change money)
    (make-change2 money
        '((100 dollar dollars)
          (50 half-dollar half-dollars)
          (25 quarter quarters)
          (10 dime dimes)
          (5  nickel nickels)
          (1  penny pennies)))))

(define (make-change2 balance currency-list)
    (cond ((zero? balance) '())
          ((null? currency-list) '())
          ((< balance (caar currency-list))
           (make-change2 balance (cdr currency-list)))
          ((>= balance (* 2 (caar currency-list)))
           (cons (list (quotient balance (caar currency-list))
                       (caddar currency-list))
                 (make-change2 (remainder balance
                                          (caar currency-list))
                               (cdr currency-list))))
          ((>= balance (caar currency-list))
           (cons (list (quotient balance (caar currency-list))
                       (cadar currency-list))
                 (make-change2 (- balance (caar currency-list))
                               (cdr currency-list)))))))
```

Exercise 4.7.6 Recursive append (p. 73)

See the definition of append2, in section refappend-def, on page pagerefappend-def.

Exercise 4.7.9 Recursive remove-duplicates (p. 74)

```
(define (remove-duplicates list)
    (cond ((null? list) nil)
          ((memq? (car list) (cdr list))
           (remove-duplicates (cdr list)))
          (else
           (cons (car list)
                 (remove-duplicates (cdr list))))))
```

Exercise 4.7.10 Recursive Check Balancing (p. 74)

```
(define (check-book balance list)
    (cond ((null? list) balance)
          ((atom? list) (cons 'error:atom-instead-of-list: list))
          ((not (number? balance))
           (cons 'error:non-numeric-balance: balance))
          (else
           (cond ((number? (car list))
                  (check-book (+ balance (car list)) (cdr list)))
                 ((and (list? (car list))
                       (number? (caar list)))
                  (check-book (* balance (caar list))
                              (cdr list)))))))
```

Exercise 4.7.11 Recursive NOW Account (p. 75)

```
(define (now-account balance list)
    (cond ((null? list) balance)
          ((atom? list) (cons 'error:atom-instead-of-list: list))
          ((not (number? balance))
           (cons 'error:non-numeric-balance: balance))
          (else
           (cond ((number? (car list))
                  (and (< balance 500)
                       (< (car list) 0)
                       (set balance (- balance .1)))
                  (now-account (+ balance (car list)) (cdr list)))
                 ((and (list? (car list))
                       (number? (caar list))
                       (>= balance 500))
                  (now-account (* balance (caar list)) (cdr list)))
                 (else (now-account balance (cdr list)))))))
```

Exercise 4.7.12 Simple Pattern Matcher (p. 75)

```
(define (match? pattern list)
    (cond ((and (null? pattern) (null? list)) T)
          ((alikev? (car pattern) (car list))
           (match? (cdr pattern) (cdr list)))
          ((eq? (car pattern) '*wild*)
           (cond ((null? list) (null? (cdr pattern)))
                 (else (or (match? (cdr pattern) list)
                           (match? pattern (cdr list))))))
          (else nil)))
```

Exercise 4.7.13 Count Occurrences (p. 76)

```
(define (count-occurrences atm lst)
    (cond ((null? lst) 0)
          ((eq? atm lst) 1)
          ((atom? lst) 0)
          (else (+ (count-occurrences atm (car lst))
                   (count-occurrences atm (cdr lst))))))
```

Exercise 4.7.14 Tree Addition (p. 77)

```
(define (tree-addition n l)
    (cond ((null? l) '())
          ((atom? l) (+ n l))
          (else (cons (tree-addition n (car l))
                      (tree-addition n (cdr l))))))
```

Exercise 4.7.15 Tree Average (p. 77)

This answer uses **let** to introduce a local variable and avoid evaluating **tree-average** twice. See chapter 5 for details.

```
(define (tree-average num-tree)
    (let ((pair (leaf-average num-tree 0 0)))
        (/ (car pair) (cdr pair))))

(define (leaf-average l count total)
    (cond ((null? l) '(0 . 0))
          ((atom? l) (cons (+ total l) (+ count 1)))
          (else (merge (leaf-average (car l) count total)
                       (leaf-average (cdr l) count total)))))

(define (merge x y)
    (cons (+ (car x) (car y))
          (+ (cdr x) (cdr y))))
```

Exercise 5.4.2 Identifying Local and Global Variables (p. 90)

- *Locals:* n

- *Globals:* x, y, add-to-x (it is a variable whose value is a procedure)

Exercise 5.4.3 Local Variables and Making Change (p. 90)

```
(define (make-change money)
  (let ((result nil))
    (cond ((not-less? money 100)
           (set result
                (cons (list (quotient money 100) 'dollars)
                      result))
           (set money (remainder money 100))))
    (cond ((not-less? money 50)
           (set result
                (cons (list (quotient money 50) 'half-dollar)
                      result))
           (set money (remainder money 50))))
    (cond ((not-less? money 25)
           (set result
                (cons (list (quotient money 25) 'quarter)
                      result))
           (set money (remainder money 25))))
    (cond ((not-less? money 10)
           (set result
                (cons (list (quotient money 10) 'dime) result))
           (set money (remainder money 10))))
    (cond ((not-less? money 5)
           (set result
                (cons (list (quotient money 5) 'nickel) result))
           (set money (remainder money 5))))
    (cond ((greater? money 0)
           (set result
                (cons (list money 'pennies) result))))
    result))
```

Exercise 5.4.4 Niece of Zeller (p. 90)

```
(define (niece-of-zeller month day year)
  (let ((days-of-the-week
          '(sunday monday tuesday wednesday thursday
            friday saturday))
```

```
        (mname (cadr (assq month
                        '((january 11)
                          (february 12)
                          (march 1)
                          (april 2)
                          (may 3)
                          (june 4)
                          (july 5)
                          (august 6)
                          (september 7)
                          (october 8)
                          (november 9)
                          (december 10))))))
    (nth days-of-the-week
         (son-of-zeller day mname year)))))
```

Exercise 6.6.2 String Procedures (p. 105)

```
(define (lastchar string)
    (cond ((string-empty? string) string)
          (else
           (string-elt string (- (string-length string) 1)))))

;  Here are three different ways.
(define (capitalize1 string)
    (list->string (cons (char-upcase (string-head string))
                        (string->list (string-tail string)))))

(define (capitalize2 string)
    (string-append (char->string (char-upcase (string-head string)))
                   (string-tail string)))

;  This method destructively alters string
(define (capitalize3 string)
    (set (string-head string)
         (char-upcase (string-head string)))
    string))
```

```
(define (case-string-equal? s-one s-two)
  (cond ((and (string-empty? s-one)      ;  both strings are empty
              (string-empty? s-two))
         T)
        ((or  (string-empty? s-one)      ;  only one string is empty
              (string-empty? s-two))
         nil)
        ((char=                          ;  if the two heads are equal
             (char-upcase (string-head s-one))
             (char-upcase (string-head s-two)))
         (case-string-equal?             ;  then compare the tails
             (string-tail s-one)
             (string-tail s-two)))
        (else nil)))                     ;  otherwise NIL

(define (string-less? first second)
  (cond ((string-empty? first) T)
        ((string-empty? second) nil)
        ((char= (string-head first)
                (string-head second))
         (string-less? (string-tail first)
                       (string-tail second)))
        ((char< (string-head first)
                (string-head second))
         T)
        (else nil)))
```

Exercise 6.6.3 Sorting Lists (p. 105)

```
(define (merge a b)
  (cond ((null? a) b)
        ((null? b) a)
        ((inorder? a b)
         (cons (car a)
               (merge (cdr a) b)))
        (else
         (cons (car b)
               (merge (cdr b) a)))))
```

```
;   inorder?  is a simple comparison predicate for numbers
(define (inorder? a b)
  (not-greater? (car a) (car b)))
```

```
;   inorder?  could be defined for other object types, such as characters
(define (inorder? a b)
    (char<= (car a) (car b)))
```

Exercise 6.6.4 Roman Numeral Characters (p. 106)

```
(define (roman-char->decimal str)
      (roman->decimal
          (string->symbol-list (string-upcase str))))

(define (string->symbol-list str)
      (cond ((string-empty? str) nil)
            (else (cons (string->symbol
                          (char->string (string-head str)))
                        (string->symbol-list
                         (string-tail str))))))
```

Exercise 6.6.5 String reverse (p. 107)

```
(define (string-reverse text)
    (list->string
      (reverse (string->list text))))

;  or slightly more efficient (when compiled)
(define (string-reverse text)
    (list->string (string-reverse2 text '())))

(define (string-reverse2 text result)
    (cond ((string-empty? text) result)
          (else
           (string-reverse2 (string-tail text)
                             (cons (string-head text)
                                   result)))))
```

Exercise 6.6.6 Spelling Correction (p. 107)

```
(define (string-swap string index1 index2)
    (cond ((or (not (string? string))
               (negative? index1)
               (negative? index2)
               (not-less? index1 (string-length string))
               (not-less? index2 (string-length string)))
           'error-in-string-swap)
```

```
        (else
          (let ((new-string (copy-string string))
                (temp-char (string-elt string index1)))
            (set (string-elt new-string index1)
                 (string-elt new-string index2))
            (set (string-elt new-string index2) temp-char)
            new-string)))))

;  We can be more efficient using exchange,
:  which is explained in section 14.7.13.
          ...
        (else
          (let ((new-string (copy-string string)))
            (exchange (string-elt new-string index1)
                      (string-elt new-string index2))
            new-string)))))

(define (string-insert string new-char index)
    (cond ((or (not (string? string))
               (not (char? new-char))
               (not (integer? index))
               (> index (string-length string))
               (negative? index))
           'error-in-string-insert)
          (else
            (string-append
                (substring string 0 index)
                (list->string (cons new-char nil))
                (string-nthtail string index)))))
```

Exercise 7.7.1 column-print (p. 124)

```
(define (column-print list indentation port)
    (cond ((null? list)
           (newline port)
           repl-wont-print)
          (else
           (indent (car list) indentation port)
           (column-print (cdr list) indentation port))))
```

Exercise 7.7.2 split Command (p. 124)

The left-text and right-text do not get printed on the same line.

```
(define (split left-text right-text port)
    (flushleft left-text port)
    (write-spaces port
                    (- (line-length port)
                       (+ (string-length left-text)
                          (string-length right-text))))
    (write-string port right-text)
    repl-wont-print)
```

Exercise 7.7.3 tab Command (p. 124)

```
(define (tab column port)
    (cond ((>= (hpos port) column)
            (newline port)))
    (write-spaces port (- column (hpos port)))
    repl-wont-print)
```

Exercise 7.7.4 pinetree-print (p. 125)

```
(define (pinetree-print text port)
  (newline port)
  (pinetree-print2 text 1 port)
  repl-wont-print)

(define (pinetree-print2 text length port)
  (let ((text-length (string-length text)))
     (cond ((>= length text-length)
             (center text port))
           (else
            (center (substring text 0 length) port)
            (pinetree-print2
                    (string-nthtail text length)
                    (+ 2 length)
                    port)))))
```

Exercise 7.7.5 peek-char Problem (p. 125)

It doesn't return a character. It returns the port value. See page 151 for a better definition.

Exercise 7.7.6 split-fill (p. 125)

```
(define (split-fill left-text char right-text port)
    (flushleft left-text port)
    (repeat-char port char
                 (- (line-length port)
                    (+ (hpos port)
                       (string-length right-text))))
    (write-string port right-text)
    repl-wont-print)

(define (repeat-char port char count)
    (cond ((zero? count) repl-wont-print)
          (else (write-char port char)
                (repeat-char port char (- count 1))))))
```

Exercise 7.7.7 Printing Recipes (p. 126)

```
(define (print-recipe recipe port)
    (let ((title (car recipe))
          (ingredients (cadr recipe))
          (instructions (caddr recipe)))
      (center title port)
      (print-recipe-ingredients ingredients port)
      (print-recipe-instructions instructions 1 port)
      repl-wont-print))

(define (print-recipe-ingredients ingredients-list port)
    (newline port)
    (cond ((null? ingredients-list)
           (newline port))
          (else
           (write-spaces port 10)
           (my-print (car ingredients-list) port)
           (print-recipe-ingredients (cdr ingredients-list)
                                     port))))
```

```
(define (print-recipe-instructions instructions count port)
  (newline port)
  (cond ((null? instructions)
         (newline port))
        (else
         (write-spaces port 4)
         (display (cons count nil) port)
         (write-spaces port 2)
         (my-print (car instructions) port)
         (print-recipe-instructions (cdr instructions)
                                    (+ count 1) port)))))

(define (my-print list port)
    (cond ((null? list) repl-wont-print)
          (else (display (car list) port)
                (write-spaces port 1)
                (my-print (cdr list) port)))))
```

Exercise 7.7.10 File Comparison (p. 128)

```
(define (compare-file file-1 file-2)
    (let ((port-1 (open file-1 '(IN)))
          (port-2 (open file-2 '(IN))))
      (port-compare port-1 port-2)
      (close port-1)
      (close port-2)
      '*end-of-file-compare*))

(define (port-compare p-1 p-2)
  (cond ((or (not (input-port? p-1))
             (not (input-port? p-2)))
         (write-string (error-output)
           "Foul port in (PORT-COMPARE)"))
        ((eof? (peek-char p-1))
         '*END-OF-PORT-COMPARE*)
        (else
         (let ((l-1 (read-line p-1))
               (l-2 (read-line p-2)))
           (cond ((not (string-equal? l-1 l-2))
                  (format T "~%1: ~S~%" l-1)
                  (format T "2: ~S~%" l-2))
                 (else nil))
           (port-compare p-1 p-2)))))
```

Exercise 8.7.3 Deck of Cards (p. 147)

```
(define (make-deck ranks suits)
  (apply append
    (map
      (lambda (suit)
        (map
          (lambda (rank)
            (cons rank suit))
          ranks))
      suits)))
```

Exercise 8.7.4 reverse with labels (p. 147)

```
(define (reverse l)
  (labels (((sub-reverse l result)
            (cond ((null? l) result)
                  (else
                    (sub-reverse (cdr l)
                                 (cons (car l) result))))))
    (sub-reverse l nil)))
```

Exercise 8.7.5 Length Problems (p. 147)

Add a third argument to **count-length** through which to pass the procedure itself!
(Thanks to Jim Meehan for this example.)

```
(define (good-length l)
  (let ((count-length
          (lambda (l n fn)
            (cond ((null? l) n)
                  (else (fn (cdr l) (+ 1 n) fn))))))
    (count-length l 0 count-length)))
```

Exercise 9.8.1 Bottles of Beer (p. 170)

Recursion and iteration are two different ways to achieve the same result. A bartender program could use either method.

Exercise 9.8.2 Iterative Average (p. 170)

```
(define (it-average nlist)
  (iterate again
      ((lst nlist)
       (count 0)
       (total 0))
      (cond ((null? lst) (/ total count))
            (else
              (again (cdr lst)
                     (+ count 1)
                     (+ (car lst) total)))))))
```

Exercise 9.8.3 More Spelling Correction: Soundex (p. 170)

```
(define (soundex word)
    (cond ((symbol? word) (set word (symbol->string word))))
    (set word (remove-pairs (string-upcase word)))
    (soundex-2 (substring word 0 1) (string-tail word)))

;;   recursive version of soundex-2
(define (soundex-2 code word)
    (cond ((or (string-empty? word)
               (equal? (string-length code) 4))
           (string->symbol code))
          (else
           (soundex-2 (string-append code (code-digit
                                           (string-head word)))
                      (string-tail word)))))

;;   iterative version of soundex-2
(define (soundex-2 code word)
    (do ((code code (string-append code (code-digit
                                         (string-head word))))
         (word word (string-tail word)))
        ((or (string-empty? word)
             (equal? (string-length code) 4))
         (string->symbol code))))
```

```
(define (code-digit character)
   (case character
     ((#\B #\F #\P #\V)               "1")
     ((#\C #\G #\J #\K #\Q #\X)       "2")
     ((#\D #\T)                       "3")
     ((#\L)                           "4")
     ((#\M #\N)                       "5")
     ((#\R)                           "6")
     ((#\S #\Z)                       "7")
     (else                            "")))

(define (tag-word word)
  (let ((word (cond ((symbol? word)
                     (symbol->string word))
                    ((string? word)
                     (string-upcase word)))))
    (put (soundex word) 'word word)))

(define (isa-word word)
   (let ((code-word (get (soundex word) 'word))
         (word (cond ((symbol? word)
                      (symbol->string word))
                     ((string? word)
                      (string-upcase word)))))
     (cond ((alikev? word code-word) T)
           ((null? code-word)
            "No match at all.")
           (else (format nil "No. How about ~A ?" code-word)))))
```

Exercise 9.8.4 Unwind protection (p. 172)

```
(catch finish
  (unwind-protect
     (block
        (step-one)
        (step-two))
     (step-three)))
```

Exercise 9.8.5 Binary Game Catch (p. 172)

Nothing. That is, the program would behave the same way. It turns out that the **catch** in **binary** is superflous since all calls to procedures that call **quit-action** are in the tail position. They are all tail-recursive calls. See chapter 16 for a discussion of tail recursion. The **catch** is still recommended here, because a small change to the program could remove this tail recursive property, and complicate the termination code.

Exercise 10.5.1 my-error (p. 189)

```
(define (my-error . args)
    (format (error-output) "~%** My error: ")
    (apply format (error-output) args)
    (breakpoint))
```

Exercise 10.5.2 Buggy fact (p. 189)

The formula expression given calls for adding the current number to the result of the recursive call instead of multiplying.

Exercise 10.5.3 bad-length Problem (p. 189)

The procedure is executing endless calls of (bad-length (cdr ())), since the cdr of the empty list is the empty list itself.

Exercise 11.6.2 repeat Macro with a Value (p. 208)

```
(define-syntax  (repeat n result . body)
  `(let ((code (lambda () ,@body))
         (result ,result)
         (n ,n))
     (do ((count n (- count 1)))
         ((<= count 0) result)
       (code))))
```

Exercise 11.6.3 repeat with iterate (p. 208)

```
(define-syntax (repeat n result . body)
  `(let ((body (lambda () ,@body))
         (result ,result))
     (iterate continue ((count ,n))
       (cond ((<= count 0) result)
             (else
              (body)
              (continue (- count 1)))))))
```

Exercise 11.6.4 Changing the T Prompt (p. 209)

These definitions require a new **repeat** macro to allow **code** to affect the value of **result**.

```
(define-syntax (repeat n result . body)
 `(let ((code (lambda () ,@body)))
    (do ((*!!*count*!!* ,n (- *!!*count*!!* 1)))
        ((<= *!!*count*!!* 0) ,result)
        (code))))

(define (my-prompt n)
   (let ((result ""))
    (repeat n (string-append "Yes, Master" result " ")
            (set result (string-append result ">")))))

(define (new-prompt str chstr)
  (lambda (n)
    (let ((result ""))
    (repeat n (string-append str result " ")
            (set result (string-append result chstr))))))
```

Exercise 11.6.5 while Macro (p. 209)

```
(define-syntax (while test result . body)
 `(let ((test (lambda () ,test))
        (body (lambda () ,@body))
        (result ,result))
    (do ()
        ((null? (test)) result)
        (body))))
```

Exercise 11.6.6 until Macro (p. 210)

```
(define-syntax (until test result . body)
 `(let ((test (lambda () ,test))
        (body (lambda () ,@body))
        (result ,result))
    (do ()
        ((test) result)
        (body))))
```

Exercise 11.6.7 block0 Macro (p. 210)

One solution is to generate a unique name for the local variable inside the lambda expression.

```
(define-syntax (block0 first . rest)
   (let ((var (generate-symbol 'block0)))
     `((lambda (,var) ,@rest ,var) ,first)))
```

Another method is to call a subprocedure from the macro. The local variables in the procedure solve the name conflict problem.

```
(define-syntax (my-block0 first . rest)
  `(*my-block0 ,first (lambda () ,@rest)))

(define (*my-block0 first rest)
   (rest)
   first)
```

Exercise 11.6.8 dpsq Macro (p. 211)

The two calls to (**pop** 1) as arguments to **put** might not be evaluated left to right, and the side-effects could result in incorrect code. Here is a safer way. We use **iterate** instead of **apply** for efficiency – avoiding consing the argument list.

```
(define (dps . l)
  (let ((node (car l)))
    (iterate next ((l (cdr l)))
        (cond ((null? l) nil)
              (else
                 (put node (car l) (cadr l))
                 (next (cddr l)))))))

(define-syntax (dpsq . l)
     `(apply dps (quote ,l)) )
```

Exercise 11.6.9 ISA Inheritance Hierarchy (p. 212)

```
(define (isa-get node prop)
    (cond ((get node prop))
  ((get node 'isa)
   =>
   (lambda (n)
     (isa-get n prop)))
  (else nil)))
```

Exercise 11.6.10 Data-Driven dpsq Macro (p. 212)

Replace **put** with **ddput** in dps.

```
(define (ddput node prop val)
 (and
  (symbol? node)
  (symbol? prop)
```

```
   (block
    (cond ((isa-get prop '!invert-property)
           (ddput prop val node)))
    (cond ((isa-get prop '!invert-value)
           (*put val prop node)))
    (cond ((isa-get prop '!invert-onto)
           =>
           (lambda (p) (ddput val p node))))
    (cond ((isa-get prop '!multiple-values)
           (add-property node prop val))
          ((and (get node prop)
                (isa-get prop '!save-property))
           (*put (or (get node 'save-node)
                     (ddput node 'save-node (generate-symbol 'save)))
                 prop
                 (get node prop))
           (*put node prop val))
          ((isa-get prop '!lambda-property)
           =>
           (lambda (fn) (apply fn (list node prop val))))
          (else
           (*put node prop val)))
      val)))

(define (*put node prop val)
   (put node '!ddprops (enter (get node '!ddprops) prop))
   (put node prop val))

(define (add-property node prop val)
    (*put node prop (enter (get node prop) val)))

(define (enter lst val)
   (cond ((memq val lst) lst)
  (else (cons val lst))))

(define (ppp node)
  (format t "~%~A" node)
  (map (lambda (prop)
 (format t "~%~4T~A ~22T~A" prop (get node prop)))
       (get node '!ddprops))
  repl-wont-print)

(define-syntax (pppq node)
   `(ppp ',node))
```

Exercise 12.4.1 Sorting Teams (p. 231)

```
(define (inorder? a b)
   (<=0? (games-behind (car a) (car b))))
```

Exercise 12.4.2 Score Updates (p. 231)

```
(define (final-score game h-score v-score)
   (set (score-home (game-score game)) h-score)
   (set (score-visitor (game-score game)) v-score)
   (cond ((> h-score v-score)
           (increment (team-won (game-home game)))
           (increment (team-lost (game-visitor game))))
          (else
           (increment (team-lost (game-home game)))
           (increment (team-won (game-visitor game)))))
   'end-of-update)
```

Exercise 12.4.7 default Macro (p. 235)

```
(define-syntax (default name . l)
  (let ((stype (concatenate-symbol name '-stype))
        (l     (default-aux name l)))
   `(*def (stype-master ,stype) ,@l)))

(define (default-aux name l)
   (cond ((null? l) nil)
         (else
           (cons (concatenate-symbol name '- (car l))
                 (cons (cadr l)
                       (default-aux name (cddr l)))))))

(define (*def master . l)
   (iterate next ((l l))
      (cond ((null? l) nil)
            (else
              (let ((selector (car l))
                    (value (cadr l)))
                (set (selector master) value)
                (next (cddr l)))))))
```

Exercise 13.6.1 Symbol Generator Revisited (p. 254)

```
> (all-symbols nodegen)
(NODE0 NODE1 NODE2 NODE3 NODE4 NODE5 NODE6 NODE7)
```

```
> (all-symbols nodegen2)
(NODE0 NODE1 NODE2 NODE3 NODE4 NODE5 NODE6
 ...       ;  lots more nodes ...
NODE994 NODE995 NODE996 NODE997 NODE998 NODE999)
```

Exercise 13.6.4 Queue Object (p. 255)

```
(define-predicate queue?)
(define-predicate queue-empty?)
(define-operation (enqueue self obj))
(define-operation (dequeue self))
(define-operation (reveal self))
(define-operation (q-head self))

(define (make-queue)
   (let ((tail nil)
         (head nil))
      (object nil
         ((reveal self)
          (list 'head head 'tail tail))
         ((print self port)
          (format port "~%#Queue ~A ~A"
          (object-hash self) head))
         ((queue? self) T)
         ((queue-empty? self) (null? head))
         ((enqueue self obj)
          (cond ((null? head)
                 (set tail (push head obj)))
                (else
                 (set (cdr tail) (cons obj nil))
                 (set tail (cdr tail)))))
         ((q-head self)  (car head))
         ((dequeue self) (pop head))  )))
```

Exercise 13.6.5 make-better-plist (p. 256)

Simply substitute all occurrences of **assq** in the code for **make-plist** with
ass alikev?.

Exercise 14.7.4 Three-Dimensional Arrays (p. 280)

```
(define-predicate 3d-array?)
(define-settable-operation (3d-ref self x y z))
(define-operation (3d-set self x y z val))
(define 3d-set (setter 3d-ref))
(define-operation (3d-array-fill self val))

(define (make-3d-array x y z)
   (labels ((3d-array (make-vector x))
            ((3d-initialize vector index sizey sizez)
             (cond ((= index 0) vector)
                   (else
                    (decrement index)
                    (set (vref vector index)
                         (make-2d-array sizey sizez))
                    (3d-initialize vector index sizey sizez)))))
      (set 3d-array (3d-initialize 3d-array x y z))
      (object nil
        ((print self port)
         (format port "#{3d-array ~A ~A}"
           (object-hash self) 3d-array))
        ((3d-array? self) T)
        ((3d-ref self x y)
         (2d-ref (vref 3d-array x) y z))
        ((3d-set self x y z val)
         (set (vref (vref (vref 3d-array x) y) z) val))
        ((3d-array-fill self val)
         (walk-vector
           (lambda (v) (2d-array-fill v val)) 3d-array)
        3d-array))))
```

Exercise 14.7.5 n-Dimensional Arrays (p. 280)

```
(define-predicate nd-array?)
(define-settable-operation (nd-ref self . d))
(define-operation (nd-set self . d))
(define nd-set (setter nd-ref))
(define-operation (walk-nd-array self proc))
(define-operation (nd-array-fill self . d))
(define-operation (dimensions-of self))

(define (make-nd-array . d)
   (labels ((dim (length d))
            (nd-array nil)
```

```
           ((nd-init vector . n)
            (cond ((null? n) vector)
                  ((null? vector)
                   (apply nd-init (make-vector (car n)) n))
                  ((or (= (car n) 0)
                       (null? (cdr n)))
                   vector)
                  (else
                   (decrement (car n))
                   (set (vref vector (car n))
                        (apply nd-init nil (cdr n)))
                   (apply nd-init vector n))))
           ((dref obj d)
            (cond ((null? (cdr d))
                   (vref obj (car d)))
                  (else
                   (dref (vref obj (car d)) (cdr d)))))
           ((dset obj d)
            (cond ((null? (cddr d))
                   (set (vref obj (car d)) (cadr d)))
                  (else
                   (dset (vref obj (car d)) (cdr d)))))
           ((dwalk proc obj dim)
            (cond ((zero? dim) (proc obj))
                  (else
                   (walk-vector
                     (lambda (v) (dwalk proc v (- dim 1)))
                     obj)))))
  (set nd-array (apply nd-init nil d))
  (object nil
    ((print self port)
     (format port "#{nd-array ~A ~A}"
        (object-hash self) nd-array))
    ((nd-array? self) T)
    ((dimensions-of self) d)
    ((nd-ref self . d)
     (dref nd-array d))
    ((nd-set self . d)
     (dset nd-array d))
    ((walk-nd-array self proc)
     (dwalk proc nd-array dim))
```

```
((nd-array-fill self val)
 (dwalk (lambda (v) (vector-fill v val))
   nd-array (- dim 1))
 nd-array) )))
```

Exercise 14.7.6 Hash Tables (p. 281)

Simply replace eq? with alikev?.

Exercise 14.7.7 Searching Hash Tables (p. 282)

```
;;  First, declare the operation.
(define-operation (table-find self value))
;;  Then, add the following method to the object clause in make-hash-table.
((table-find self value)
 (cond ((vector-pos
          (lambda (m b)
           (alikev? m (cdr b))) value table)
        =>
        (lambda (index) (car (vref table index))))
       (else nil)))
```

Exercise 14.7.8 Random Hash Tables (p. 282)

The main advantage would be minimizing collisions for insertions. The primary disadvantage would be reducing the odds of ever retrieving data. A random hash table is an example of a write-only data structure.

Exercise 14.7.9 More Hash Tables (p. 282)

```
(define (make-hash-table size)
  (labels ((table (vector-fill (make-vector size) nil))
           ((get-bucket key)
            (let ((bucket-number (mod (tree-hash key) size)))
              (or (vref table bucket-number)
                  (set (vref table bucket-number)
                       (copy-tree '(((())))))))))
    (object nil
      ((reveal self) (vector->list table))
      ((hash-table? self) T)
      ((table-get self key)
       (cdr (ass alikev? key (get-bucket key)))))
```

```
    ((table-put self key value)
     (let ((bucket (get-bucket key)))
       (cond  ((ass alikev? key bucket)
                =>
                (lambda (x) (set (cdr x) value)))
              (else
               (set (cdr bucket)
                    (cons (cons key value)
                          (cdr bucket)))
                value)))))
    ((print self port)
     (format port "#{Hash table ~A}"
       (object-hash self))
     repl-wont-print) )))
```

Exercise 14.7.10 new-hash (p. 283)

```
(define (new-hash tree)
  (labels (((string-hash string)
            (cond ((string-empty? string) 1)
                  (else
                   (+ (char->ascii (string-head string))
                      (* (string-hash
                          (string-tail string)) 2)))))
           ((hash tree)
            (cond ((pair? tree)
                   (+ (hash (car tree))
                      (* (hash (cdr tree)) 2)))
                  ((symbol? tree)
                   (string-hash (symbol->string tree)))
                  ((string? tree)
                   (string-hash tree))
                  ((null? tree) 31415926)
                  ((vector? tree)
                   (hash (vector->list tree)))
                  ((char? tree)
                   (char->ascii tree))
                  ((integer? tree)
                   tree)
                  (else (hash (error "unhashable leaf~%  (~s ~s)"
                                     'tree-hash
                                     tree))))))
    (hash tree)))
```

Exercise 14.7.12 Generalized Chi-Squared (p. 284)

```
(define (chi-sq vec exp)
   (cond ((number? exp)
          (set exp (vector-fill
                       (make-vector (vector-length vec))
                       exp))))
   (labels ((range (vector-length vec))
            ((square-dif x y)
             (let ((dif (- x y)))
               (* dif dif)))
            ((do-next count)
             (cond ((= count range) 0)
                   (else
                    (+ (do-next (+ count 1))
                       (/ (square-dif
                            (vref vec count)
                            (vref exp count))
                          (vref exp count)))))))
      (->float (do-next 0)))))
```

Exercise 14.7.13 Shuffling Cards (p. 285)

```
(define (shuffle lst n)
   (let ((vec (list->vector lst))
         (rand (make-random (length lst))))
      (do ((count 0 (+ count 1)))
          ((= count n) (vector->list vec))
         (exchange (vref vec (rand)) (vref vec (rand))))))
```

Exercise 14.7.15 Chance Music (p. 286)

```
(define (music pitches durations count)
   (labels ((pitch-vec (list->vector pitches))
            (dur-vec   (list->vector durations))
            (note-vec  (make-vector count))
            (rand-pitch (make-random (length pitches)))
            (rand-dur   (make-random (length durations)))
            ((get-pitch)
             (vref pitch-vec (rand-pitch)))
            ((get-dur)
             (vref dur-vec (rand-dur)))
```

```
      ((get-notes n)
       (cond ((= n count) (vector->list note-vec))
             (else
              (set (vref note-vec n)
                   (cons (get-pitch) (get-dur)))
              (get-notes (+ n 1)))))))
   (get-notes 0)))
```

Exercise 14.7.16 New Math (p. 287)

Here are two ways. First, let the small number be some random number modulus the bigger number.

```
(define (prob func size)
  (labels ((rand (make-random size))
           ((make-prob lastbig lastsmall)
            (let* ((big (rand))
                   (small (mod (rand) big))
                   (ans (func big small)))
              . . .
```

The second way is to choose both numbers at random, then compare them and assign the bigger number to big.

```
(define (prob func size)
  (labels ((rand (make-random size))
           ((make-prob lastbig lastsmall)
            (let* ((big (rand))
                   (small (rand))
                   (ans (func big small)))
              (cond ((> small big)
                     (set ans (abs ans))
                     (exchange big small)))
              . . .
```

Exercise 14.7.17 Lazy n-Dimensional Arrays (p. 287)

```
(define-predicate nd-larray?)
(define-settable-operation (nd-ref self . d))
(define-operation (nd-set self . d))
(define nd-set (setter nd-ref))
(define-operation (nd-larray-fill self . d))
(define-operation (dimensions-of self))
```

```
(define (make-nd-larray . d)
   (labels ((dim (length d))
            (nd-larray nil)
            (nd-fill-value 0)
            (nd-fill-flag nil)
            ((nd-init vector . n)
             (cond ((null? n) vector)
                   ((null? vector)
                    (delay
                      (apply nd-init
                             (make-vector (car n)) n)))
                   ((or (= (car n) 0)
                        (null? (cdr n)))
                    vector)
                   (else
                    (decrement (car n))
                    (set (vref vector (car n))
                         (apply nd-init nil (cdr n)))
                    (apply nd-init vector n))))
            ((dref obj d)
             (cond ((delay? (vref obj (car d)))
                    nd-fill-value)
                   ((null? (cdr d))
                    (vref obj (car d)))
                   (else
                    (dref (vref obj (car d)) (cdr d)))))
            ((dset obj d)
             (cond ((delay? (vref obj (car d)))
                    (set (vref obj (car d))
                         (force (vref obj (car d))))
                    (cond ((and nd-fill-flag (null? (cdddr d)))
                           (vector-fill (vref obj (car d))
                                        nd-fill-value)))
                    (dset (vref obj (car d)) (cdr d)))
                   ((null? (cddr d))
                    (set (vref obj (car d)) (cadr d)))
                   (else
                    (dset (vref obj (car d)) (cdr d)))))
```

```
      ((dwalk proc obj dim)
       (cond ((delay? obj) (proc obj))
             ((zero? dim) (proc obj))
             (else
              (walk-vector
                (lambda (v) (dwalk proc v (- dim 1)))
                obj)))))
  (set nd-larray (apply nd-init (make-vector (car d)) d))
  (object nil
    ((print self port)
     (format port "#{nd-larray ~A ~A}"
       (object-hash self) nd-larray))
    ((nd-larray? self) T)
    ((dimensions-of self) d)
    ((nd-ref self . d)
     (dref nd-larray d))
    ((nd-set self . d)
     (dset nd-larray d))
    ((nd-larray-fill self val)
     (dwalk
       (lambda (v)
         (cond ((delay? v)
                (set nd-fill-flag T)
                (set nd-fill-value val))
               (else
                (vector-fill v val))))
       nd-larray (- dim 1))
     nd-larray))))
```

Exercise 14.7.18 Executable Data Structures (p. 288)

To make the data structures settable and executable, add a **(setter self)** method and replace the initial null argument to **object** with an accessor procedure. Here are code fragments for the two examples.

```
;; hash table
   (object
     (lambda (key)
       (cdr (ass alikev? key (get-bucket key))))
     ((setter self)
      (lambda (key value)
        (table-put self key value)))
```

```
;;  nd-array
    (object
      (lambda d (dref nd-array d))
      ((setter self)
       (lambda d (dset nd-array d)))
```

Note that the lambda variables in the **nd-array** example are not enclosed in a list. This notation indicates that the variable is itself bound to a list of unknown length. This is analogous to the dot notation.

Exercise 15.7.1 Export (p. 312)

```
(define-syntax (export env . vars)
  (let ((g (generate-symbol 'export)))
    `(let ((,g ,env))
       ,@(map (lambda (var) `(*define ,g ',var ,var))
              vars))))
```

Exercise 15.7.2 Cleaning the Slate (p. 312)

```
(define (clean-slate)
  (let ((env (repl-env)))
    (define *clean-env* (make-locale standard-env '*clean-env*))
    (*define *clean-env* 'dirty-slate
        (lambda () (set (repl-env) env)))
    (set (repl-env) *clean-env*)))
```

Exercise 15.7.3 Making Transcripts (p. 313)

```
(define (my-transcript-on filename)
  (catch stop
    (format t "Starting transcript.  End with (my-transcript-off)~%")
    (labels ((port (open filename '(out)))
             (ws-prompt (repl-prompt))
             ((ws-fn? input)
              (cond ((eq? (car input) 'my-transcript-off)
                     (close port)
                     (stop nil)))))
      (format port ";;; Transcript file. ~A~%" filename)
      (iterate loop ()
        (format t "~%~A" ws-prompt)
        (format port "~%~A" ws-prompt)
```

```
        (let ((input (read (standard-input))))
          (cond ((list? input)
                 (ws-fn? input)))
          (format port "~%~A" input)
          (let ((val (eval input (repl-env))))
            (print val port)
            (print val (standard-output))
            (loop)))))))
    (format t "~%Transcript logged on file: ~A~%" filename)
  'end-transcript)
```

This method does not properly log errors, nor does it handle terminal input and output other than that involved in the read-eval-print loop. For example, the results of most **format** statements will not make it to the log file.

Exercise 15.7.4 Workspace Editor (p. 313)

```
(define (ed id)
  (catch stop
    (labels ((def (get id 'definition))
             (ed-prompt "ED> ")
             (input nil)
             ((print-help)
              (map (lambda (str) (format t "~%~A" str))
                '("?         print help information"
                  "car | <   move context down by car"
                  "cdr | >   move context down by cdr"
                  "del       delete car of current context"
                  "exit      save current definition and exit"
                  "(exp)     evaluate given expression"
                  "find      move context to matching expression"
                  "i         insert at current context"
                  "p         print current context"
                  "pd        print definition"
                  "quit      exit editor without saving"
                  "rep       replace car of current context"
                  "save      save current definition"
                  "set       set current definition"
                  "subst     global substitution in definition"
                  "top       move context to top definition"
                  "u | ^     move context up" )))
```

```
      ((find pat tree)
       (cond ((atom? tree) nil)
             ((alikev? pat (car tree)) tree)
             (else (or (find pat (car tree))
                       (find pat (cdr tree))))))
      ((end-ed)
       (format t "~%Exiting editor.")
       (stop nil))
      ((save-def id def)
       (eval def (repl-env))
       (put id 'definition def)
       (cond ((memq id *ws-definitions*) nil)
         (else (push *ws-definitions* id)))))
  (cond (def
          (format t "Modifying definition of: ~A~%" id))
        (else
          (format t "Creating definition of: ~A~%" id)))
  (iterate loop
    ((context-stack (cons def nil))
     (context def))
   (format t "~%~A" ed-prompt)
   (set input (read (standard-input)))
   (cond
    ((pair? input)
     (print (eval input (repl-env)) (standard-output)))
    (else
     (case input
      ((? help) (print-help))
      ((cdr >)  (push context-stack context)
                (set context (cdr context)))
      ((car <)  (push context-stack context)
                (set context (car context)))
      ((del)    (format t "~%Deleting: ~A" (car context))
                (set (car context) (cadr context))
                (set (cdr context) (cddr context)))
      ((exit)   (save-def id def)
                (end-ed))
      ((find)   (push context-stack context)
                (format t "~%Expression: ")
                (set context
                    (find (read (standard-input)) context)))
```

```
          ((i ins)  (format t "~%Expression: ")
                    (set (cdr context) (cons (car context)
                                             (cdr context)))
                    (set (car context) (read (standard-input))))
          ((p)      (pretty-print context (standard-output)))
          ((pd)     (pretty-print def (standard-output)))
          ((q quit) (end-ed))
          ((rep)    (format t "~%Expression: ")
                    (set (car context) (read (standard-input))))
          ((save)   (save-def id def))
          ((set)    (format t "~%Definition: ")
                    (set def (read (standard-input)))
                    (set context def)
                    (push context-stack context))
          ((subst)  (let ((old (block
                                  (format t "~%Old Expression: ")
                                  (read (standard-input))))
                           (new (block
                                  (format t "~%New Expression: ")
                                  (read (standard-input)))))
                      (set def (subst alikev? new old def)))
                    (set context def))
          ((top t)  (push context-stack context)
                    (set context def))
          ((u ^)    (set context (pop context-stack)))
          (else     (format t "~%Unknown command: ~A" input)
                    (format t "~%Type ? for help.~%")))))
      (loop context-stack context))))
    repl-wont-print)

(define *ws-definitions* nil)

(define (save-ws filename)
  (let ((port (open filename '(out))))
    (format port "(herald workspace)~%")
    (map (lambda (id)
           (format port "~%;; Ed definition: ~A~%" id)
           (pretty-print (get id 'definition) port))
         *ws-definitions*)
    (close port)
    (format t "~%Workspace saved in file: ~A~%" filename)
    repl-wont-print))
```

Exercise 15.7.6 The Rest of t-eval (p. 318)

```
(define (t-eval-cond exp env)
   (t-eval-cond-aux (cdr exp) env))

(define (t-eval-cond-aux exp env)
   (cond ((t-eval (caar exp) env)
          (t-eval-sequence (cdar exp) env))
         (else
          (t-eval-cond-aux (cdr exp) env))))

(define (t-eval-case exp env)
   (t-eval-case-aux
          (t-eval (cadr exp) env)
          (cddr exp)
          env))

(define (t-eval-case-aux key clauses env)
   (cond ((null? clauses) nil)
         ((or (eq? 'else (caar clauses))
              (memq key (caar clauses)))
          (t-eval-sequence (cdar clauses) env))
         (else
          (t-eval-case-aux key (cdr clauses) env))))

(define (t-eval-and exp env)
   (t-eval-and-aux (cdr exp) env))

(define (t-eval-and-aux exp env)
   (if (null? (cdr exp))
       (t-eval (car exp) env)
       (if (t-eval (car exp) env)
           (t-eval-and-aux (cdr exp) env)
           nil)))

(define (t-eval-or exp env)
   (t-eval-or-aux (cdr exp) env))

(define (t-eval-or-aux exp env)
   (cond ((null? exp) nil)
         ((t-eval (car exp) env))
         (else
          (t-eval-or-aux (cdr exp) env))))
```

```
(define (t-eval-let exp env)
  (apply
    (lambda args
      (t-eval-sequence (cddr exp)
           (bind-variables (map car (cadr exp))
                                 args env)))
      (map cadr (cadr exp)))))
```

Exercise 16.8.2 Tail Recursive reverse (p. 336)

When compiled, this definition runs 30% faster than T's own version of **reverse**.

```
(define (tr-reverse lst)
  (labels (((tr-reverse-aux lst result)
            (cond ((null? lst) result)
                  (else
                    (tr-reverse-aux (cdr lst)
                                    (cons (car lst) result)))))))
    (tr-reverse-aux lst nil)))
```

Exercise 16.8.4 Tail Recursive last (p. 336)

The normal definition is already tail recursive.

```
(define (tr-last lst)
  (cond ((null? (cdr lst)) (car lst))
        (else (tr-last (cdr lst)))))
```

Exercise 16.8.6 Tail Recursive remove-duplicates (p. 336)

```
(define (tr-remove-duplicates lst)
  (labels
    (((tr-remove-duplicates-aux lst result)
      (cond ((null? lst) (reverse result))
            ((memq? (car lst) (cdr lst))
             (tr-remove-duplicates-aux (cdr lst) result))
            (else
              (tr-remove-duplicates-aux (cdr lst)
                        (cons (car lst) result)))))))
    (tr-remove-duplicates-aux lst nil)))
```

Exercise 17.5.1 Either or (p. 346)

If the first element is not false, it gets evaluated twice, which could be a problem if it produces side-effects. For example,

```
(or (zero? (set x (- x 1)))
    (zero? (set y (- y 1)))))
```

If x were 1 before this code is evaluated, it could end up being set to −1, instead of 0.

Exercise 17.5.2 Another block (p. 346)

There could be a naming conflict with the lambda variable **v** – it might occur inside the body of **rest**, referring to another value of **v**.

Appendix D

References

> *You will find it a very good practice*
> *always to verify your references, sir.*

◇ MARTIN JOSEPH ROUTH, *From* J. W. Burgon, *Memoir of Dr. Routh (1878)*

> *The reason why so few good books are written is,*
> *that so few people that can write know anything.*

◇ WALTER BAGEHOT, *Literary Studies (1853)*

[1] Abelson, H. and Sussman, G., *The MIT Electrical Engineering and Computer Science Series: Structure and Interpretation of Computer Programs,* MIT Press and McGraw-Hill Book Company, Cambridge, Mass., 1985.

[2] Abelson, H., et al., *The Revised Revised Report on SCHEME: An UnCommon Lisp,* AI Memo 848, MIT Artificial Intelligence Laboratory, August 1985. To appear in *SIGPLAN Notices.*

[3] Charniak, E., Riesbeck, C.K., and McDermott, D.V., *Artificial Intelligence Programming,* Lawrence Erlbaum Associates, Hillsdale, N.J., 1980.

[4] Church, A., *Annals of Mathematics Studies Number 6: The Calculi of Lambda Conversion,* Princeton University Press, Princeton, N.J., 1941.

[5] Dahl, O.J. and Nygaard, K., *SIMULA - an ALGOL-based simulation language,* Communications of the ACM, 9/9 September (1966), pp. 671–682.

[6] Ellis, J.R., *The ACM Doctoral Dissertation Award Series: Bulldog: A Compiler for VLIW Architectures,* MIT Press, Cambridge, Mass., 1985.

[7] Fisher, J.A., *Very Long Word Architectures,* Technical Report 253, Yale University Department of Computer Science, New Haven, Conn., December 1982.

[8] Gabriel, R.P., *Performance and Evaluation of Lisp Systems,* The MIT Press, Cambridge, Mass., 1985.

[9] Goldberg, A., and Robson, D., *Smalltalk-80: The Language and Its Implementation,* Addison-Wesley, Reading, Mass., 1983.

[10] Hofstadter, D.R., *Gödel, Escher, Bach: An Eternal Golden Braid,* Vintage Books, New York, 1979.

[11] Kernighan, B.W. and Plauger, P.J., *Software Tools,* Addison-Wesley, Reading, Mass., 1976.

[12] Knuth, D., *The Art of Computer Programming, Volume 1: Fundamental Algorithms,* Addison-Wesley, Reading, Mass., 1973.

[13] Knuth, D., *The Art of Computer Programming, Volume 3: Sorting and Searching,* Addison-Wesley, Reading, Mass., 1978.

[14] Knuth, D., *The Art of Computer Programming, Volume 2: Seminumerical Algorithms,* Addison-Wesley, Reading, Mass., 1981.

[15] Kranz, D., Kelsey, R., Rees, J., Hudak, P., Philbin, J., and Adams, N., ORBIT: An Optimizing Compiler for Scheme, *Proceedings of the SIGPLAN '86 Symposium on Compiler Construction,* ACM, 1986.

[16] Rees, J., Adams, N., and Meehan, J., The T Manual, Fourth Edition, Yale University Department of Computer Science, New Haven, Conn., 1984.

[17] Steele, G.L. and Sussman, G.J., *LAMBDA: The Ultimate Imperative,* AI Memo 353, MIT Artificial Intelligence Laboratory, March 1976.

[18] Steele, G.L. and Sussman, G.J., *The Revised Report on SCHEME: A Dialect of LISP,* AI Memo 452, MIT Artificial Intelligence Laboratory, January 1978.

[19] Steele, G.L. and Sussman, G.J., *The Art of the Interpreter or, The Modularity Complex (Parts Zero, One, and Two),* AI Memo 453, MIT Artificial Intelligence Laboratory, May 1978.

[20] Steele, G.L., *LAMBDA: The Ultimate Declarative,* AI Memo 379, MIT Artificial Intelligence Laboratory, November 1976.

[21] Steele, G.L., *Rabbit: A Compiler for Scheme,* AI Technical Report 474, MIT Artificial Intelligence Laboratory, May 1978.

[22] Steele, G.L., *Common LISP: The Language,* Digital Press, Burlington, Mass., 1984.

[23] Stefik, M., and Bobrow, D., *Object-Oriented Programming: Themes and Variations,* AI Magazine, VI/4 Winter (1986), pp. 40–62.

[24] Sussman, G.J. and Steele, G.L., *SCHEME: An Interpreter for Extended Lambda Calculus*, AI Memo 349, MIT Artificial Intelligence Laboratory, December 1975.

[25] Wulf, W., Johnson, R., Weinstock, C., Hobbs, S., and Geschke, C., *The Design of an Optimizing Compiler*, American Elsevier Publishing Company, Inc., New York, 1975.

Index

Items in (typewriter font and parentheses) are T system names. For convenient reference, these are given with their normal arguments, e.g., (cons object object). Special forms are indicated by "*SF" and settable procedures are marked "*SET." Items in [typewriter font and square brackets] are names of procedures given as examples or exercises in the text. Generally, they are not the same as T system names.